T0106153

THE EVERYTHING®

Kakuro Super Challenge Book

Dear Reader,

I've authored more than fifty puzzle books and love all kinds of puzzles. But kakuro would be my pick if I could have only one type of puzzle while stranded on a desert island. Kakuro is a personal favorite because it is easy to start, yet it has an intriguing depth that makes it hard to put down. I like the idea that every puzzle in this book can be completed using simple logical reasoning. As the book progresses, the puzzles become more challenging (and maybe not so simple).

If you've already had the joy of playing with kakuro, then you know that it is a hidden gem in the world of puzzles. Perhaps you started with sudoku and wanted something more. You probably found that kakuro can be addictive, which is why I've loaded these pages with a huge number of puzzles. So keep this book handy, just in case you're ever stranded on a desert island!

Welcome to the EVERYTHING® Series!

These handy, accessible books give you all you need to tackle a difficult project, gain a new hobby, comprehend a fascinating topic, prepare for an exam, or even brush up on something you learned back in school but have since forgotten.

You can choose to read an *Everything®* book from cover to cover or just pick out the information you want from our four useful boxes: e-questions, e-facts, e-alerts, and e-ssentials. We give you everything you need to know on the subject, but throw in a lot of fun stuff along the way, too.

We now have more than 400 *Everything®* books in print, spanning such wide-ranging categories as weddings, pregnancy, cooking, music instruction, foreign language, crafts, pets, New Age, and so much more. When you're done reading them all, you can finally say you know *Everything®*!

PUBLISHER Karen Cooper

DIRECTOR OF ACQUISITIONS AND INNOVATION Paula Munier

MANAGING EDITOR, EVERYTHING® SERIES Lisa Laing

COPY CHIEF Casey Ebert

ASSISTANT PRODUCTION EDITOR Jacob Erickson

ACQUISITIONS EDITOR Lisa Laing

EDITORIAL ASSISTANT Ross Weisman

EVERYTHING® SERIES COVER DESIGNER Erin Alexander

LAYOUT DESIGNERS Colleen Cunningham, Elisabeth Lariviere, Ashley Vierra, Denise Wallace

THE EVERYTHING® KAKURO SUPER CHALLENGE BOOK

More than 300 entertaining puzzles
to boost your brain power

Charles Timmerman
Founder of Funster.com

Adams Media
New York London Toronto Sydney New Delhi

Dedicated to Suzanne, Calla, and Meryl

An Everything® Series Book.
Everything® and everything.com® are registered trademarks of F+W Media, Inc.

Published by
Adams Media, a division of F+W Media, Inc.
57 Littlefield Street, Avon, MA 02322. U.S.A.
www.adamsmedia.com

ISBN 10: 1-4405-1233-7
ISBN 13: 978-1-4405-1233-9
eISBN 10: 1-4405-1234-5
eISBN 13: 978-1-4405-1234-6

Printed in the United States of America.

10 9 8 7 6 5 4 3 2 1

Contents

Acknowledgments

I would like to thank each and every one of the more than half a million people who have visited my website, *www.funster.com*, to play word games and puzzles. You have shown me how much fun puzzles can be, and how addictive they can become!

It is a pleasure to acknowledge the folks at Adams Media who made this book possible. I particularly want to thank my editor Lisa Laing for so skillfully managing the many projects we have worked on together.

Introduction

The History of Kakuro

▶ KAKURO WAS BORN in America and later acquired a Japanese name. It first appeared in 1966 in an American puzzle magazine published by Dell Magazines. They gave it the name "Cross Sums," which is still used today. In fact, these puzzles have always been popular with hard-core puzzlers. Recently cross sums (or kakuro) puzzles have gained more of a mainstream following.

In 1980 a Japanese man named Maki Kaji was in the United States on business. He was a puzzle connoisseur, so naturally he sampled some of the local fare. The ubiquitous crossword puzzles were not to his liking, as his English was not that good. However, he was able to devour cross-sum puzzles right away as they contained only numbers. Maki was so taken with these puzzles that he started creating and publishing them back in Japan. He renamed the puzzle "kasan kurosu," a combination of the Japanese word for "addition" and the Japanese pronunciation of the English word "cross." Soon it was abbreviated to kakuro, or sometimes kakro. Within a few years it became a craze in puzzle-obsessed Japan. Maki and his company, Nikoli, went on to sell about 1 million kakuro books.

Interestingly, kakuro has followed a course similar to its popular cousin, sudoku. Sudoku is also a puzzle that was invented in the United States and then made popular under a different name in Japan. The next step in both puzzles' conquest was England, another country filled with puzzle lovers. First sudoku and then kakuro were printed in British newspapers and popular books. As for the rest of the world, sudoku has led the way to an increased interest in puzzles across the globe. Following right along, kakuro is gaining fans all over the world, including back in the United States where it began.

The Rules of Kakuro

Kakuro is played on a grid that looks much like a crossword puzzle. In kakuro, the clues are sums located above or to the left of each entry. The object is to fill in the blank squares using the numbers 1 to 9 so that they add up to the sums. No number can be used more than once in a sum. There will always be just one solution for each puzzle.

How to Solve Kakuro Puzzles

There are many ways to solve a kakuro puzzle. This section explains the basic strategy to get you started. No doubt you will discover more techniques as you become a kakuro master.

Sum Combinations

Here's a quick puzzle: What three numbers from 1 to 9 will add up to 7 without repeating any number? In this case, there is only one answer: 1 + 2 + 4 = 7. So if a kakuro puzzle has 3 spaces and requires a sum of 7, then the numbers must be a 1, a 2, and a 4. We do not know the order of these numbers, but we will deal with this detail later. The table in Appendix B lists all of the possible combinations for any given number of spaces and sums. This table will tell us the possible numbers for any entry in a kakuro puzzle.

In many cases, there are numerous possible combinations of numbers, and the numbers can be arranged in any order. So this table will not really tell us all of the answers, of course. But it does give us a good starting point to work from. The real trick is to use logic to determine what number must go where. This is usually done by the process of elimination. Answers are determined by ruling out all but one possibility.

Learning by Example

This example will illustrate the basic approach to solving kakuro puzzles. We will completely solve a smaller kakuro puzzle.

The same strategies can be used in various ways to solve the puzzles in this book.

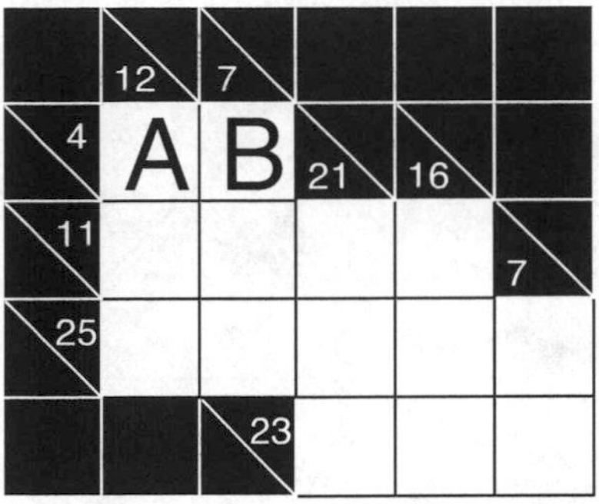

Figure 1-1

First we will determine AB in Figure 1-1. Using the table in Appendix B (or our own reasoning) we know that the three-number entry for the sum of 7 down must be 1, 2, and 4 (1 + 2 + 4). Similarly, the two-number entry for the sum of 4 across must be 1 and 3 (1 + 3). These two entries intersect at B and have only one number in common: a 1. Therefore, B must be a 1. No other number will work for both the down and across sums. It is easy to see that A must now be a 3, so that A + B will equal 4.

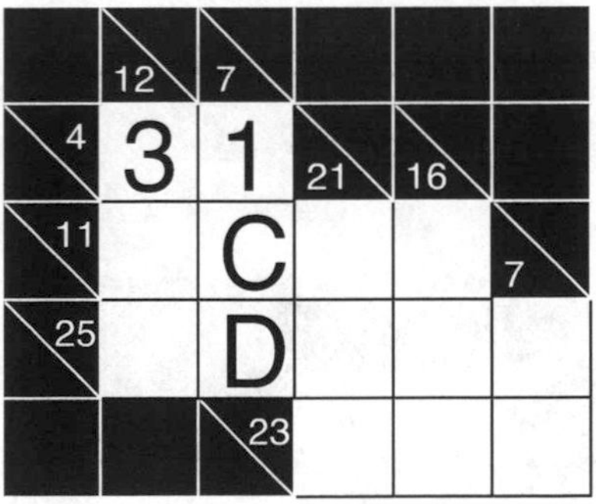

Figure 1-2

Moving on, let's determine CD in Figure 1-2. We know that C must be either a 2 or a 4 to complete the sum of 7 down. Let's try to find a clue to help us pick one of these two numbers for C. Notice the four-number entry for the sum of 11 across must be 1, 2, 3, 5. Since C is one of these digits, we must pick the 2 because the 4 is not possible. And D must be a 4, to complete the sum for 7 down.

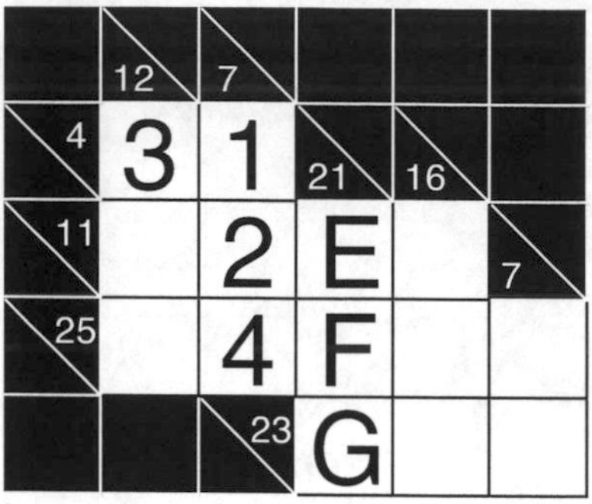

Figure 1-3

It is now possible to figure out EFG in Figure 1-3. From our previous entry, we know that E must be a 1, 5, or 3 as part of the sum of 11 across. There are multiple possibilities for the three-number entry for the sum of 21 down: 4, 8, 9; 5, 7, 9; or 6, 7, 8. We can see that E must be a 5, because it is the only number in common with both the across sum and the possible down sums. This means that the entry for the sum of 21 down can only be 5, 7, 9. Let's determine if G is the remaining 7 or 9. The three-number entry for the sum of 23 across must be 6, 8, 9. So G must be a 9, because it is the only number that will work for both the across sum and the down sum. Obviously F must be a 7 to complete the sum for 21 down.

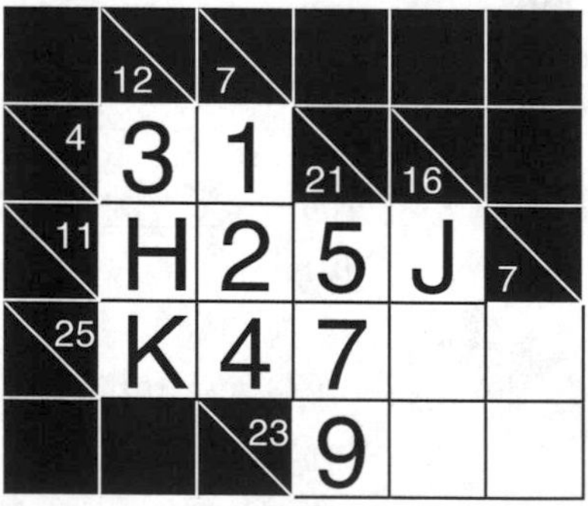

Figure 1-4

Now we can determine HJK in Figure 1-4. Since H is part of the sum of 11 across, it must be either the remaining 1 or 3. We can rule out the 3 because it is already found in the box above H. Of course, numbers can only be used once in any sum. Thus, H must be a 1. Therefore, J must be a 3 and K an 8 to complete the sums.

Figure 1-5

We can figure out entry LMNP in Figure 1-5. There are fully twelve possibilities for a five-number entry for the sum of 25 across, but only one of the twelve includes 8, 4, 7 as is required from our previous results. That only possibility is 1, 4, 5, 7, and 8, which leaves either a 1 or a 5 for L. Now let's look at the possibilities for L's column, a three-number entry for the sum of 16 down that must include a 3: 3, 4, 9; 3, 5, 8; and 3, 6, 7. This narrows the possibility for L to just a 5. It is a simple matter to complete the sums: M must be a 1, N an 8, and P a 6.

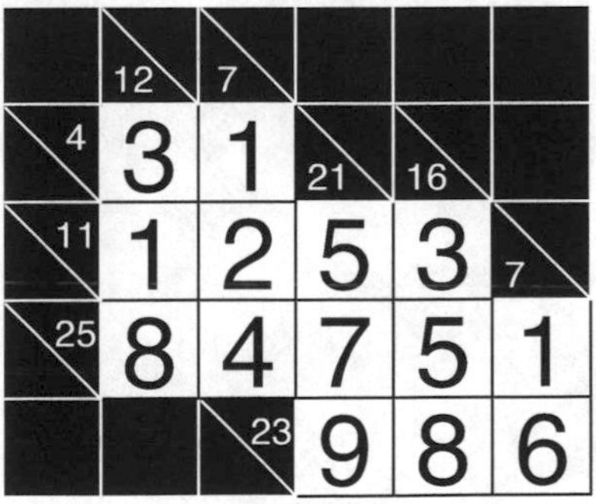

Figure 1-6

Figure 1-6 shows the completed puzzle. Admittedly, we made this example look somewhat easy by analyzing paths we knew would pay off. In the real world, a lot of trial and error is required to unlock the answers. Your persistence and ingenuity will solve any of these puzzles!

Tips

- Start with the shortest entries.
- Look for the smallest and largest sums; they will have the fewest possible combinations of answers.
- Use the Sum Combinations table in Appendix B as a starting point to determine the possible combinations for an entry.
- For each space, use the sums from both the row and the column to narrow down the possibilities.
- Write down possible combinations in the margins or on scrap paper.
- Use a pencil and an eraser. Changes are common!
- Don't dwell on just one section of the puzzle, especially if you get stumped.
- Follow the numbers: One answer will often unlock more answers.
- Never give up! Put the board aside and you might be surprised how easy it is to solve later with a fresh look.
- Teach yourself! One of the joys of kakuro is discovering new strategies and methods that work for you.

PART 1

Mildly Challenging Puzzles

1

2

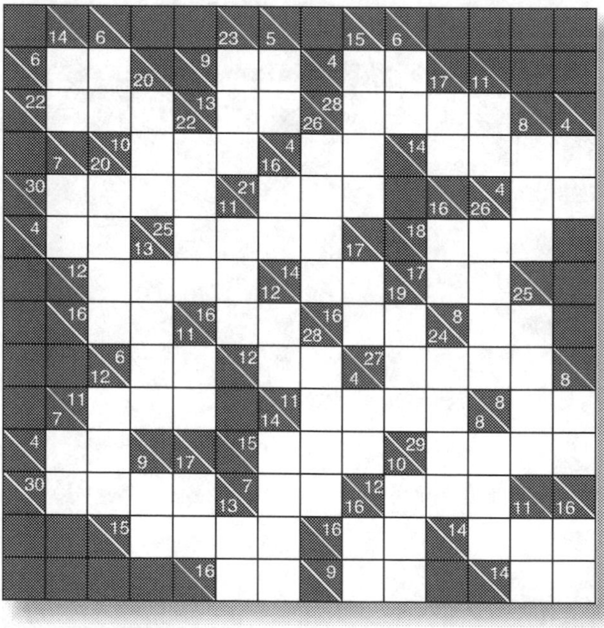

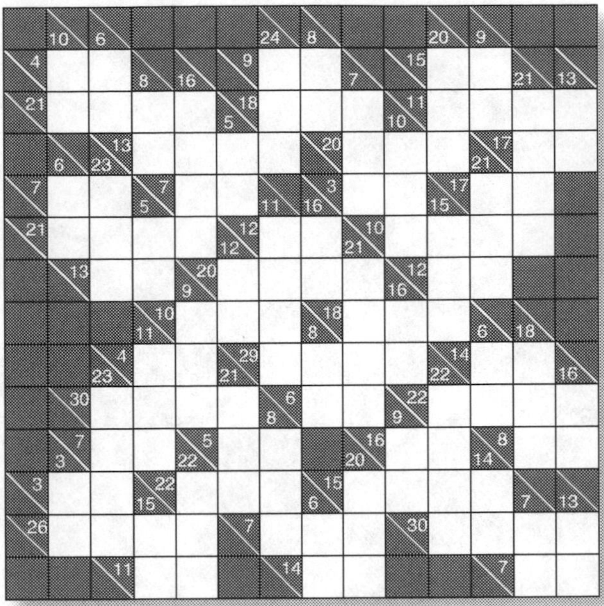

3

4

5

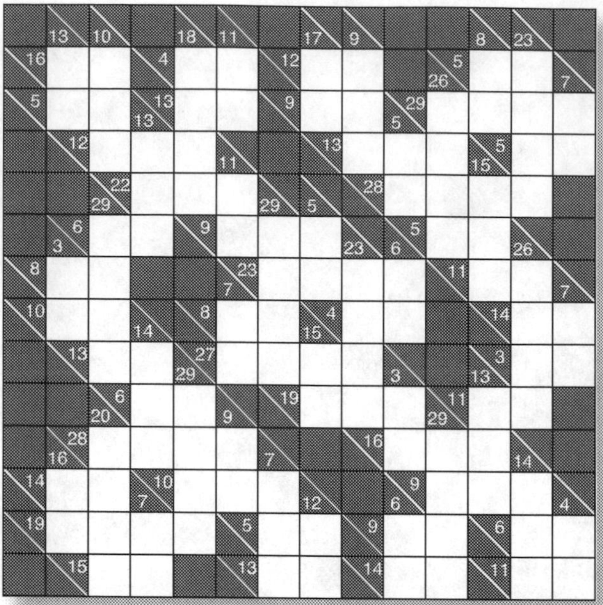
13 10 18 11 17 9 8 23
16 4 12 5 26 7
5 13 13 9 29 5
12 11 13 5 15
22 29 29 5 28
6 3 9 23 5 6 26
8 23 7 11 7
10 14 8 4 15 14
13 27 29 3 3 13
6 20 9 19 11 29
28 16 7 16 14
14 10 7 12 9 6 4
19 5 9 6
15 13 14 11

6

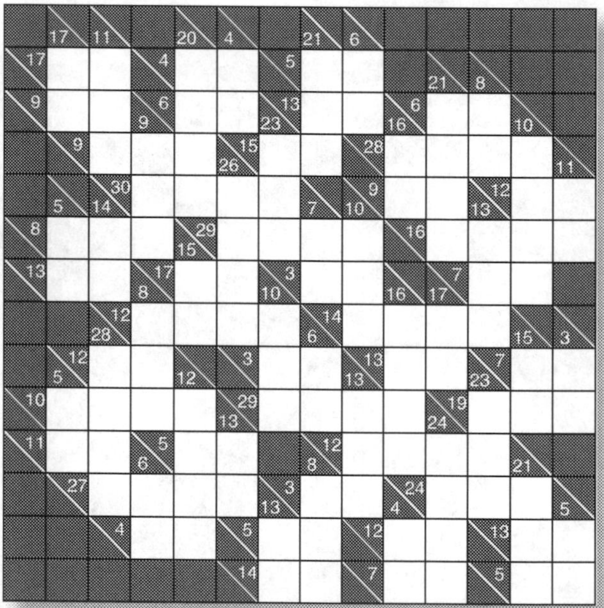
17 11 20 4 21 6
17 4 5 21 8
9 6 9 13 23 6 16 10
9 15 26 28 11
5 30 14 7 9 10 12 13
8 29 15 16
13 17 8 3 10 16 7 17
12 28 14 6 15 3
12 5 12 3 13 13 7 23
10 29 13 19 24
11 5 6 12 8 21
27 3 13 24 4 5
4 5 12 13
14 7 5

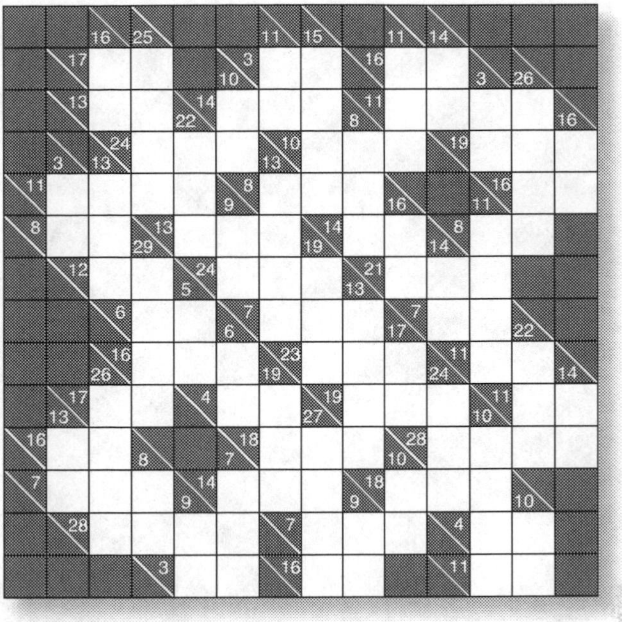

7

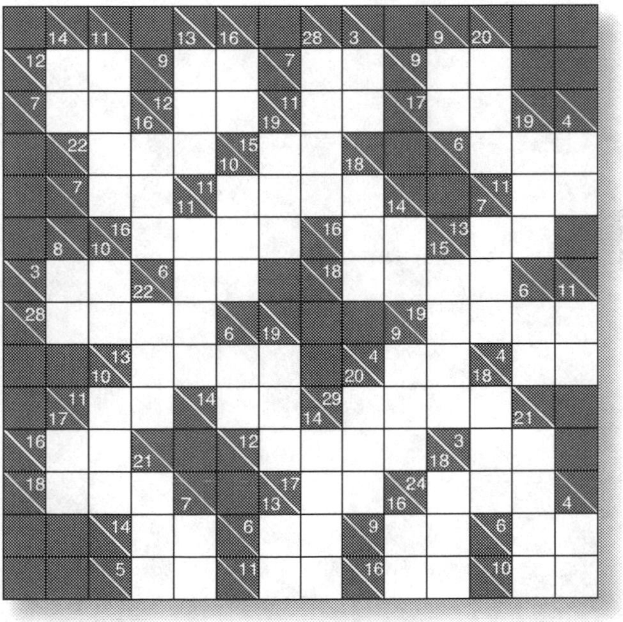

8

9

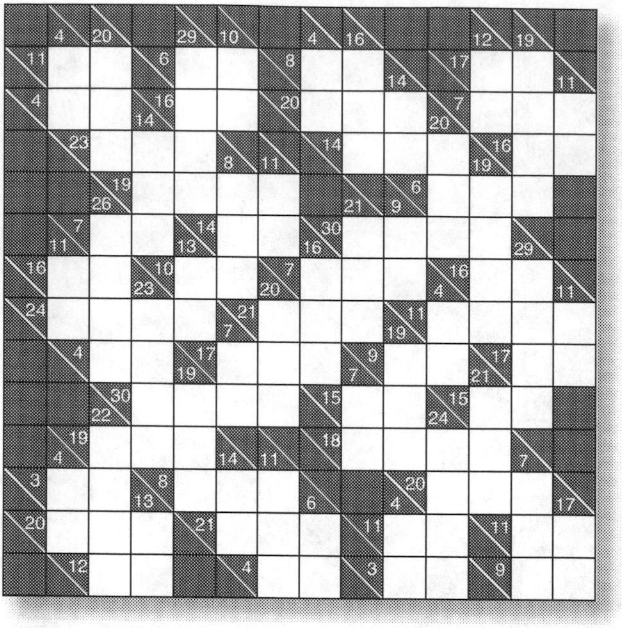

10

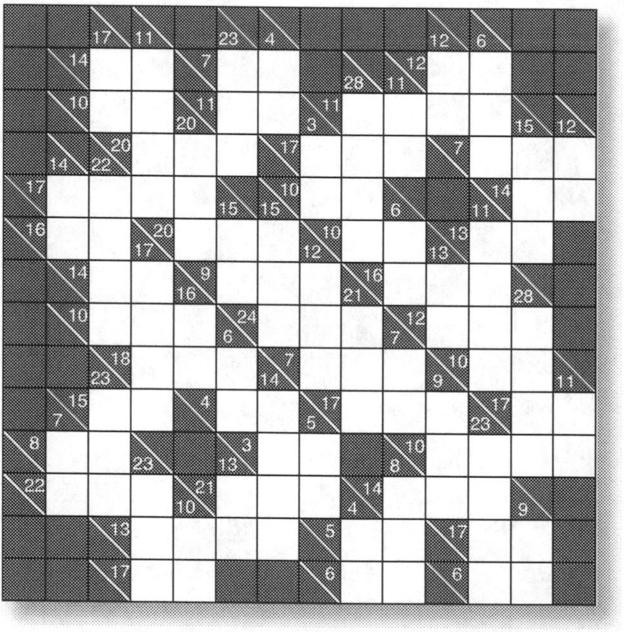

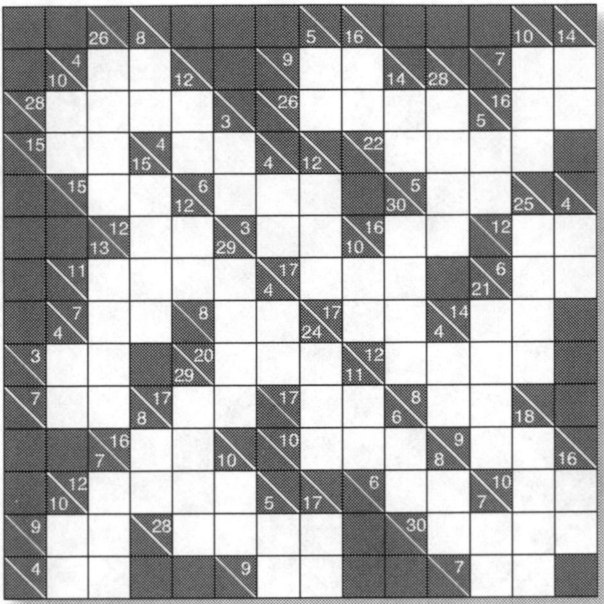

11

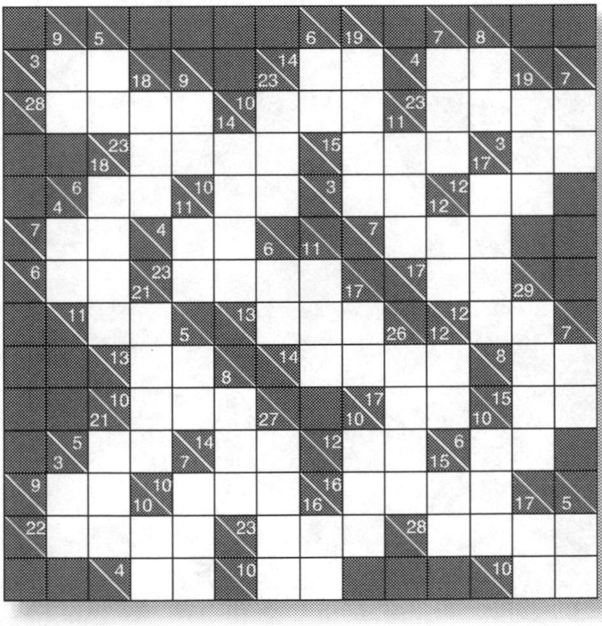

12

13

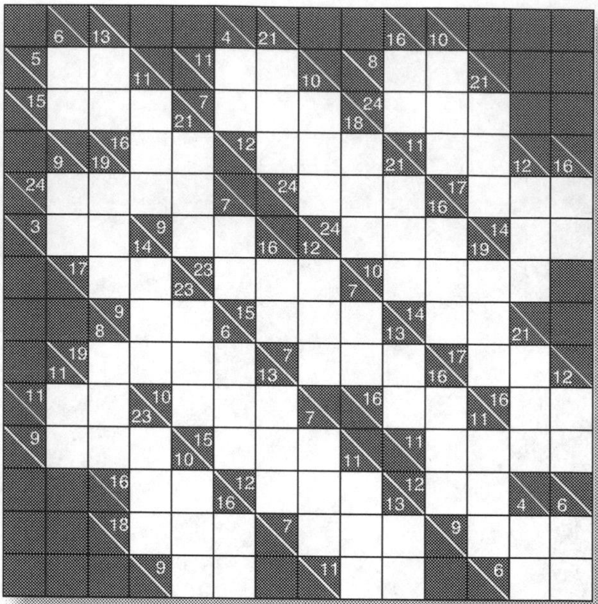

14

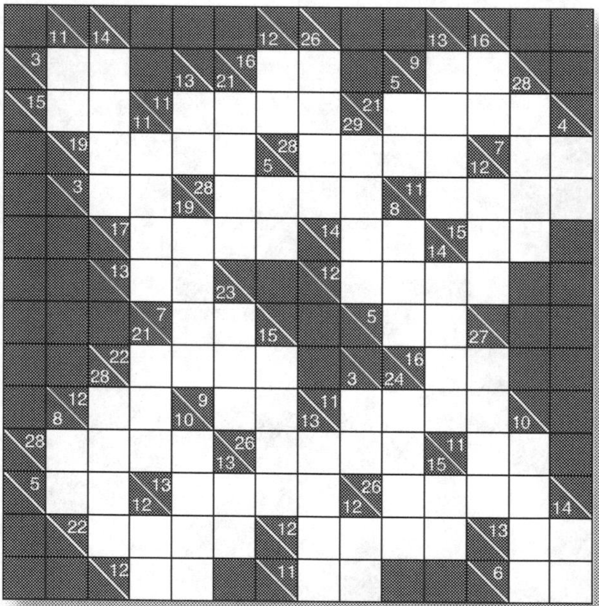

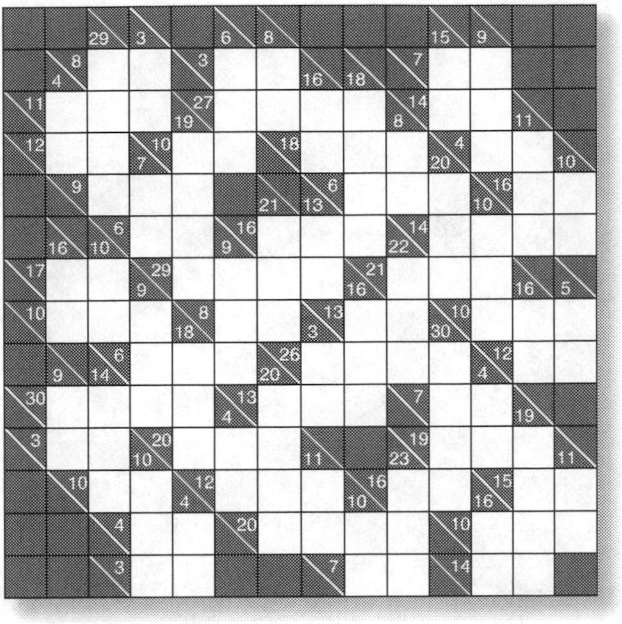

15

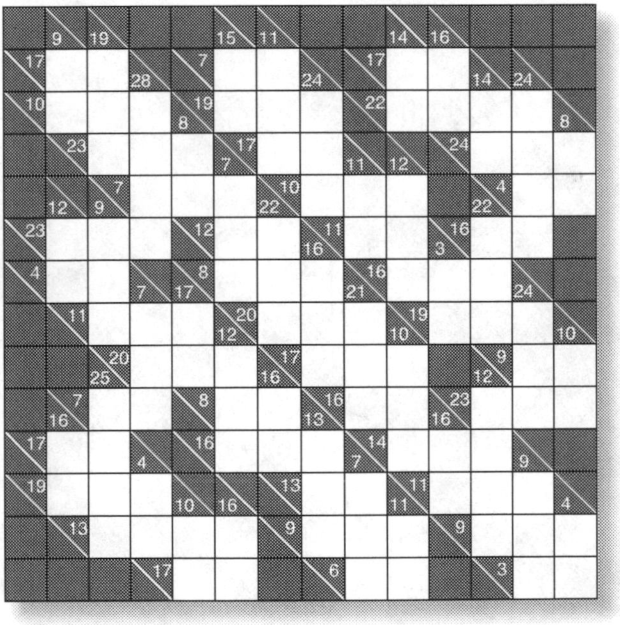

16

17

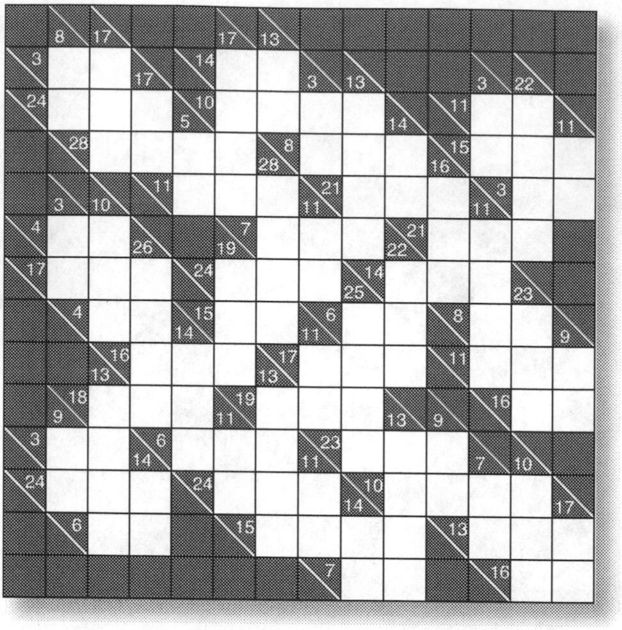

18

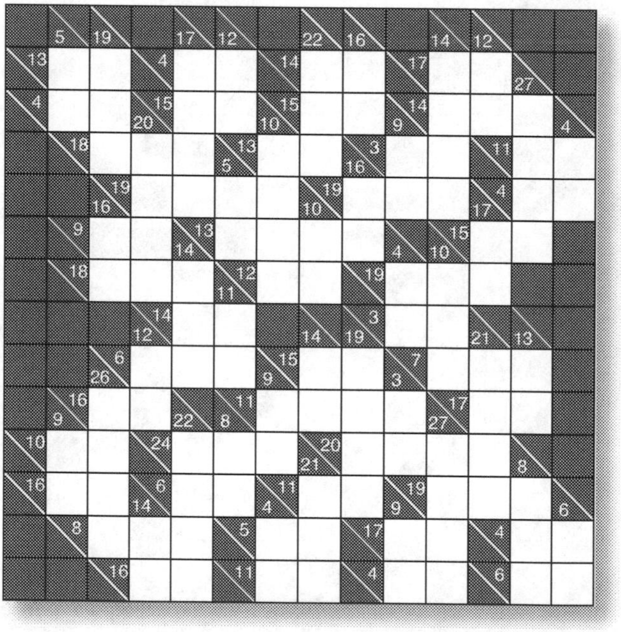

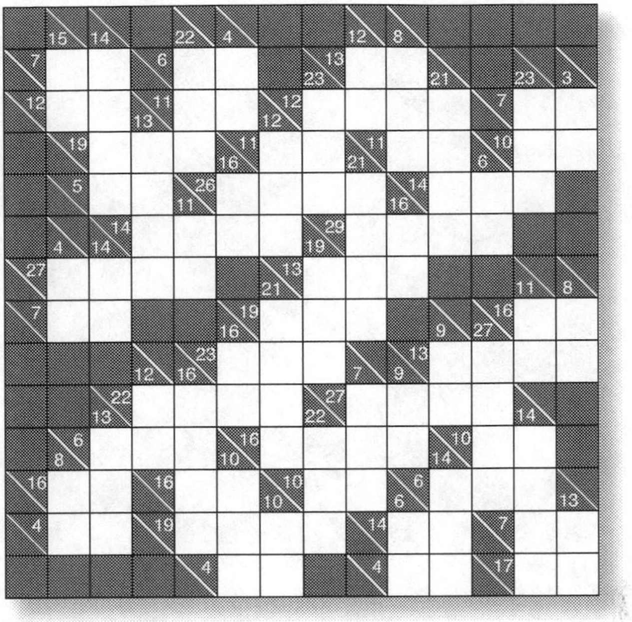

19

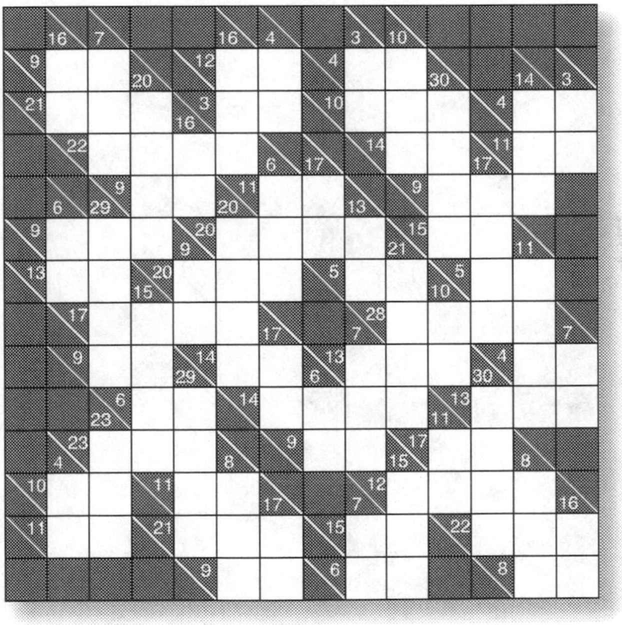

20

21

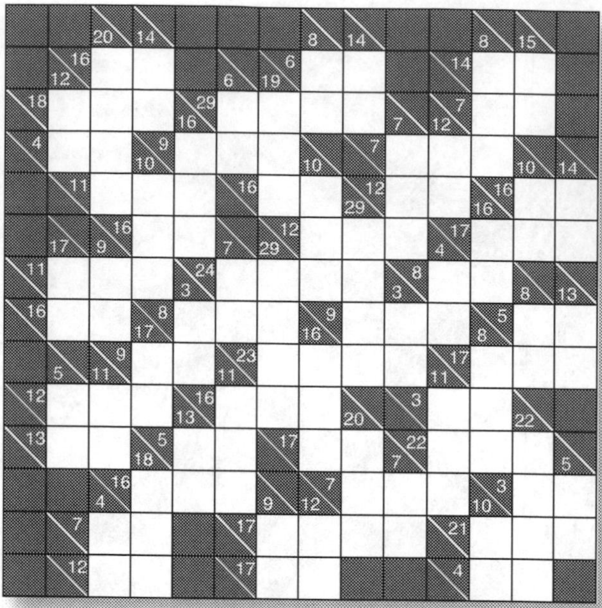
20 14 8 14 8 15
16 12 6 19 6 14
18 29 16 7 12 7
4 9 10 10 7 10 14
11 16 12 29 16 16
16 17 9 7 12 29 17 4
11 24 3 8 3 8 13
16 8 17 9 16 5 8
9 5 11 23 11 17 11
12 16 13 20 3 22
13 5 18 17 22 7 5
16 4 7 9 12 3 10
7 17 21
12 17 4

22

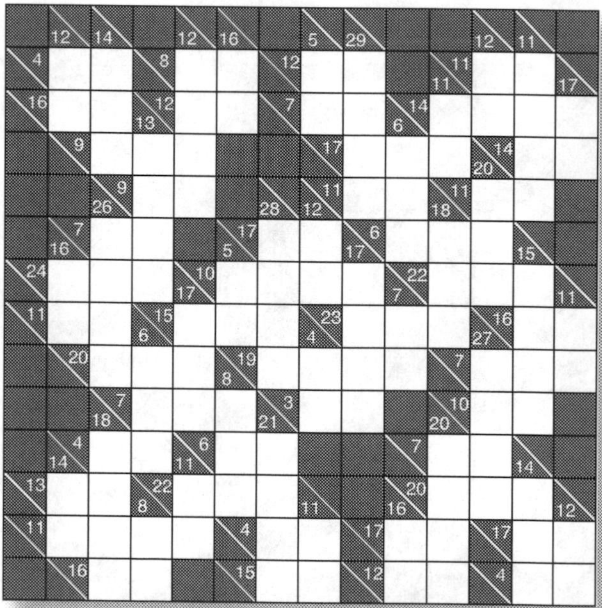
12 14 12 16 5 29 12 11
4 8 12 11 11 17
16 12 13 7 14 6
9 17 14 20
9 26 28 11 12 11 18
7 16 17 5 6 17 15
24 10 17 22 7 11
11 15 6 23 4 16 27
20 19 8 7
7 18 3 21 10 20
4 14 6 11 7 14
13 22 8 11 20 16 12
11 4 17 17
16 15 12 4

23

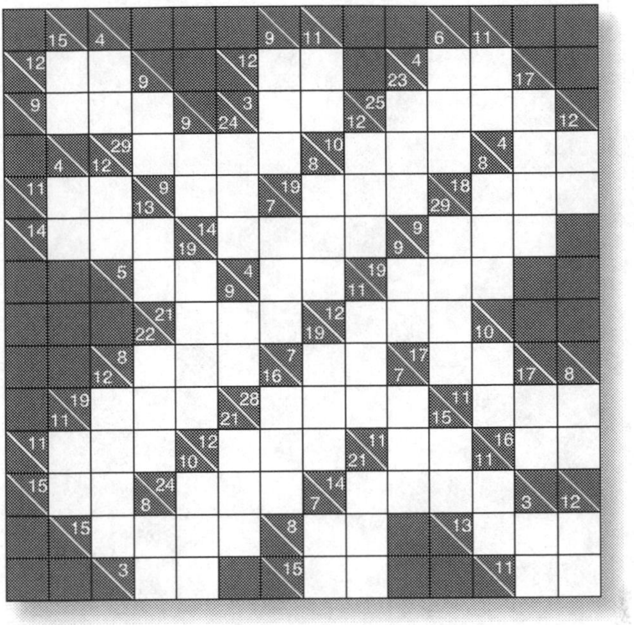

24

25

26

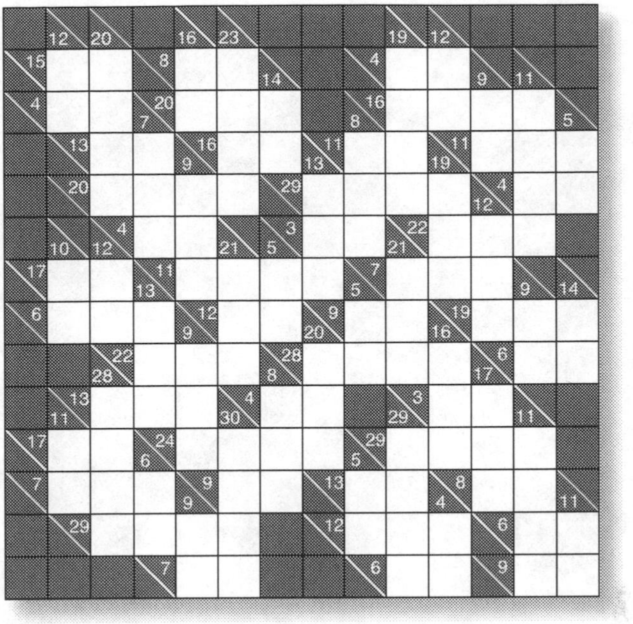

27

28

29

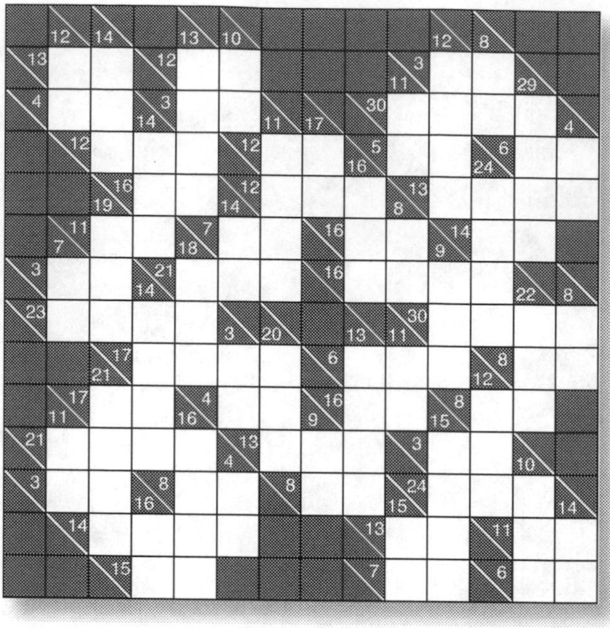

30

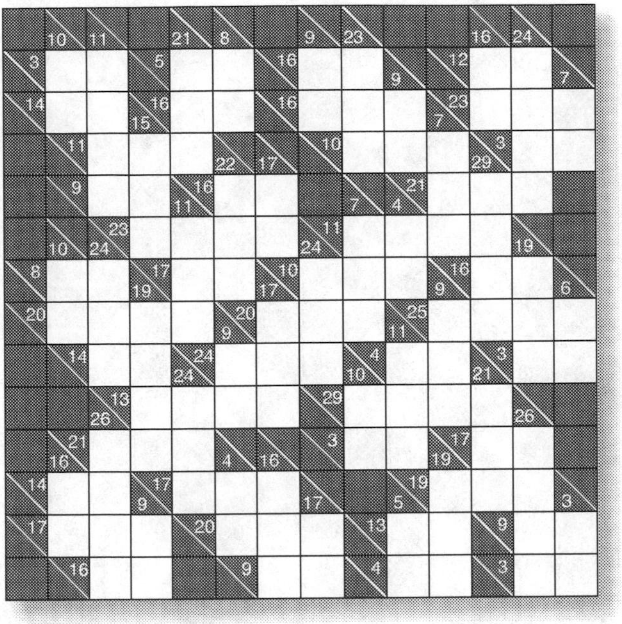

31

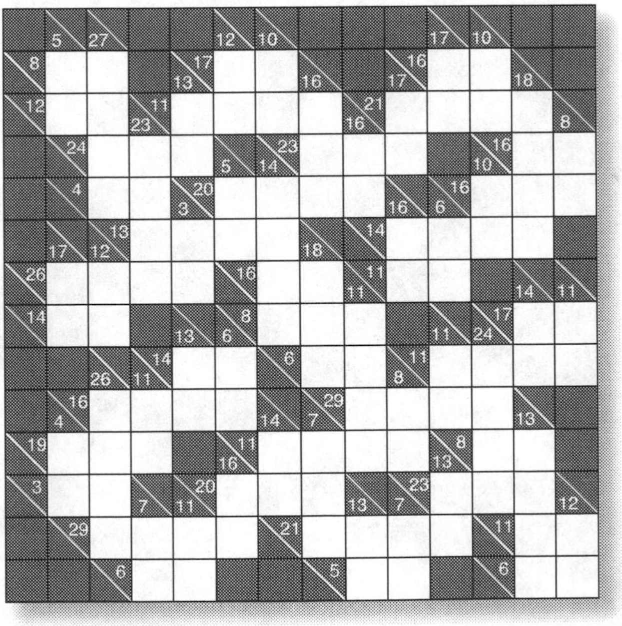

32

33

7 7 19 17 14 11 11 11
6 17 12 9 13 16
4 16 23 8 14
15 13 15 12 8 25
8 7 28 3 11 17 15
24 13 7 13 14
5 21 19 20 16
14 12 6 21 12 12
11 14 7 4 16
23 10 16 16 15 13
6 10 10 4 16 21
13 6 10 15 12 6 4
7 9 4 12
3 10 7 5

34

9 26 8 11 11 16 11 16
17 3 12 10
8 14 22 4 9 10
13 11 11 21 11 12 7
28 12 13 4 4 30
5 15 21 4 10 23 13
12 8 11 10 13
7 8 23 3 4 7
11 9 5 13 17 14 19 9
22 12 12 16 12 29
4 23 14 11 15
10 9 17 22 6 17
3 12 12 17
16 10 4 15

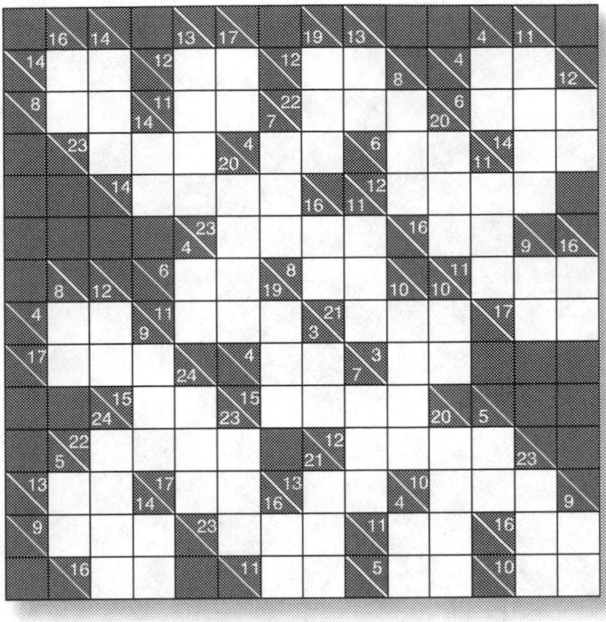

35

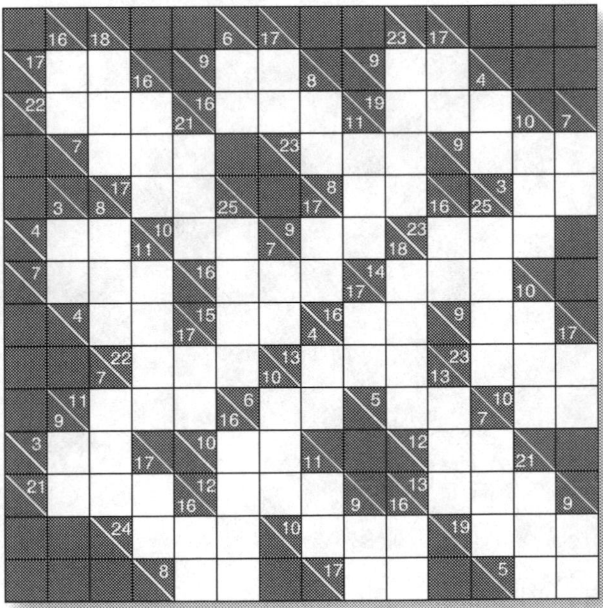

36

37

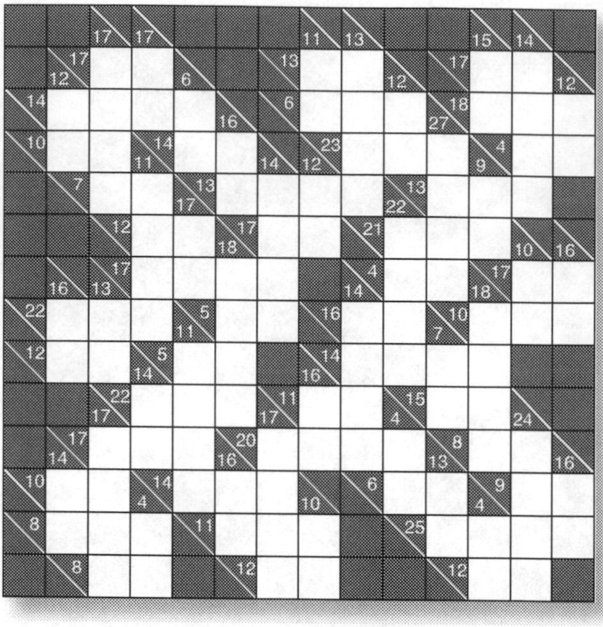

38

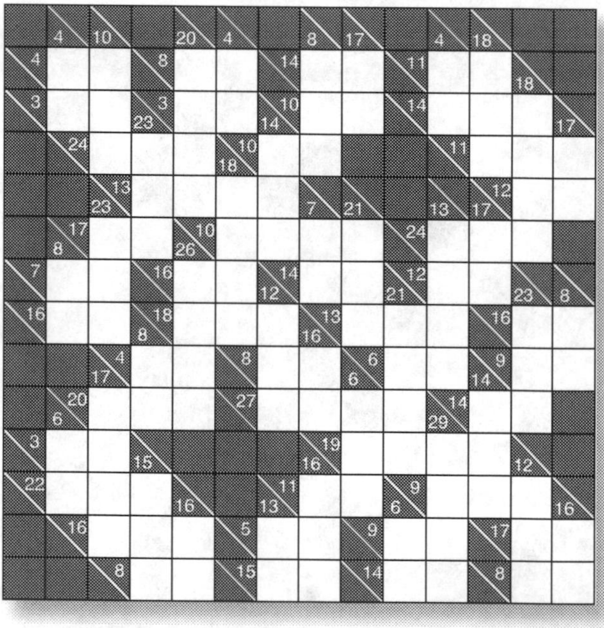

39

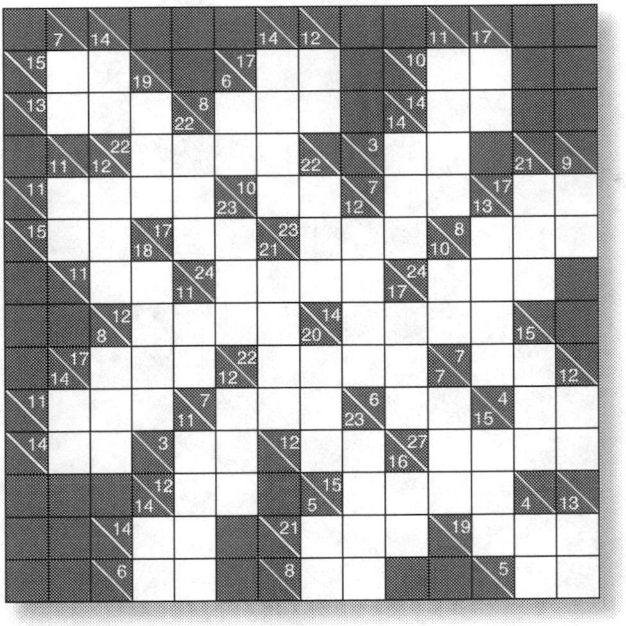

40

41

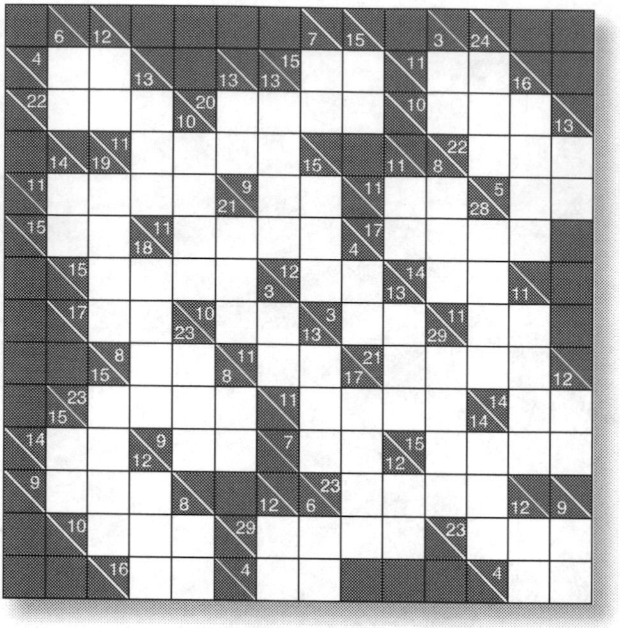

42

43

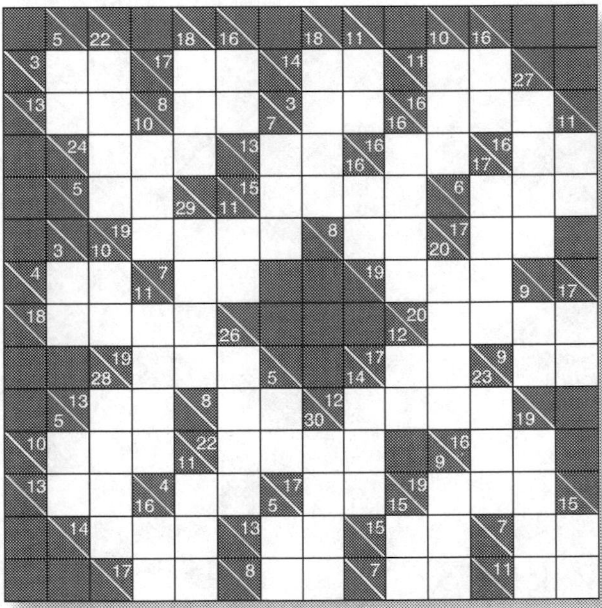

44

45

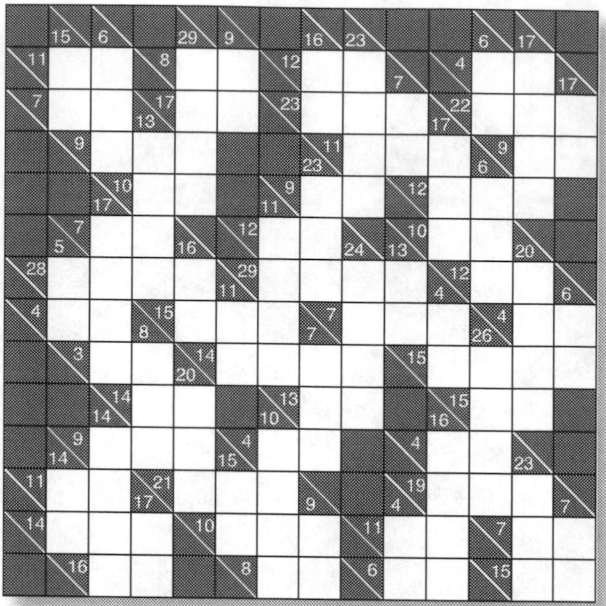

46

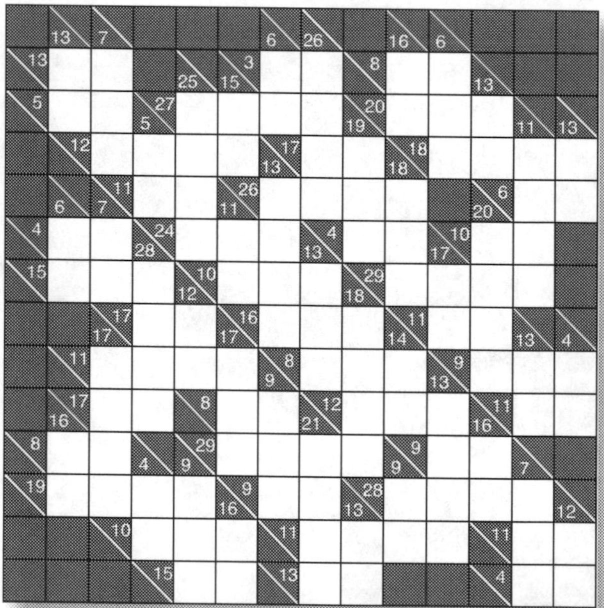

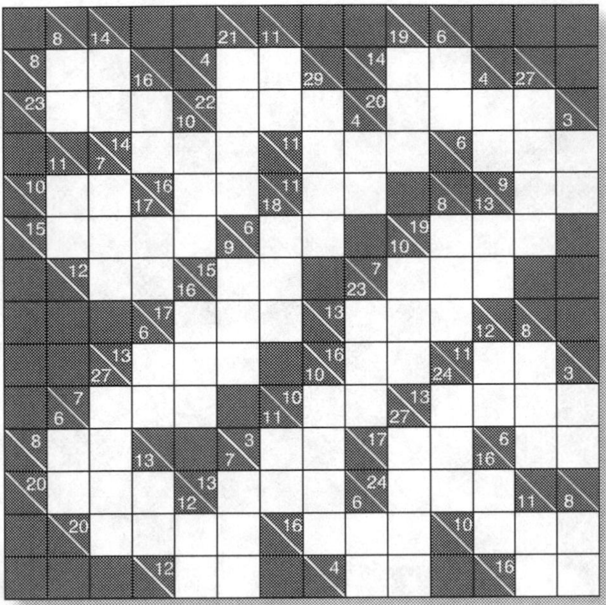

47

48

49

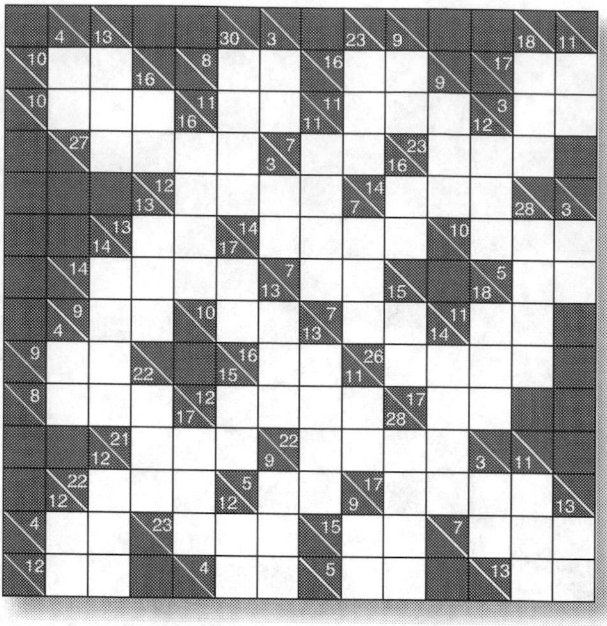

50

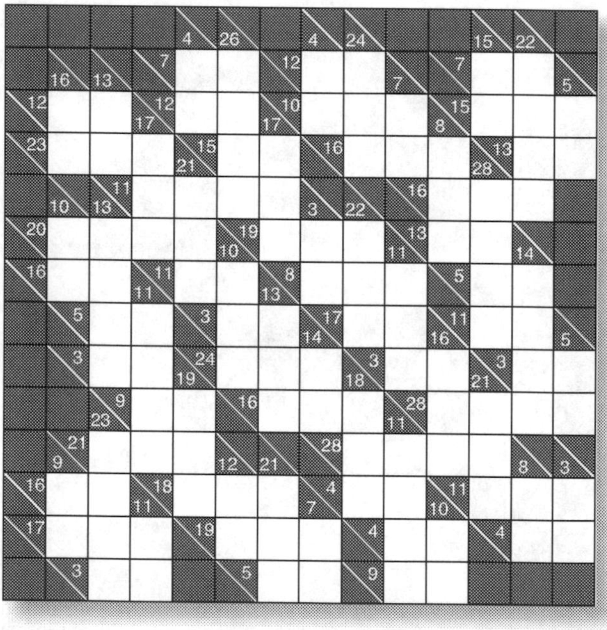

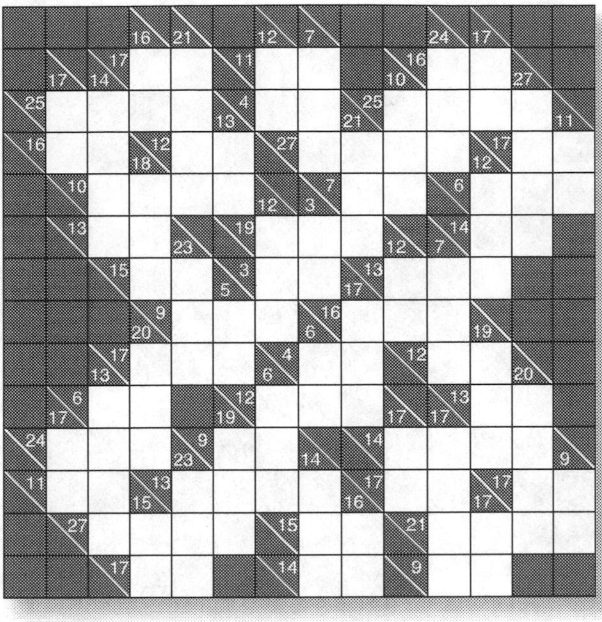

51

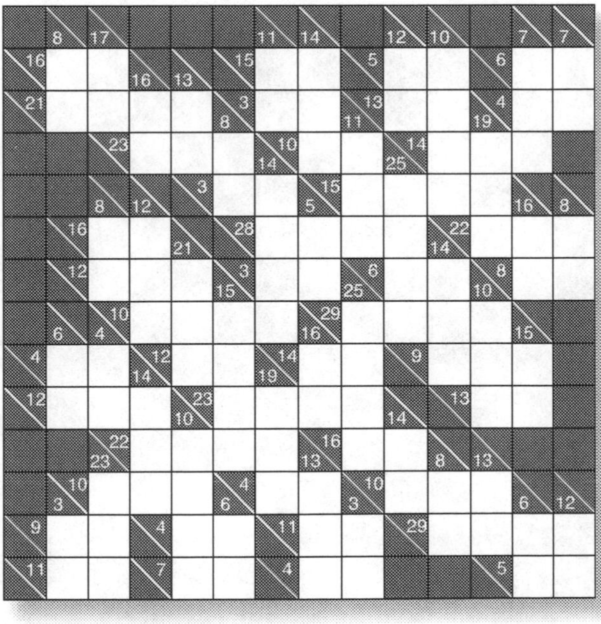

52

53

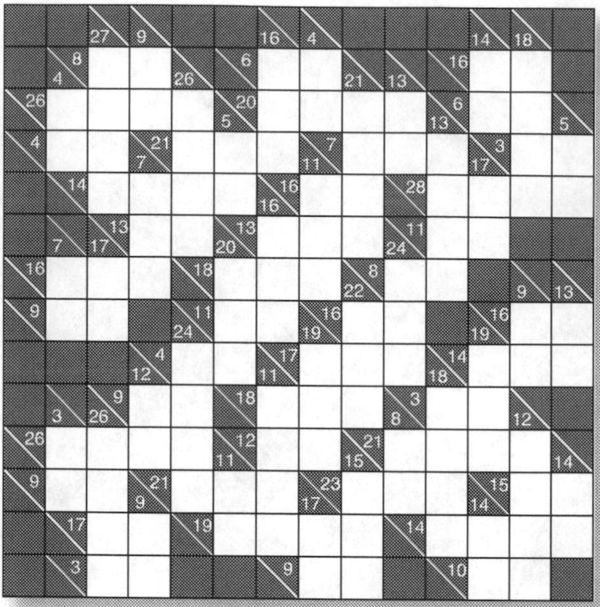

54

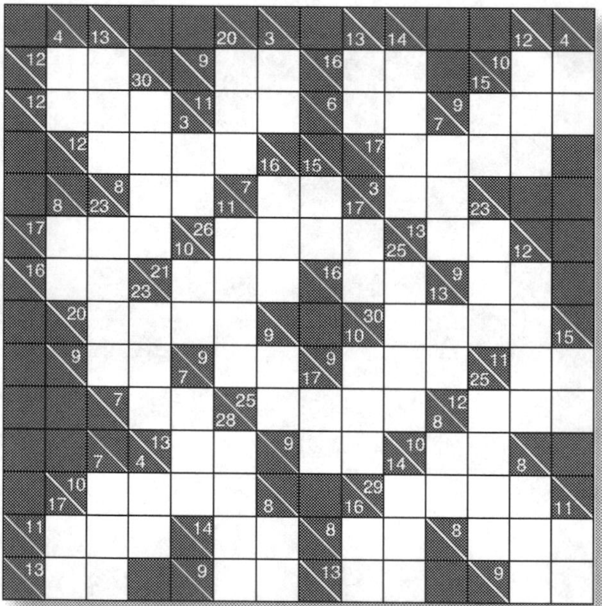

55

56

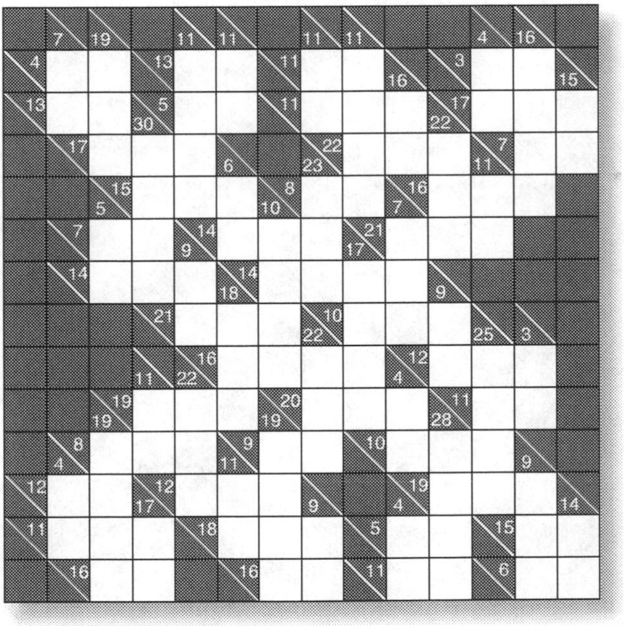

57

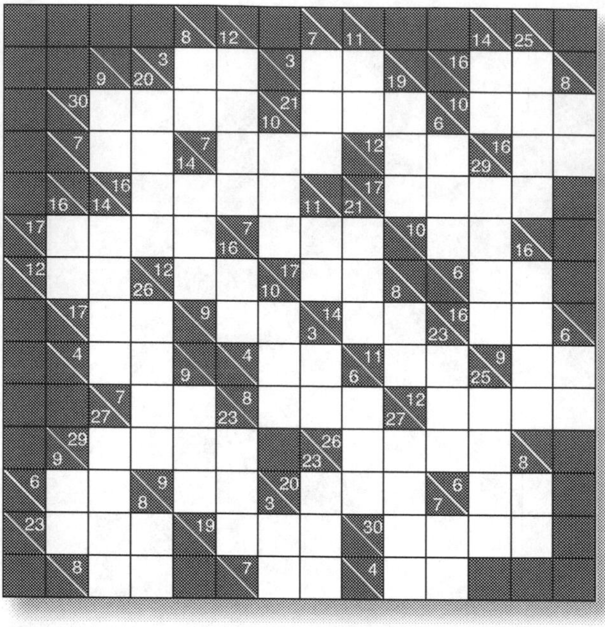

58

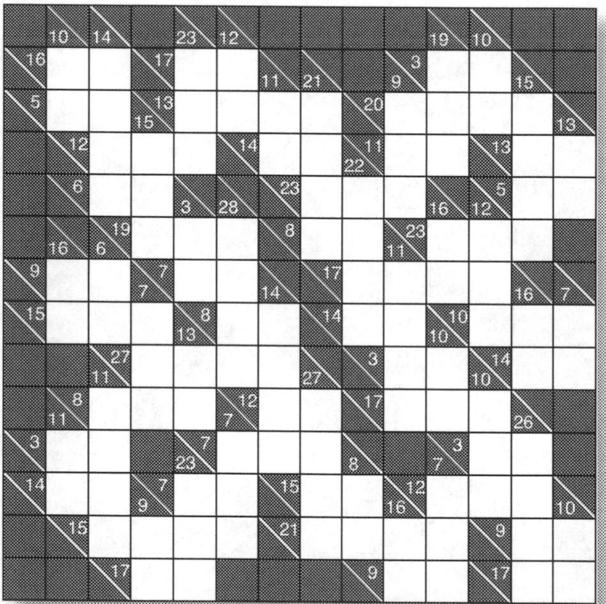

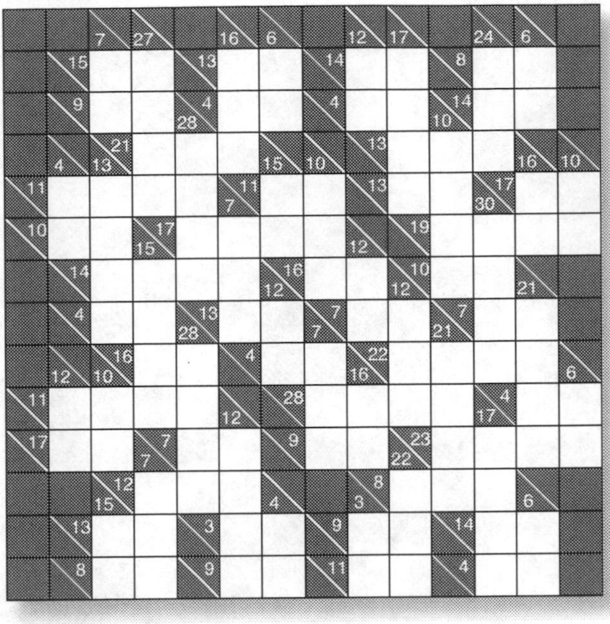

59

60

61

62

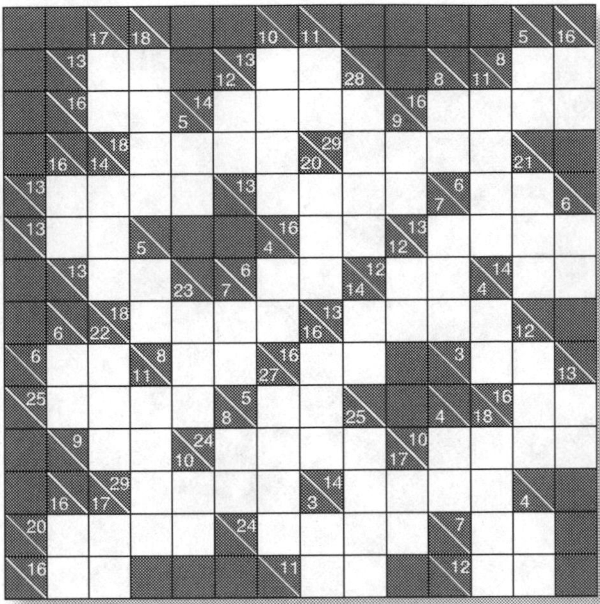

63

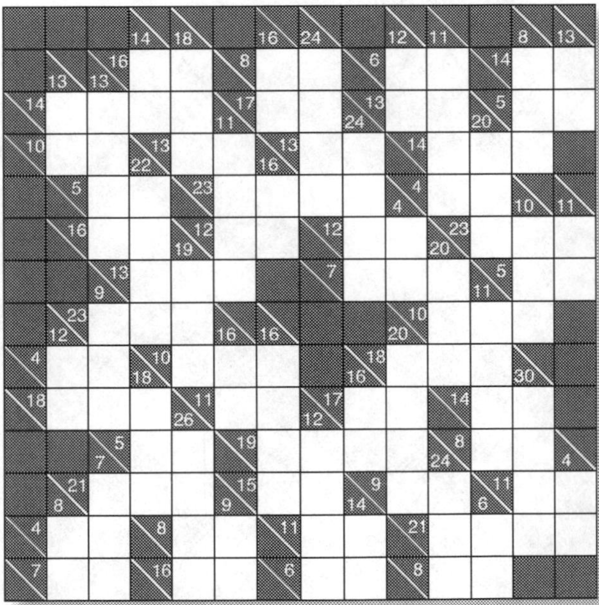

64

65

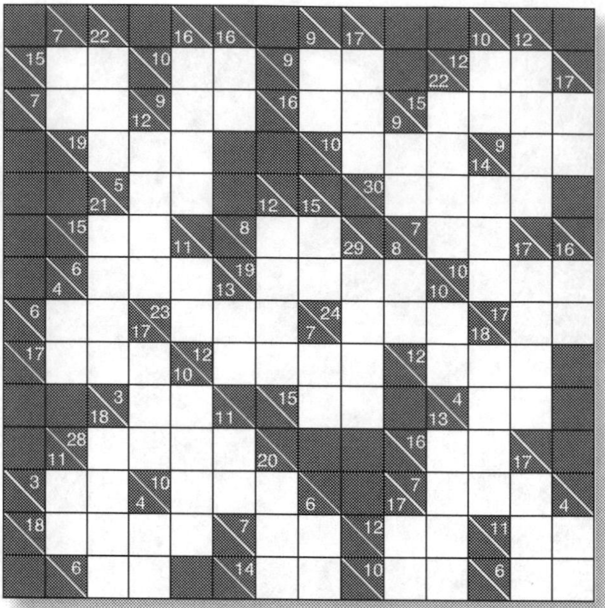

66

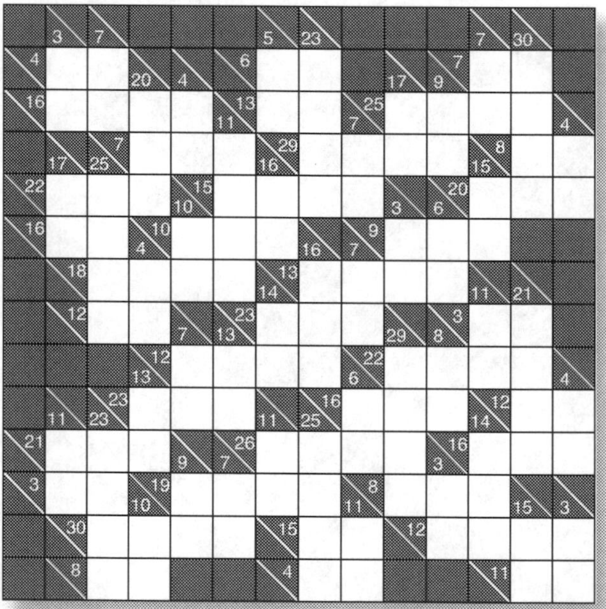

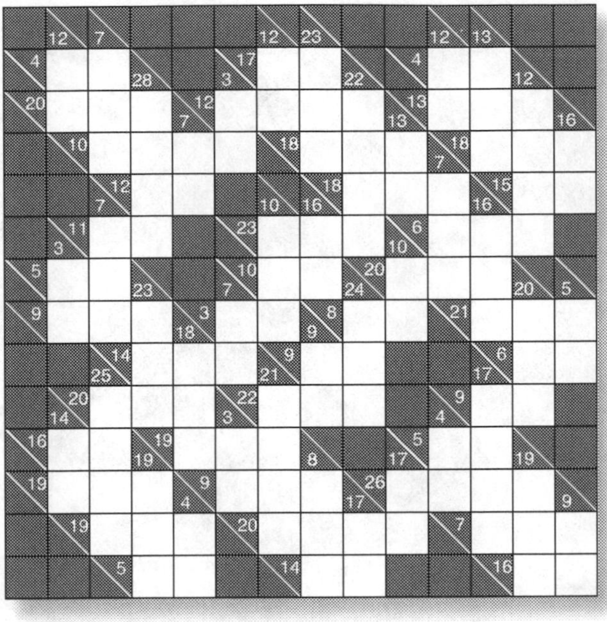

67

68

69

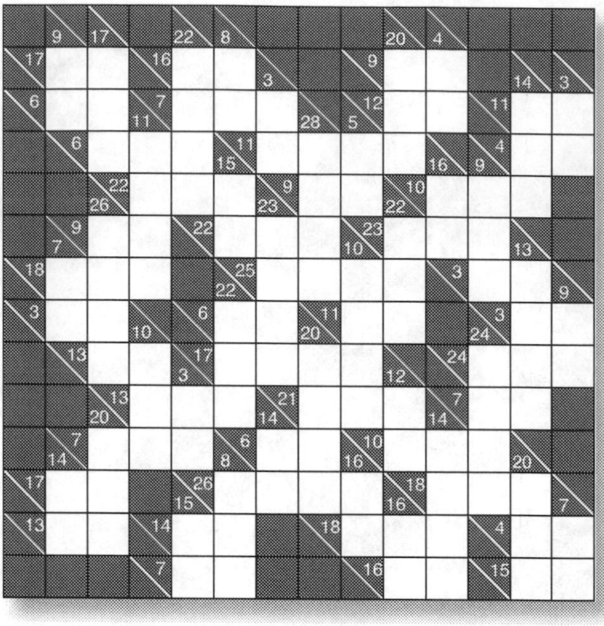

70

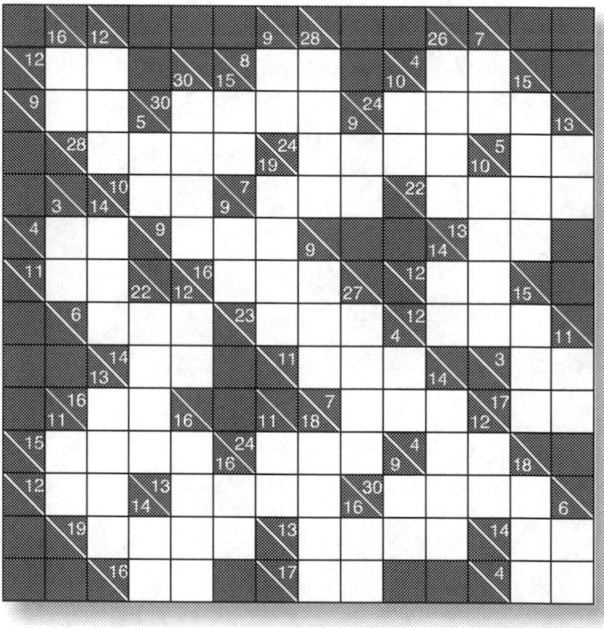

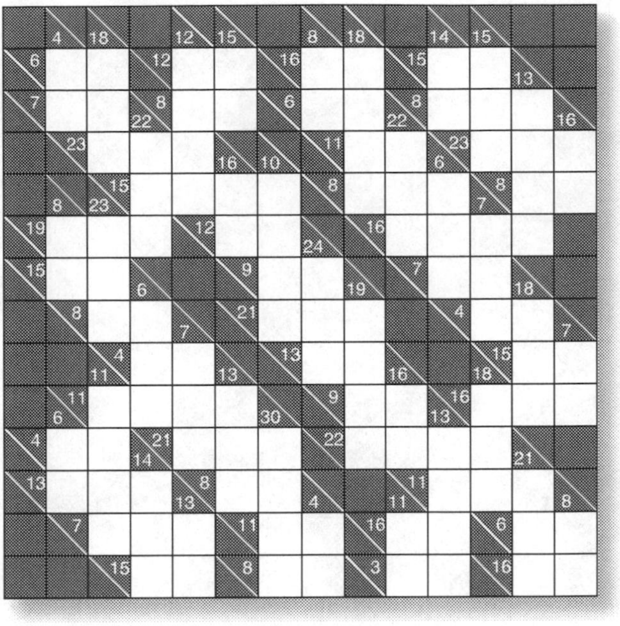

71

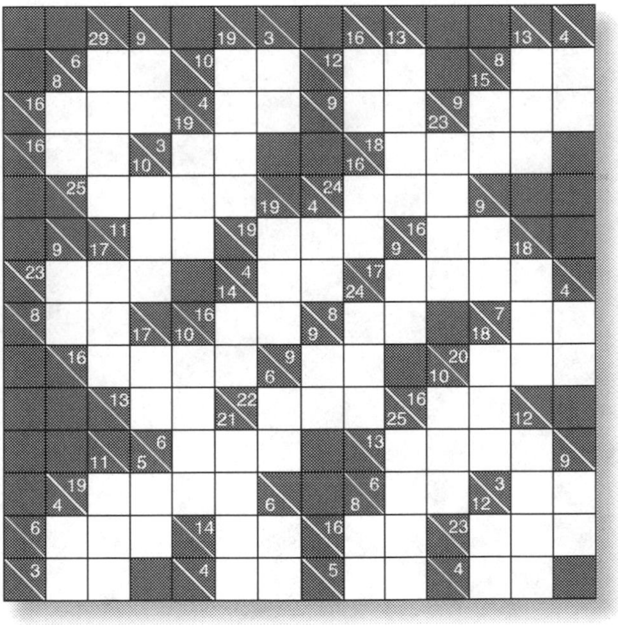

72

73

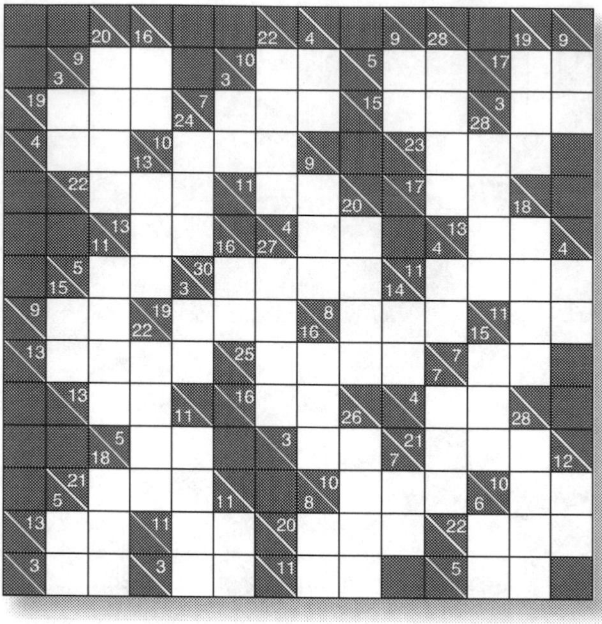

74

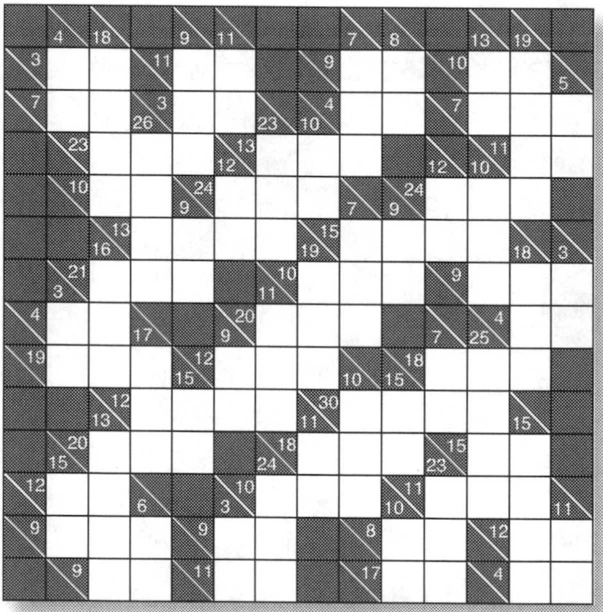

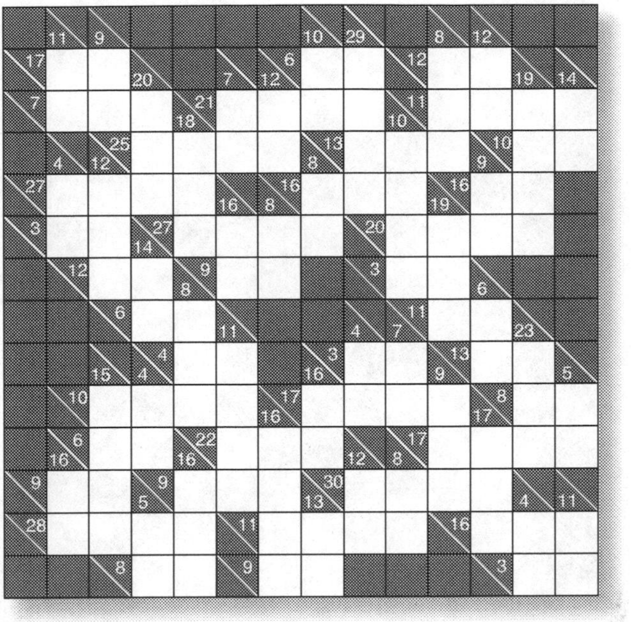

75

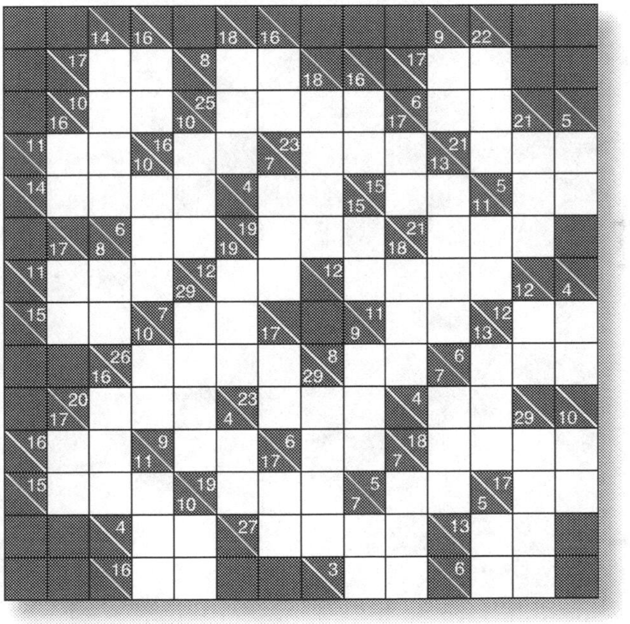

76

77

78

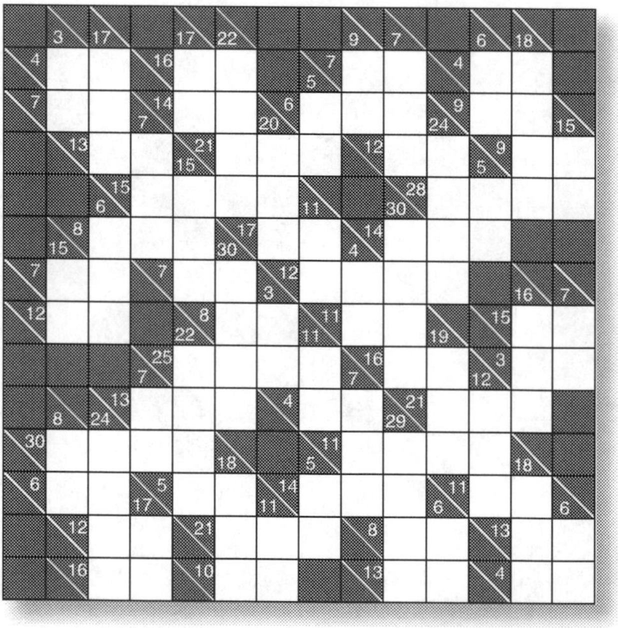

79

80

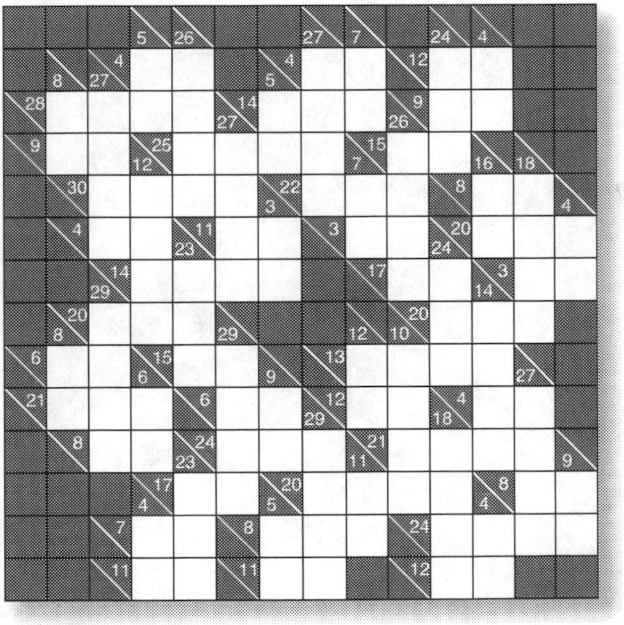

81

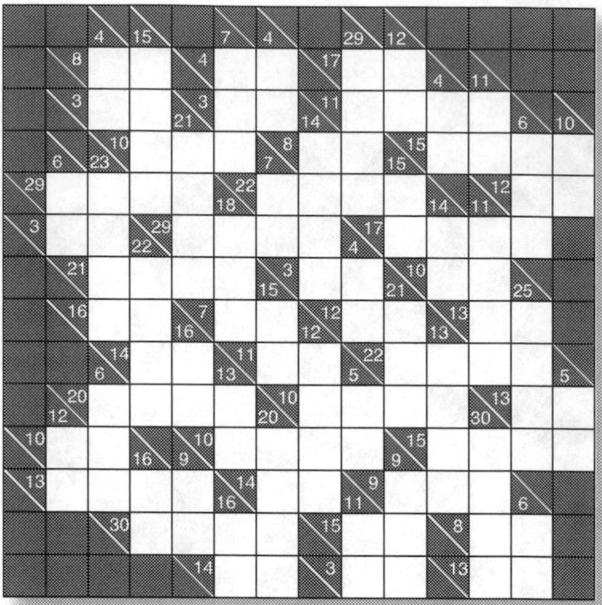

82

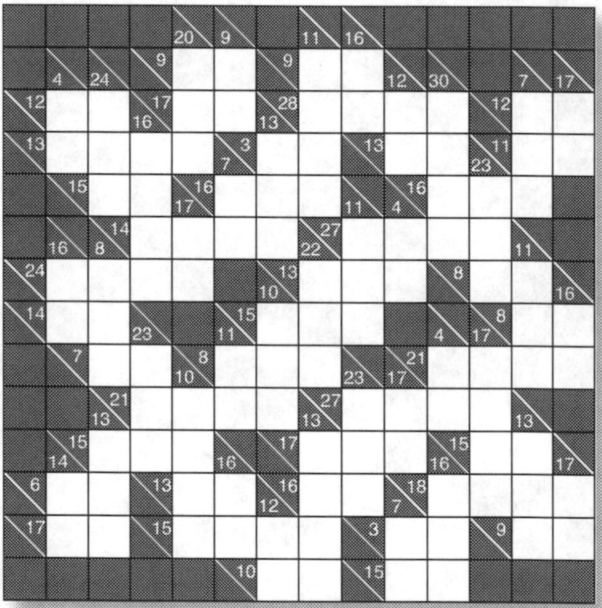

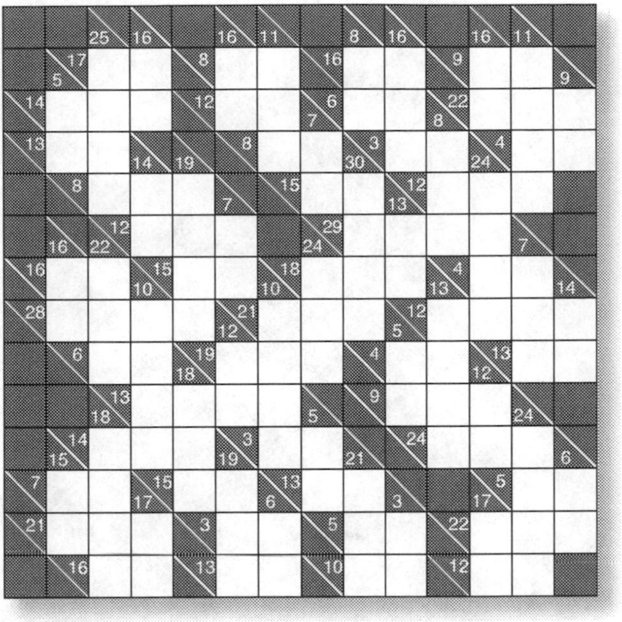

83

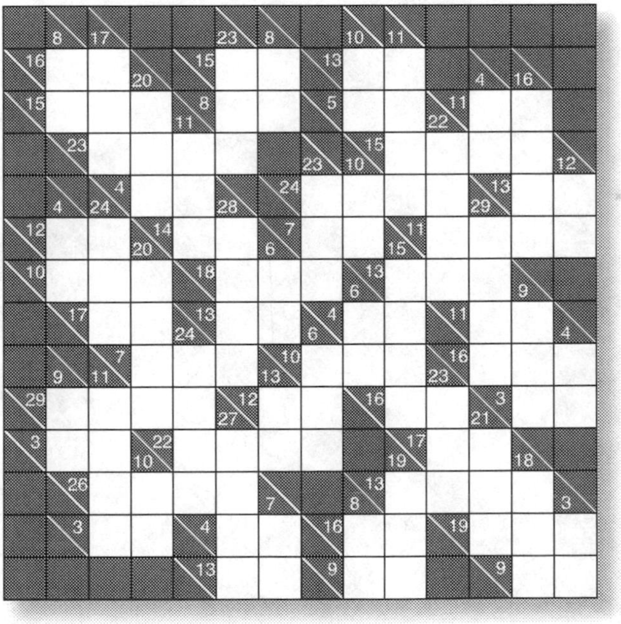

84

85

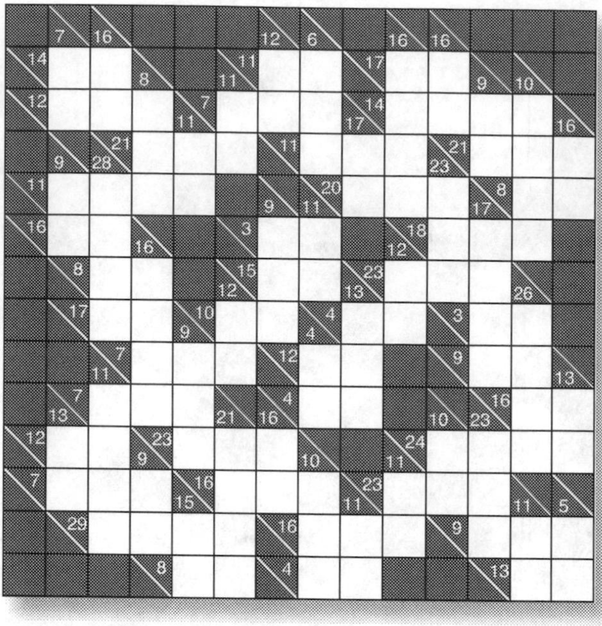

86

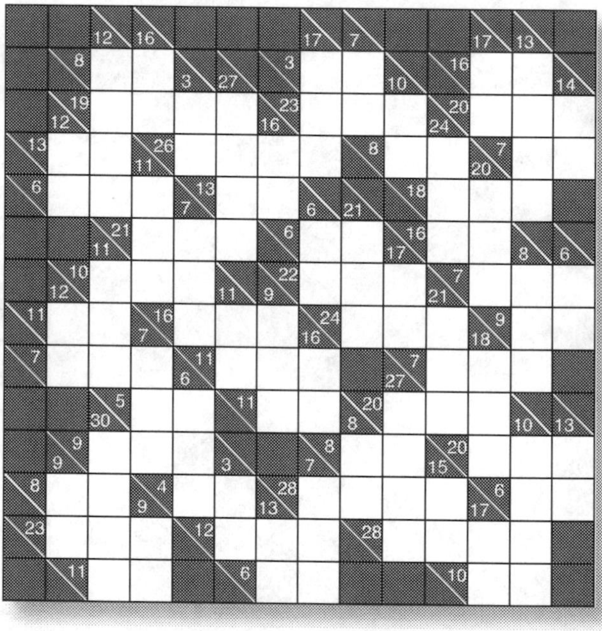

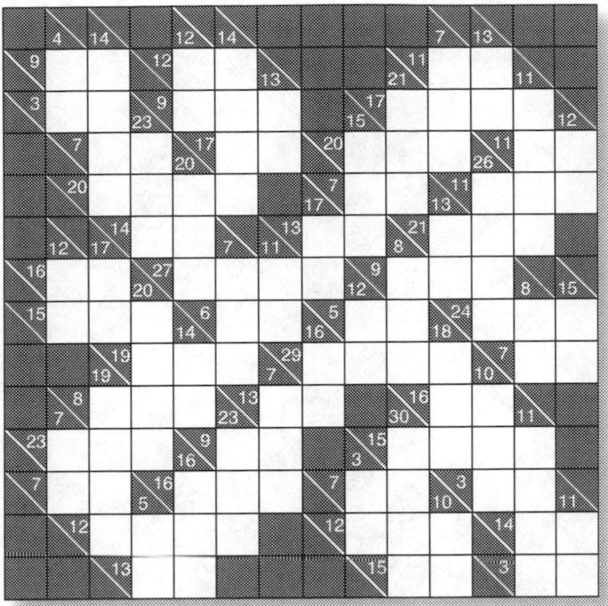

87

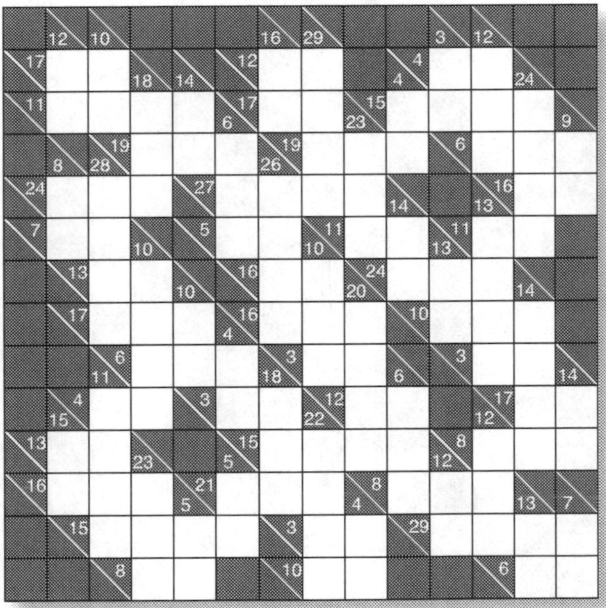

88

89

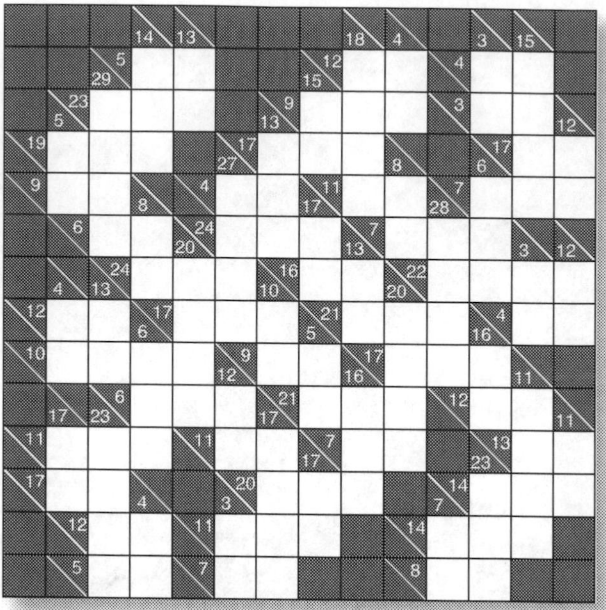

90

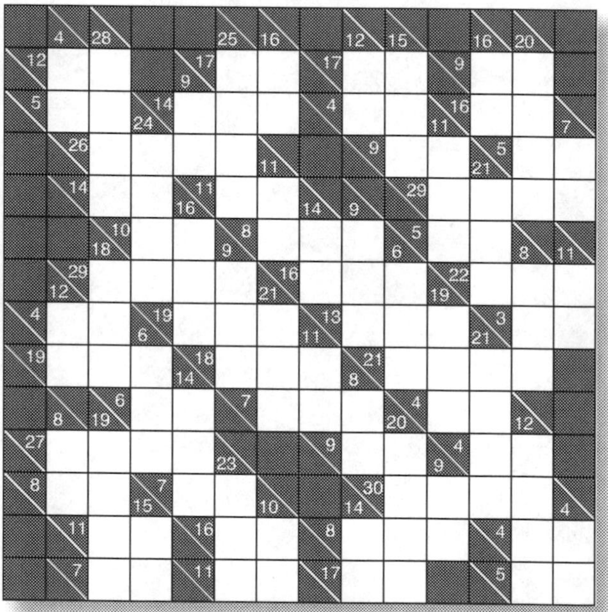

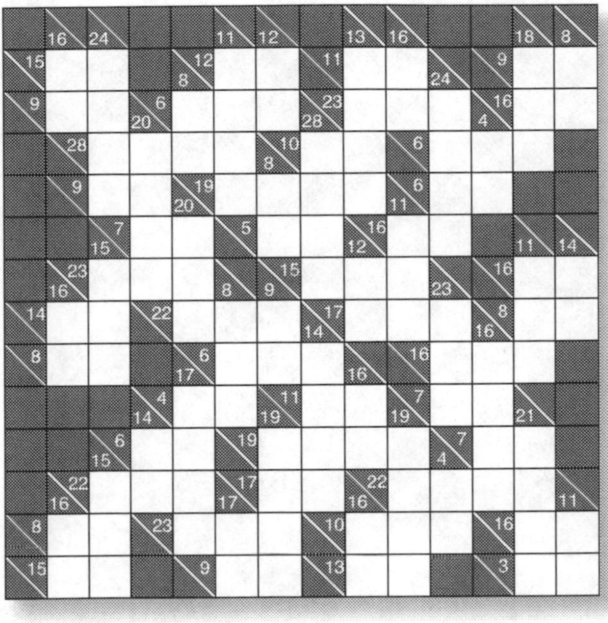

91

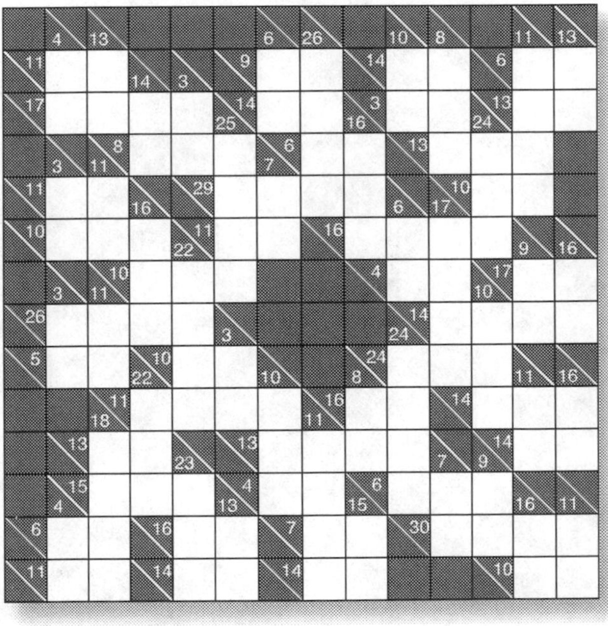

92

93

94

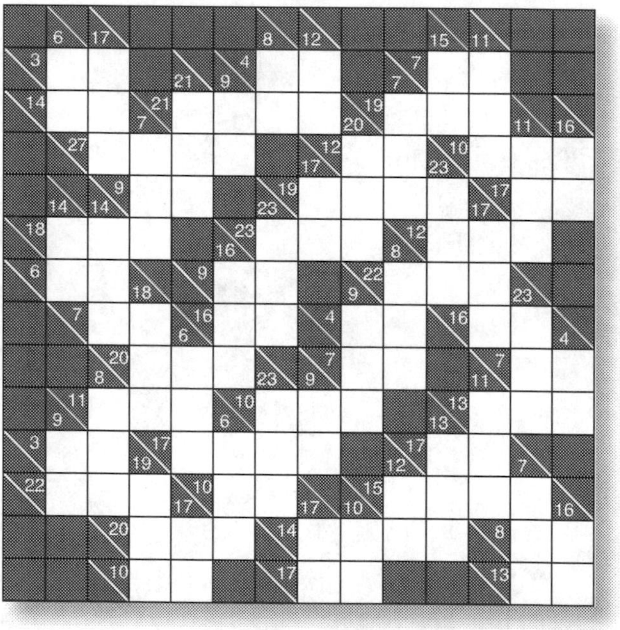

95

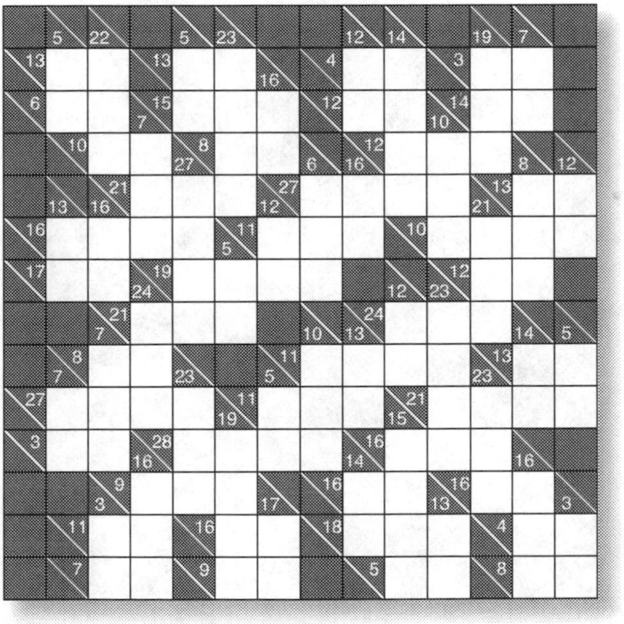

96

97

98

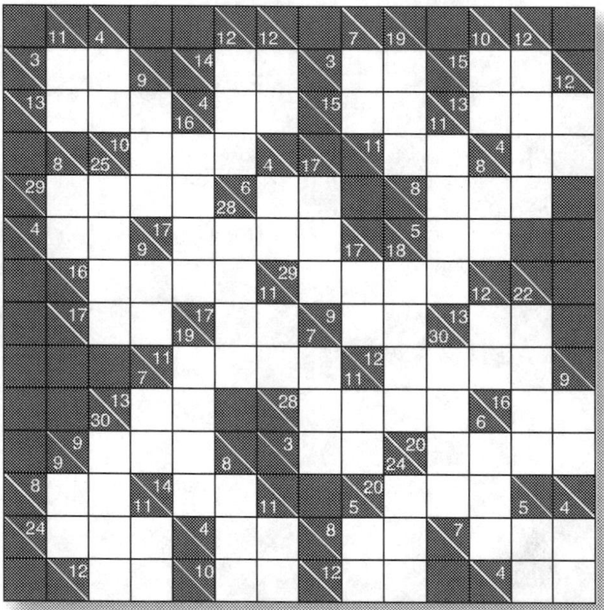

99

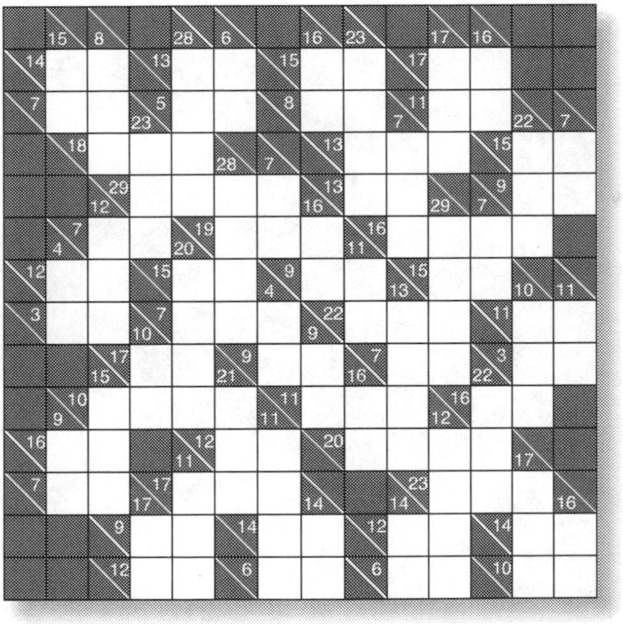

100

PART 2

Moderately Challenging Puzzles

1

2

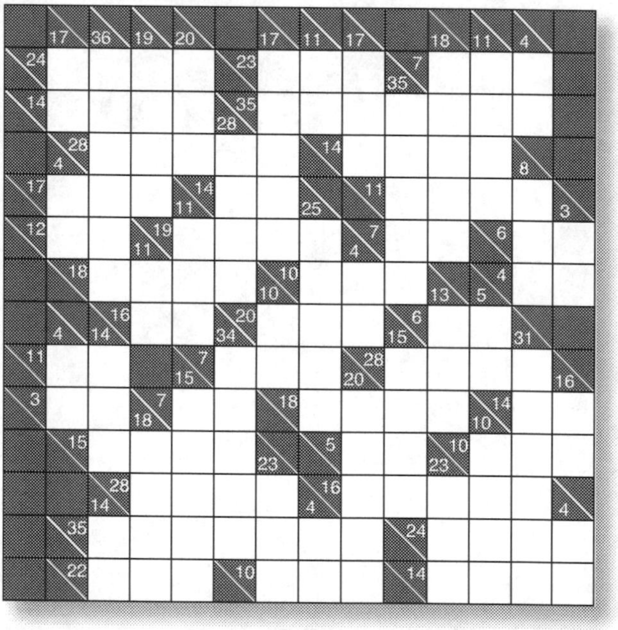

3

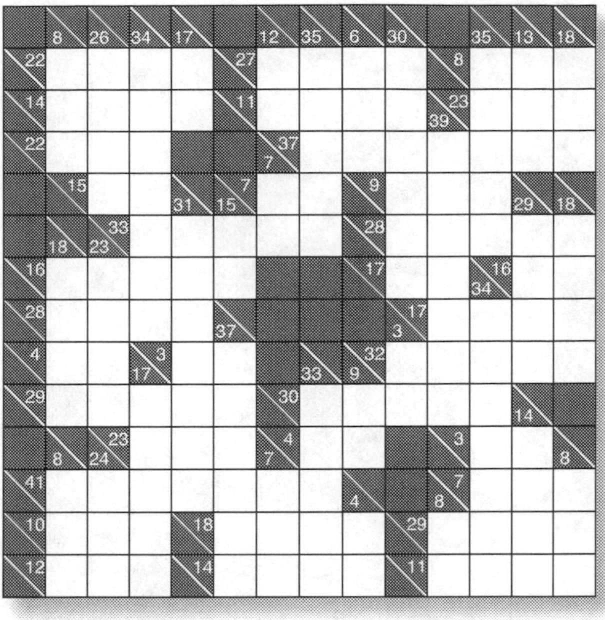
8 26 34 17 12 35 6 30 35 13 18
22 27 8
14 11 23 39
22 37 7
15 31 7 15 9 29 18
33 18 23 28
16 17 16 34
28 37 17 3
4 3 17 33 32 9
29 30 14
23 8 24 4 7 3 8
41 4 7 8
10 18 29
12 14 11

4

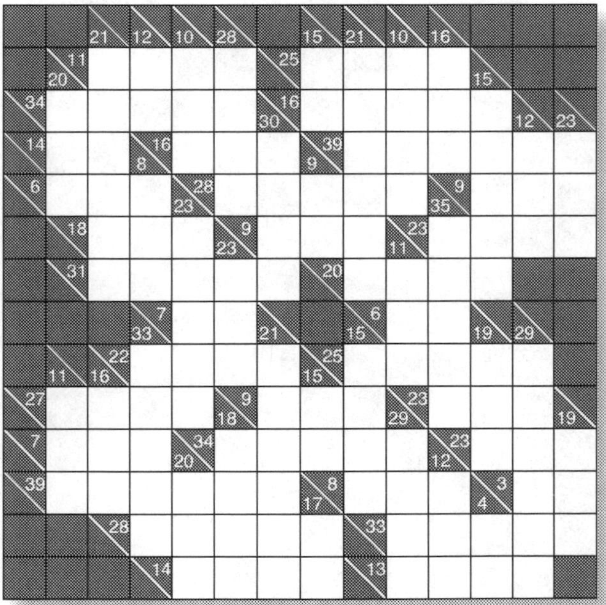
21 12 10 28 15 21 10 16
11 20 25 15
34 16 30 12 23
14 16 8 39 9
6 28 23 9 35
18 9 23 23 11
31 20
7 33 21 6 15 19 29
22 11 16 25 15
27 9 18 23 29 19
7 34 20 23 12
39 8 17 3 4
28 33
14 13

5

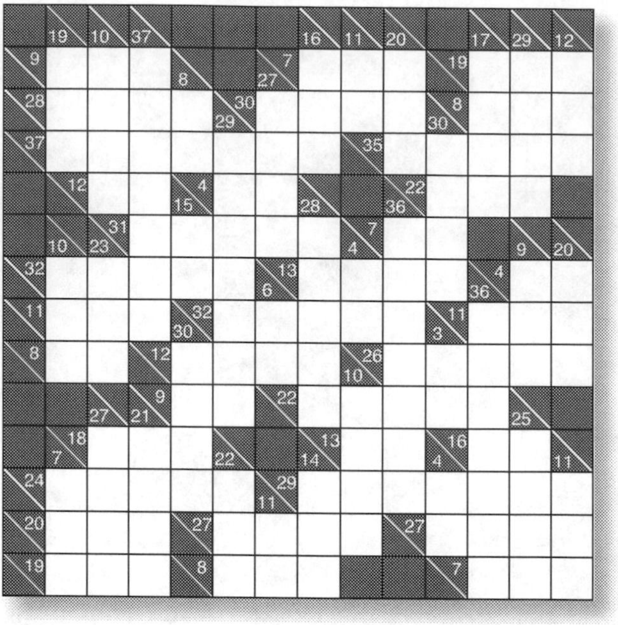

6

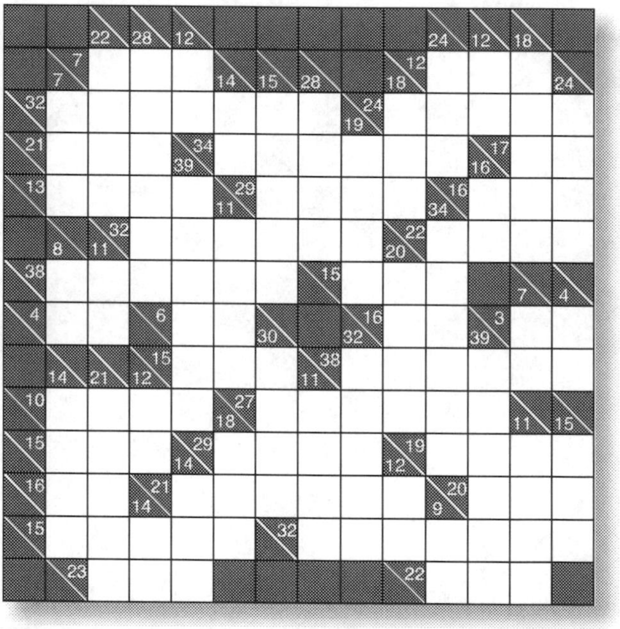

7

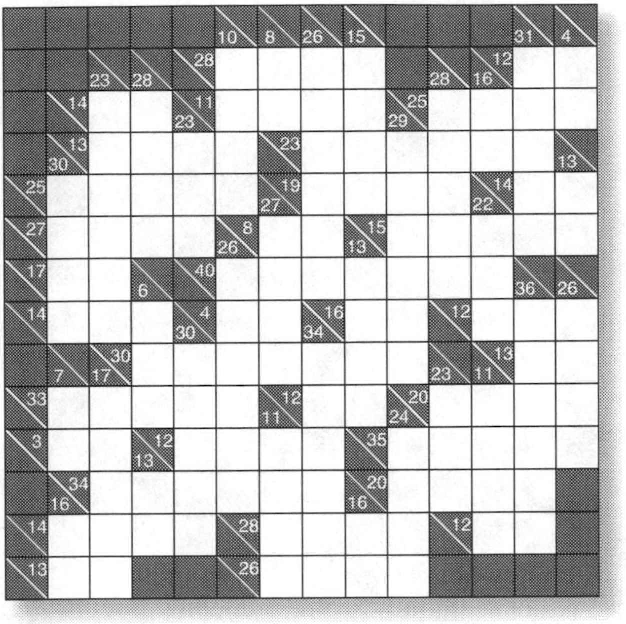

8

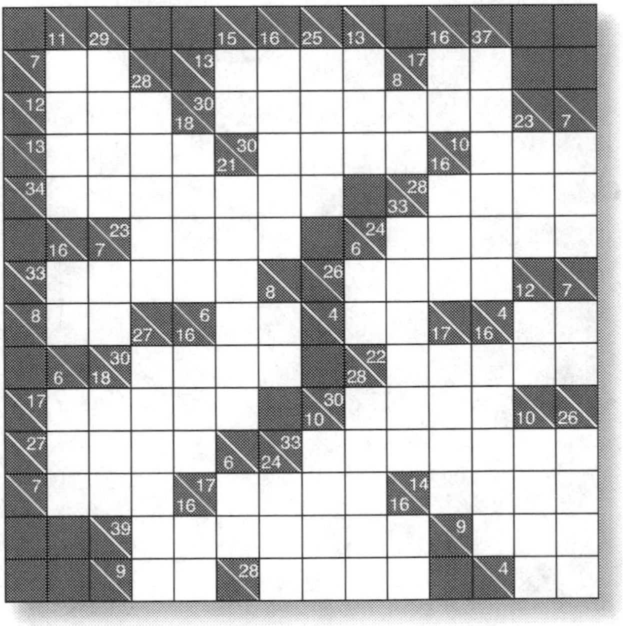

9

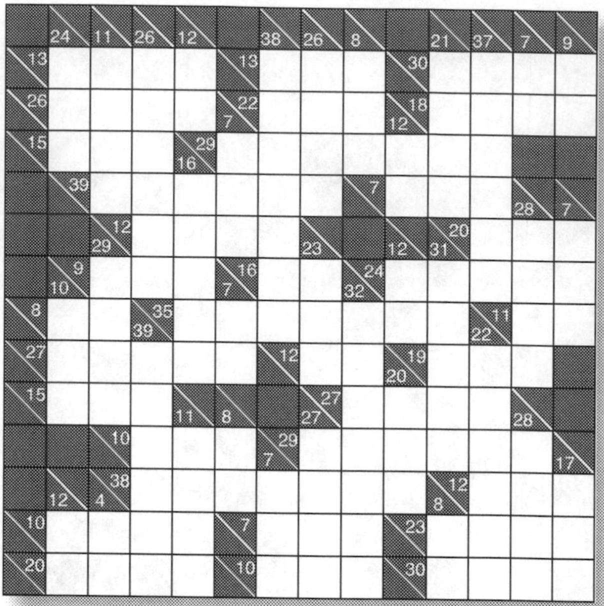

10

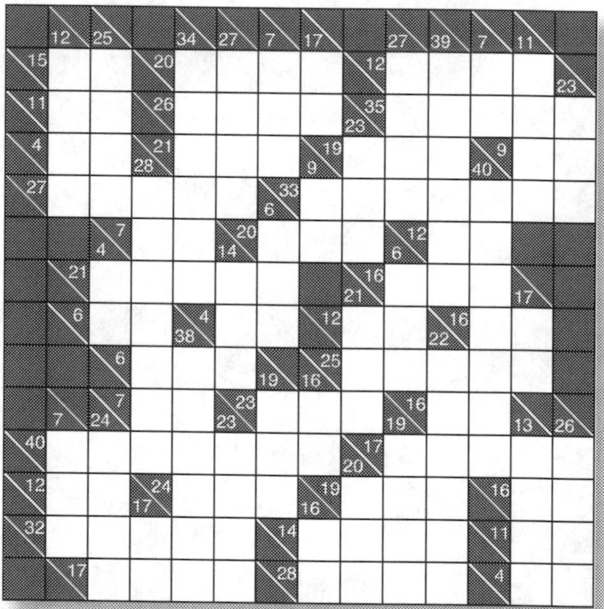

11

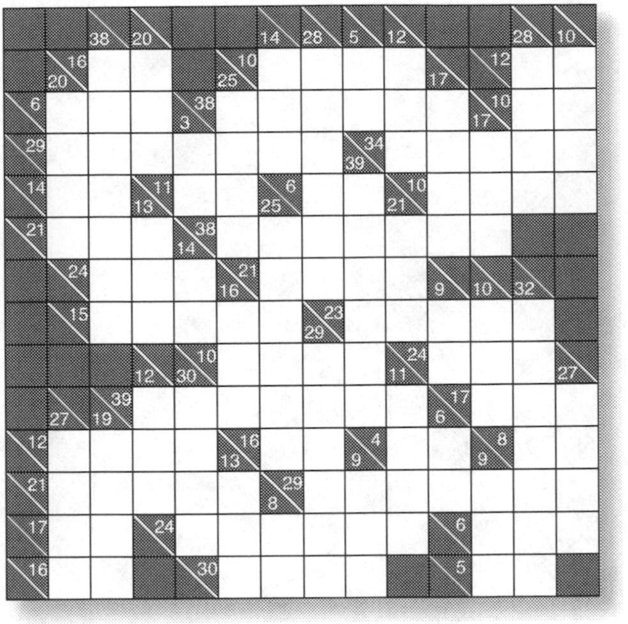

12

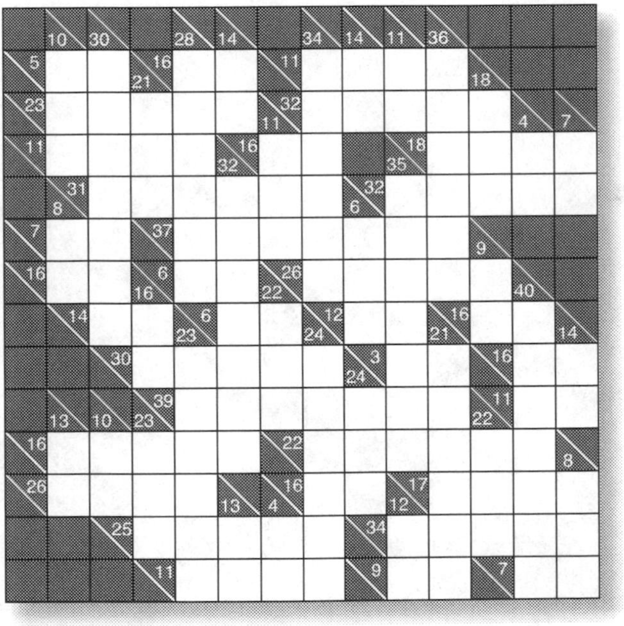

13

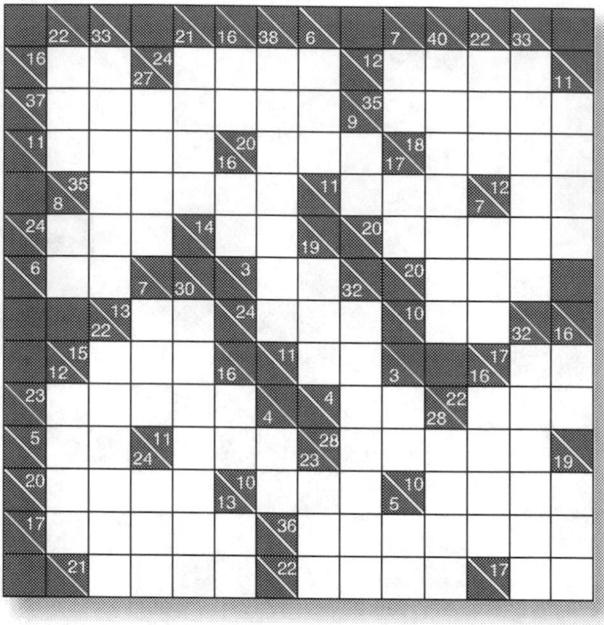

14

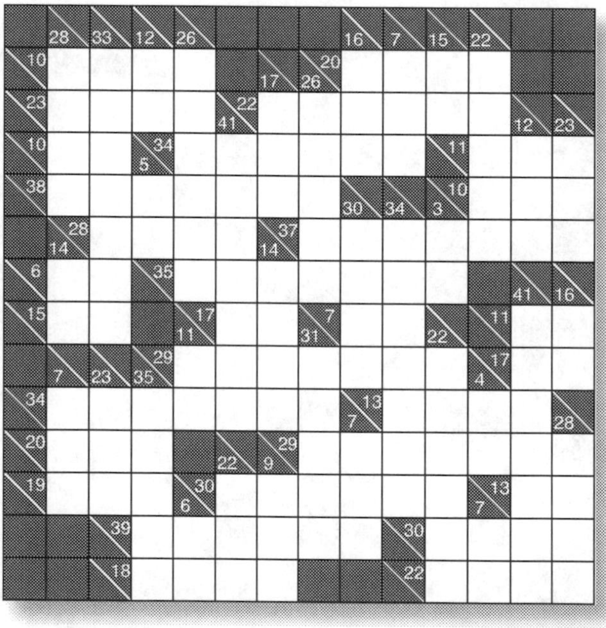

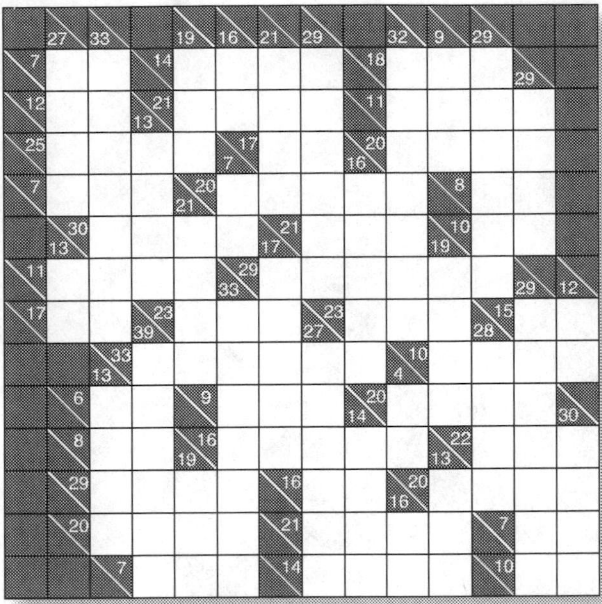

15

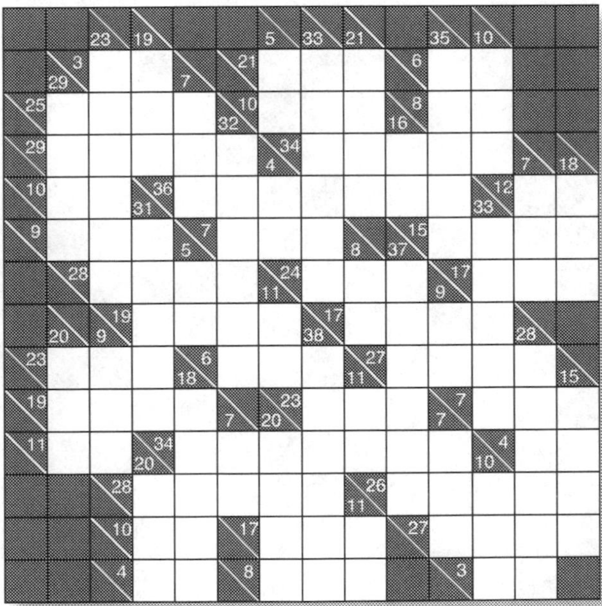

16

17

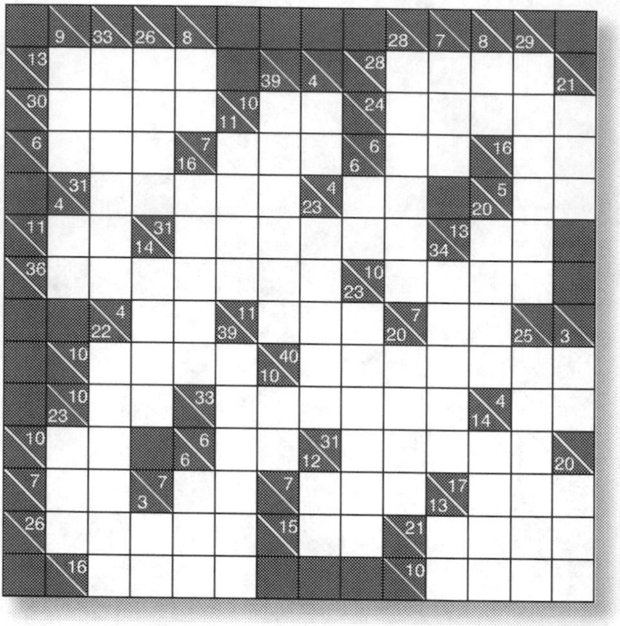
9 33 26 8 28 7 8 29
13 39 4 28 21
30 10 11 24
6 7 16 6 6 16
31 4 4 23 5 20
11 31 14 13 34
36 10 23
4 22 11 39 7 20 25 3
10 40 10
10 23 33 4 14
10 6 6 31 12 20
7 7 3 7 17 13
26 15 21
16 10

18

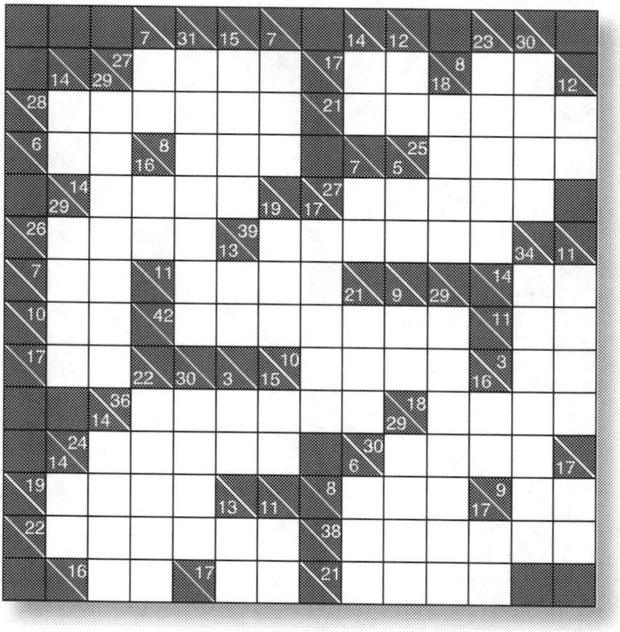
7 31 15 7 14 12 23 30
14 27 29 17 8 18 12
28 21
6 8 16 7 25 5
14 29 19 27 17
26 39 13 34 11
7 11 21 9 29 14
10 42 11
17 22 30 3 10 15 3 16
36 14 18 29
24 14 30 6 17
19 13 11 8 9 17
22 38
16 17 21

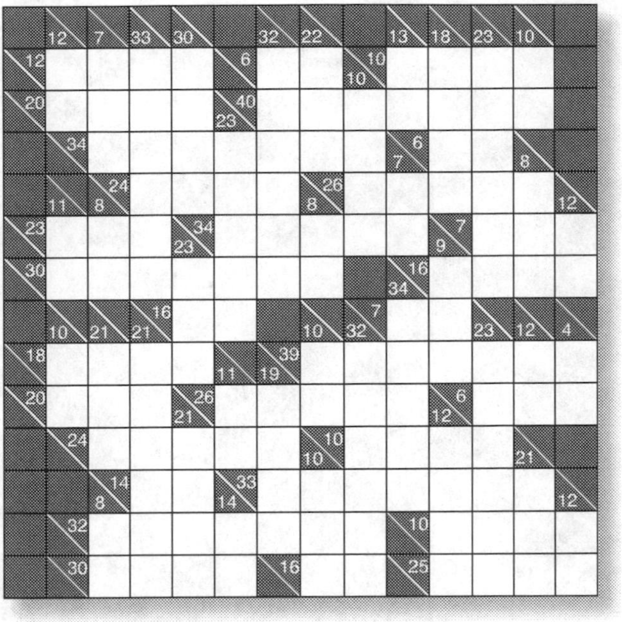

19

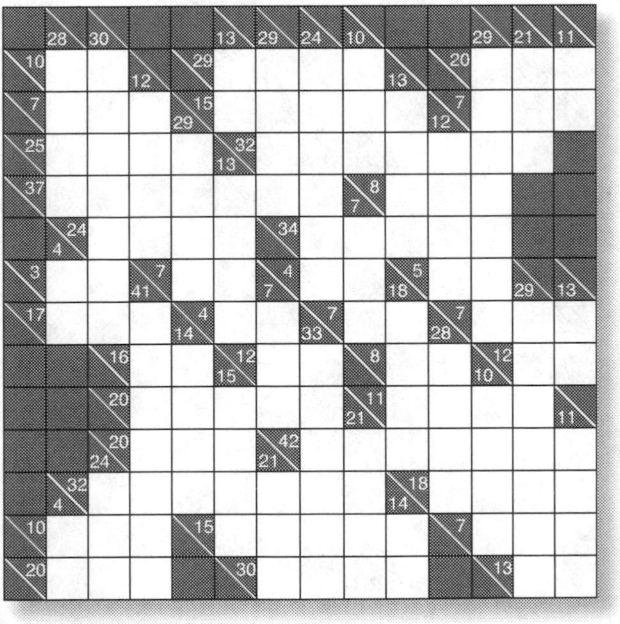

20

21

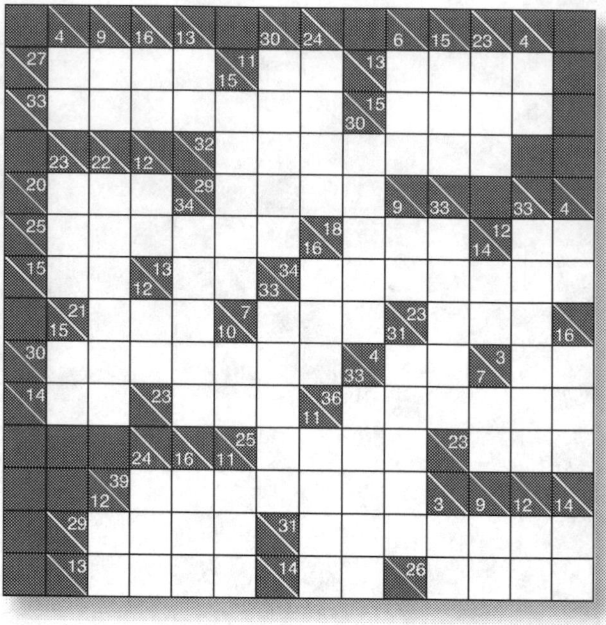

22

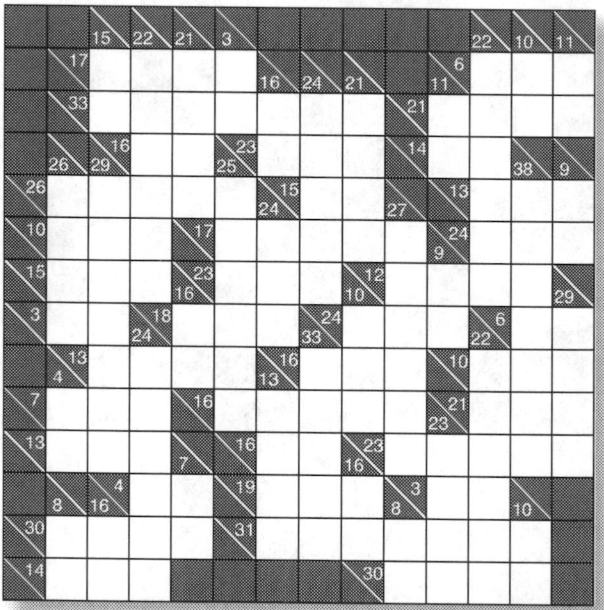

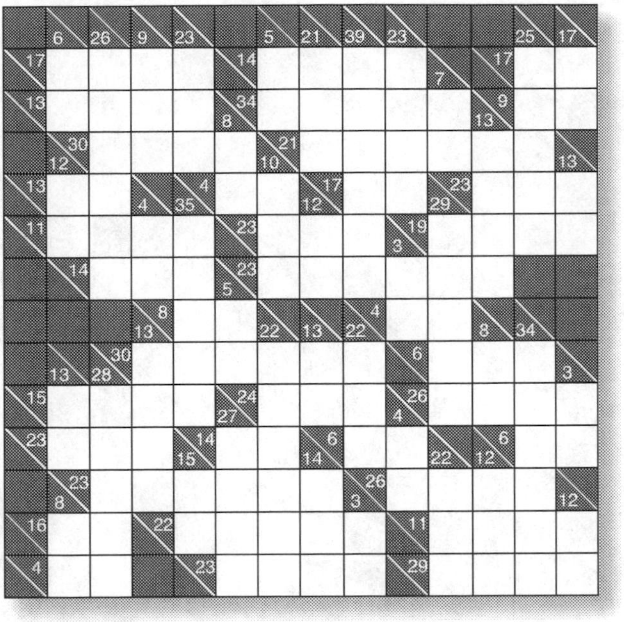

23

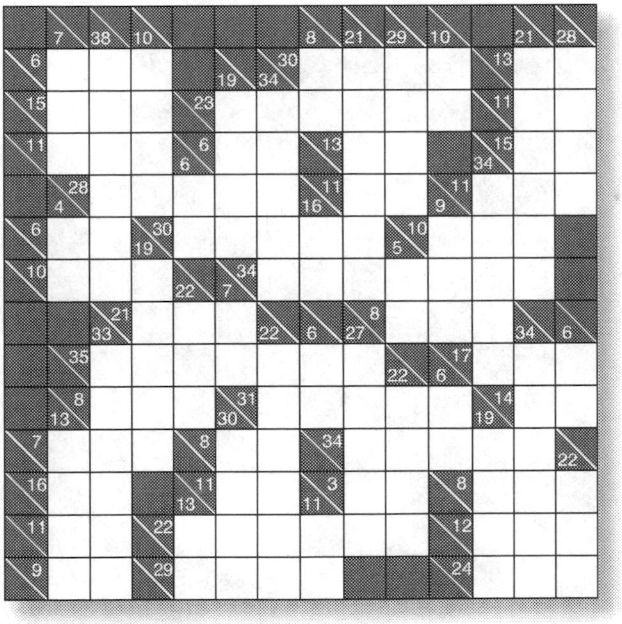

24

25

26

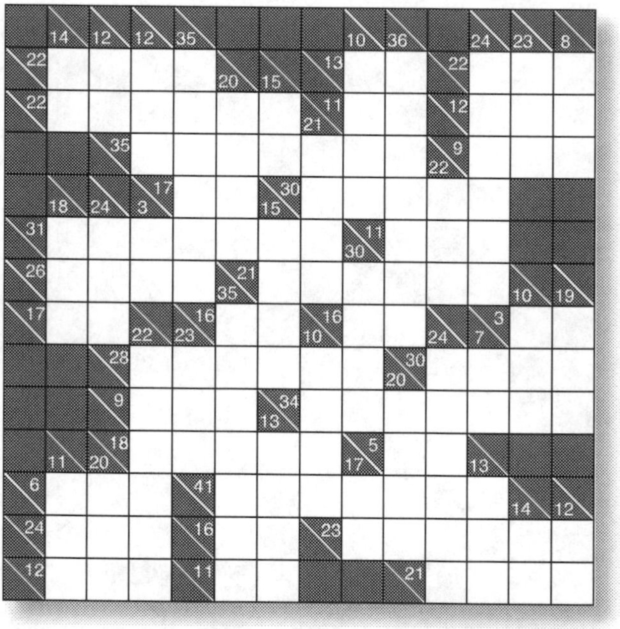

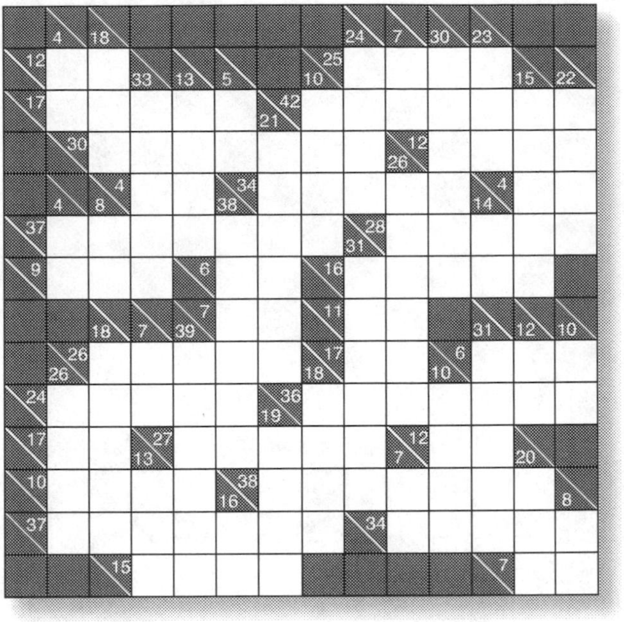

27

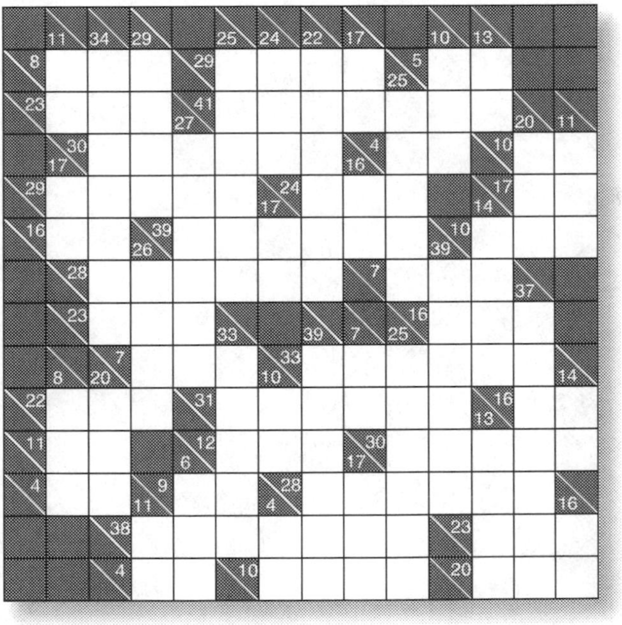

28

29

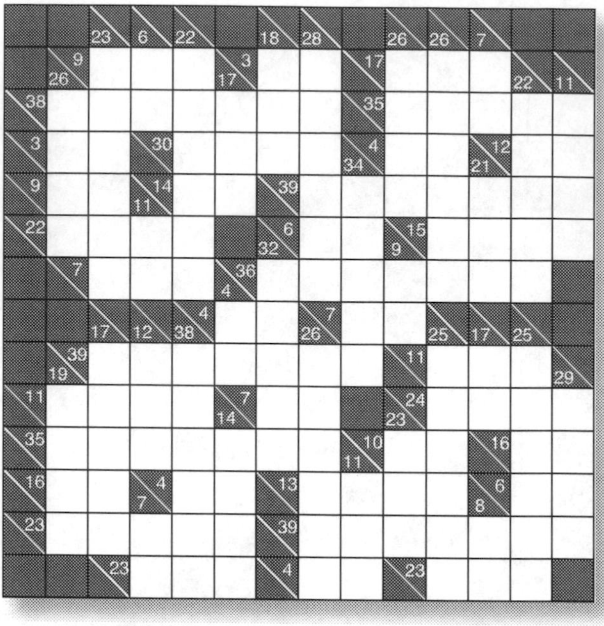

30

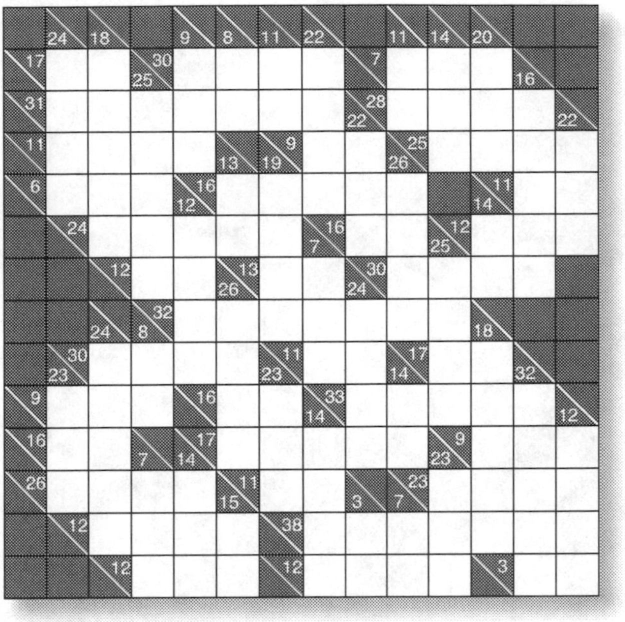

31

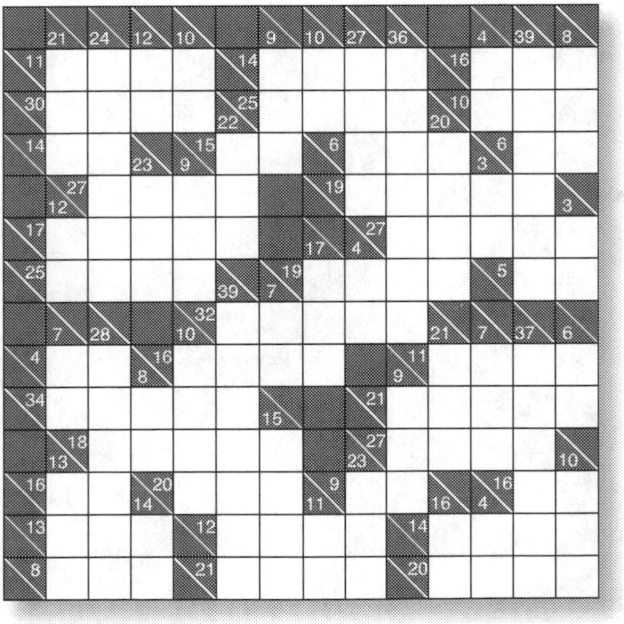

32

33

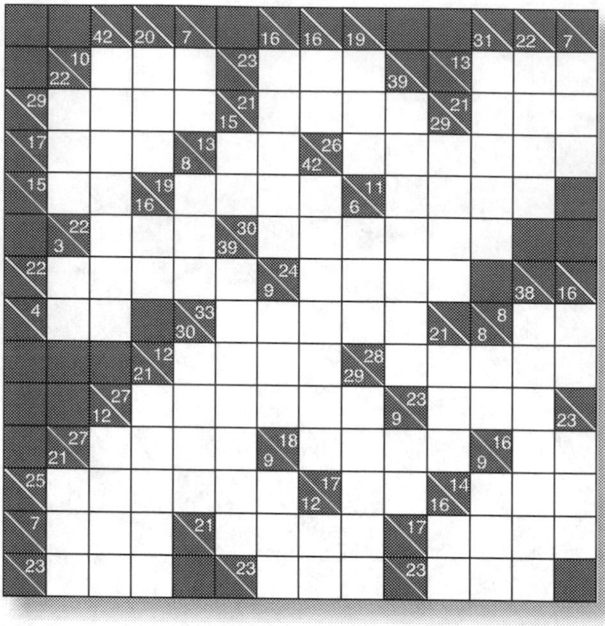
42 20 7 16 16 19 31 22 7
10 22 23 39 13
29 21 15 21 29
17 13 8 26 42
15 19 16 11 6
22 3 30 39
22 24 9 38 16
4 33 30 21 8 8
12 21 28 29
27 12 23 9 23
27 21 18 9 16 9
25 17 12 14 16
7 21 17
23 23 23

34

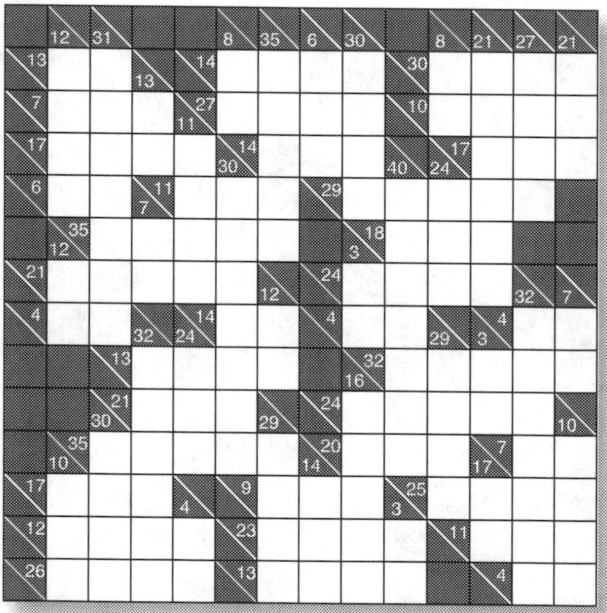
12 31 8 35 6 30 8 21 27 21
13 13 14 30
7 27 11 10
17 14 30 40 17 24
6 11 7 29
35 12 18 3
21 12 24 32 7
4 32 14 24 4 29 4 3
13 32 16
21 30 29 24 10
35 10 20 14 7 17
17 4 9 25 3
12 23 11
26 13 4

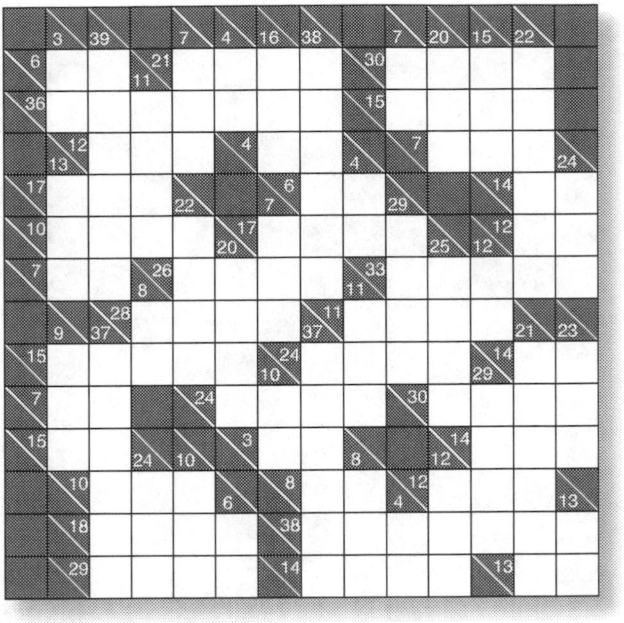

35

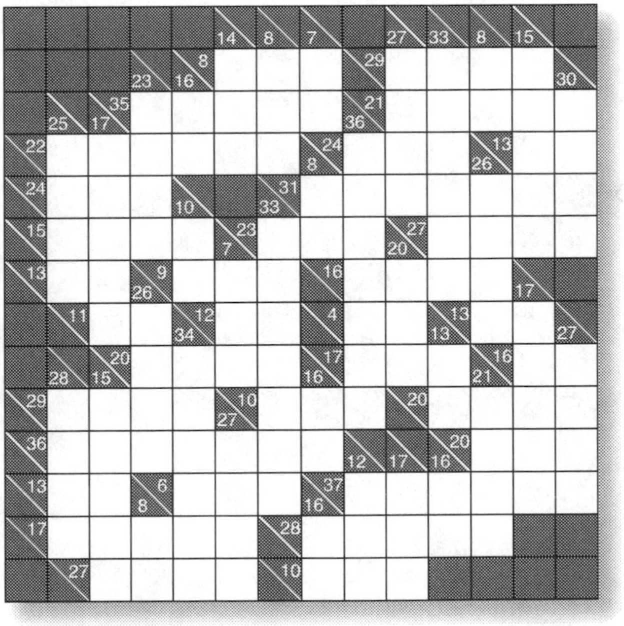

36

37

38

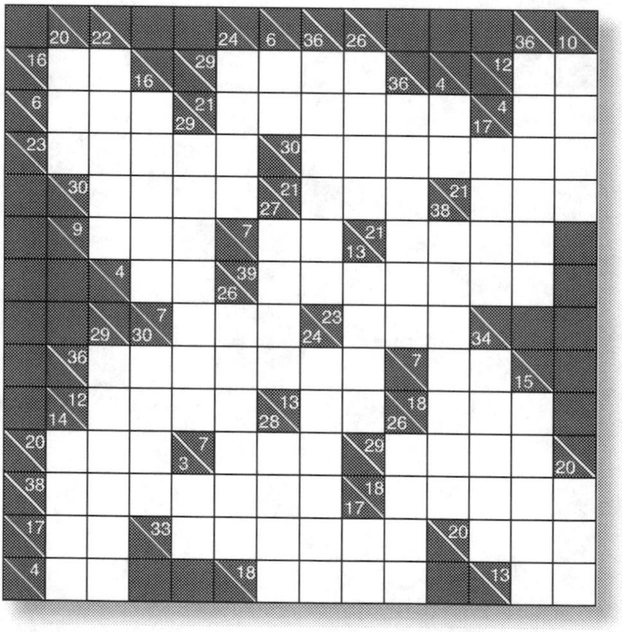

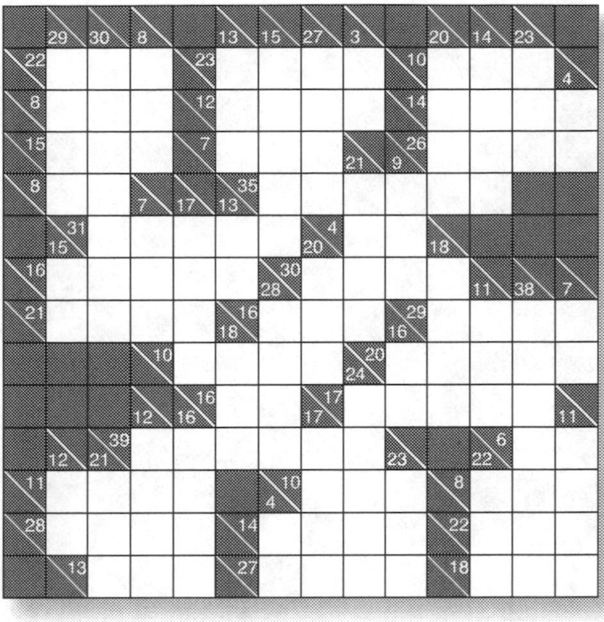

39

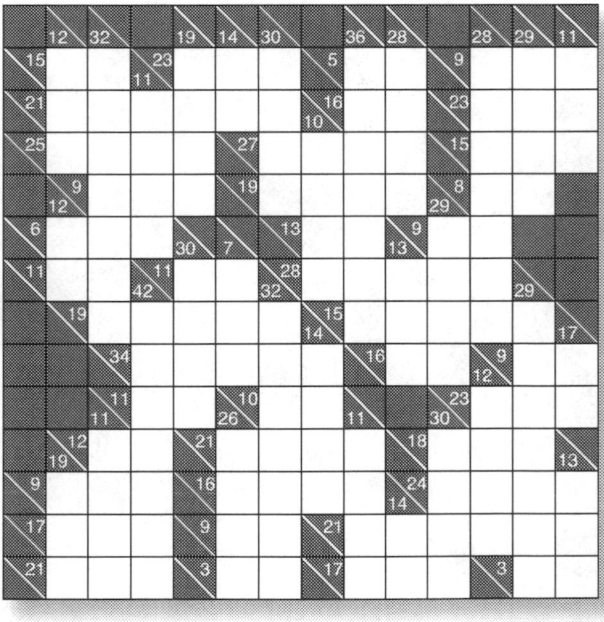

40

41

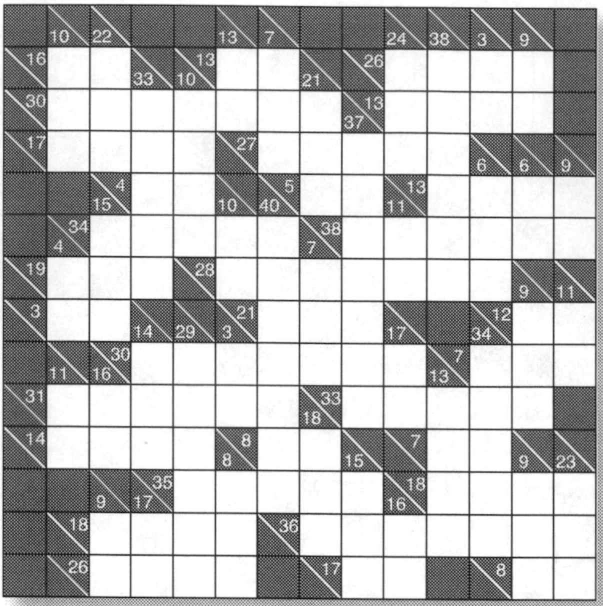
10 22 13 7 24 38 3 9
16 13 33 10 21 26
30 13 37
17 27 6 6 9
4 15 10 5 40 13 11
34 4 38 7
19 28 9 11
3 14 29 21 3 17 12 34
11 30 16 7 13
31 33 18
14 8 8 15 7 9 23
9 35 17 18 16
18 36
26 17 8

42

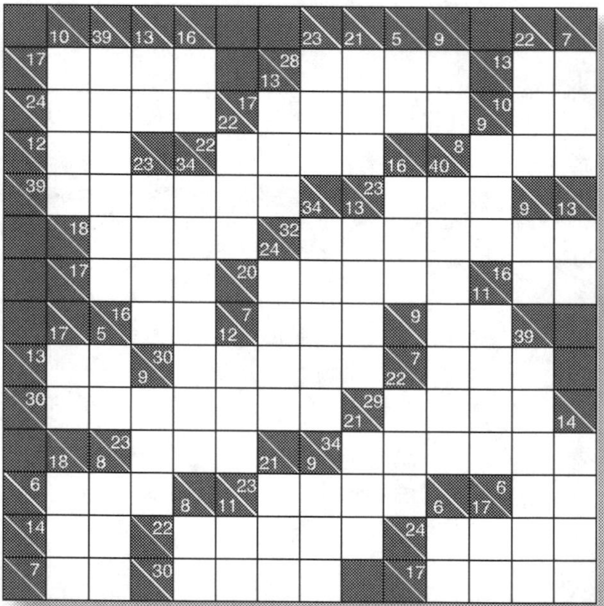
10 39 13 16 23 21 5 9 22 7
17 28 13 13
24 17 22 10 9
12 23 22 34 16 8 40
39 34 23 13 9 13
18 32 24
17 20 16 11
17 16 5 7 12 9 39
13 30 9 7 22
30 29 21 14
18 23 8 21 34 9
6 8 23 11 6 6 17
14 22 24
7 30 17

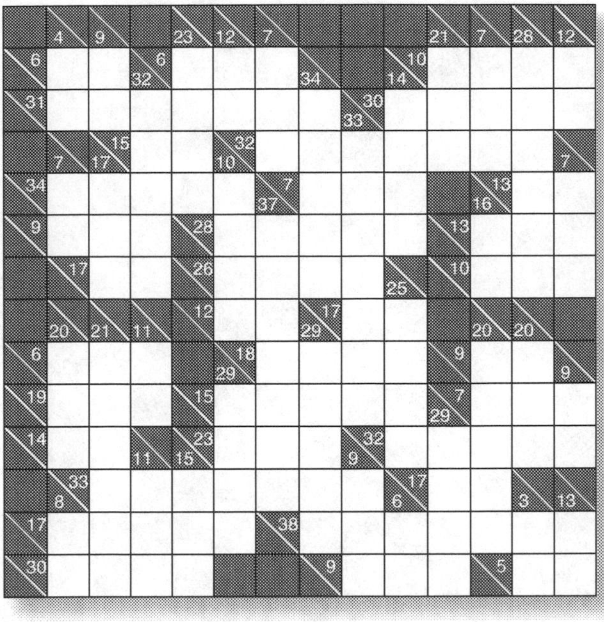

43

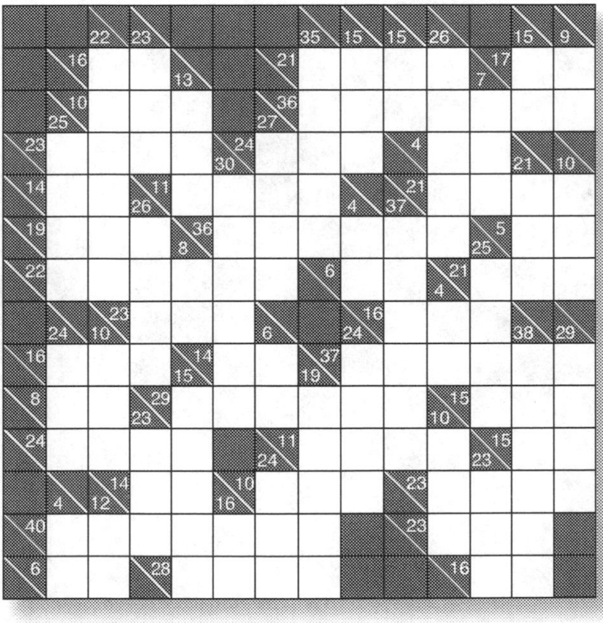

44

45

46

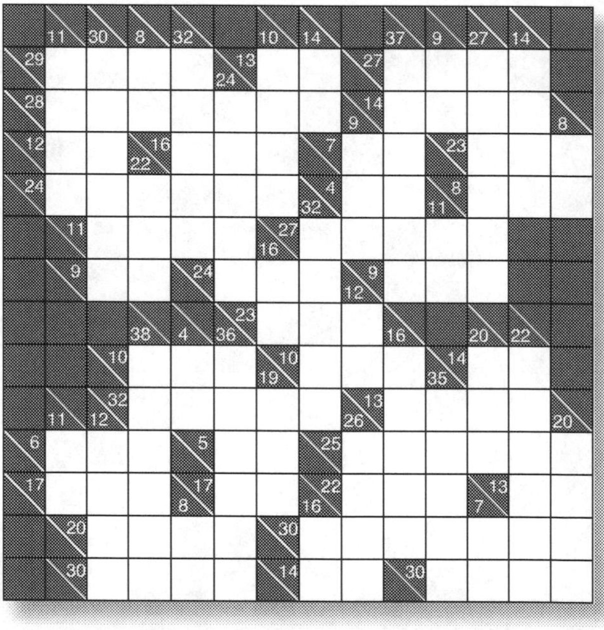

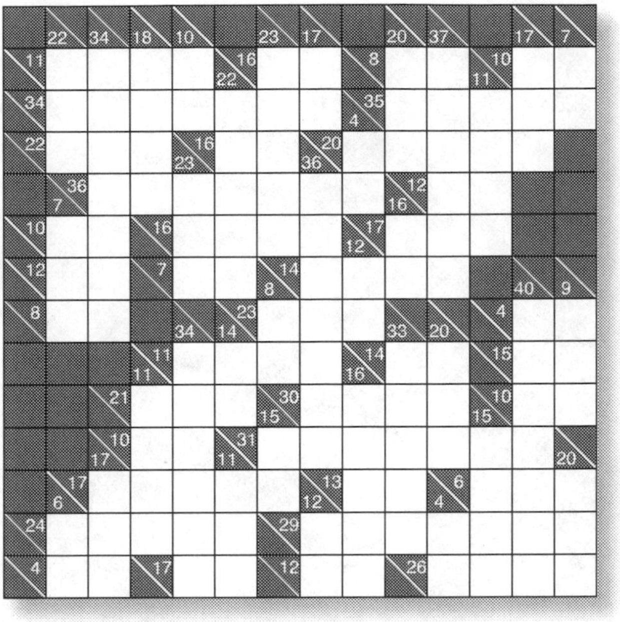

47

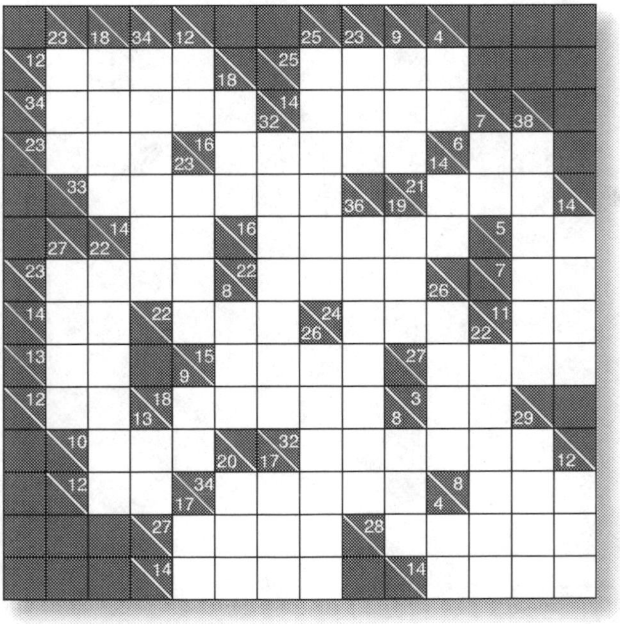

48

49

50

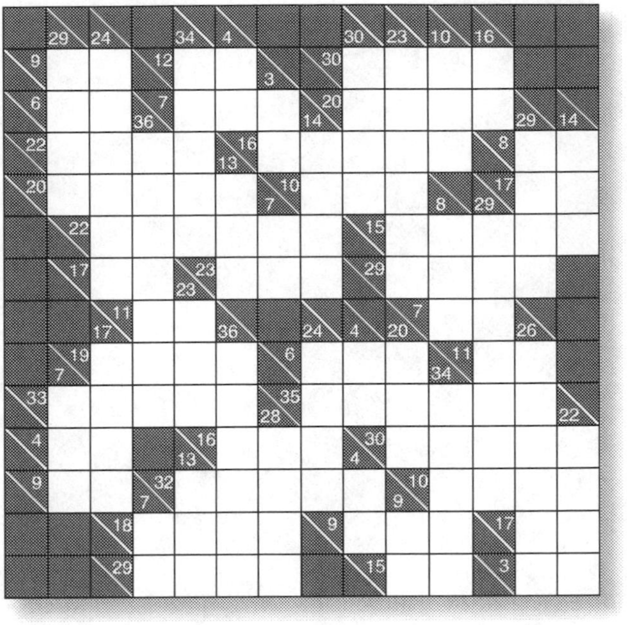

51

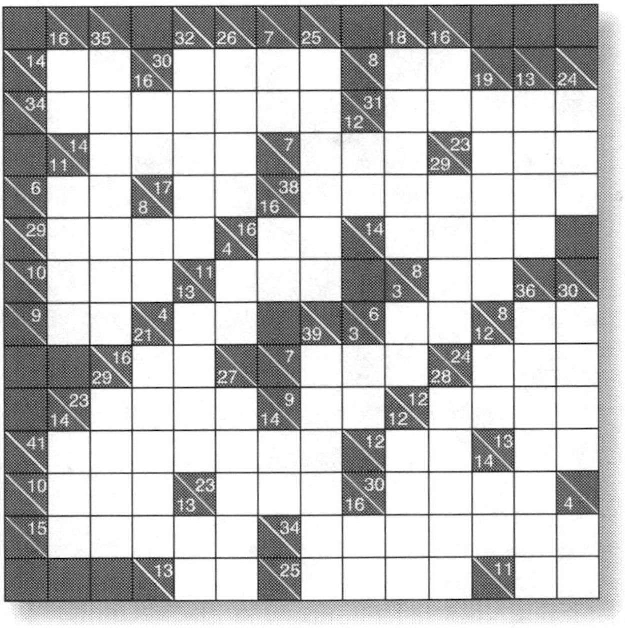

52

53

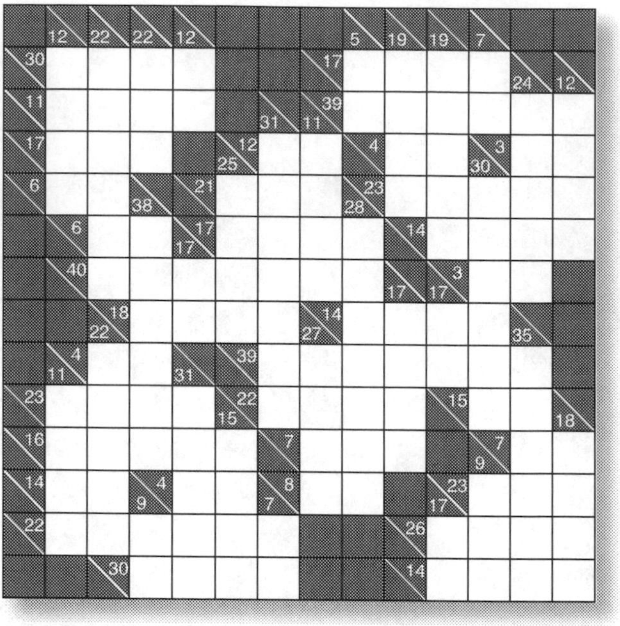
12 22 22 12 5 19 19 7
30 17 24 12
11 39 31 11
17 12 25 4 3 30
6 38 21 23 28
6 17 17 14
40 17 3 17
18 22 14 27 35
4 11 31 39
23 22 15 15 18
16 7 7 9
14 4 9 8 7 23 17
22 26
30 14

54

34 7 7 9 16 15 38 24
11 3 12 14 13 8 6
34 22 22 13
20 16 16 22 30
6 3 39 16 10 4 14 5
32 15 5
10 3 5 21 20
21 12 9 21 26 14 26
22 13 25 11 3 21
22 30 41
12 10 11 4 4 12 16 14
23 16 13 16 11 14
27 30
8 5 17 16

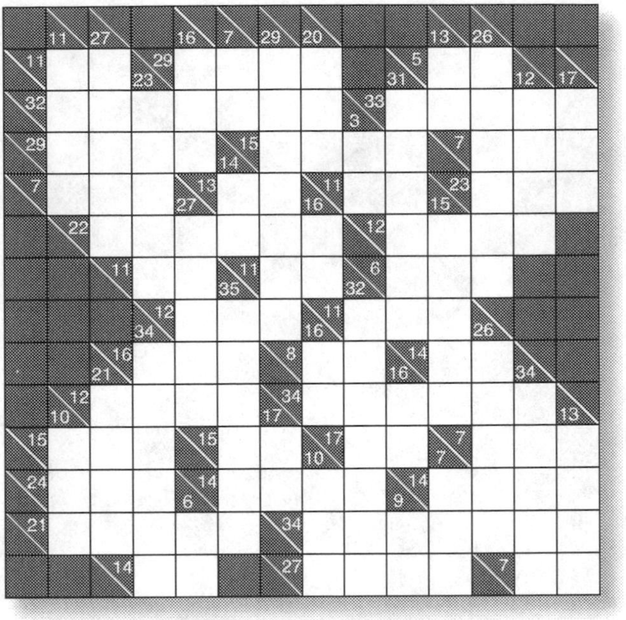

55

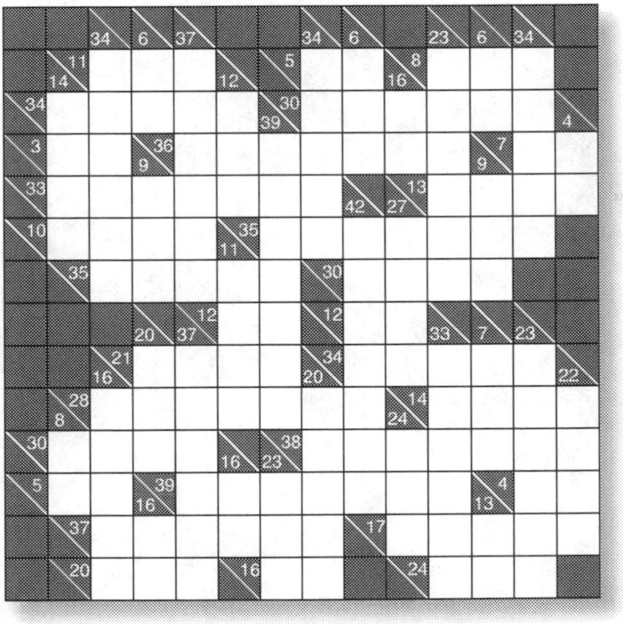

56

57

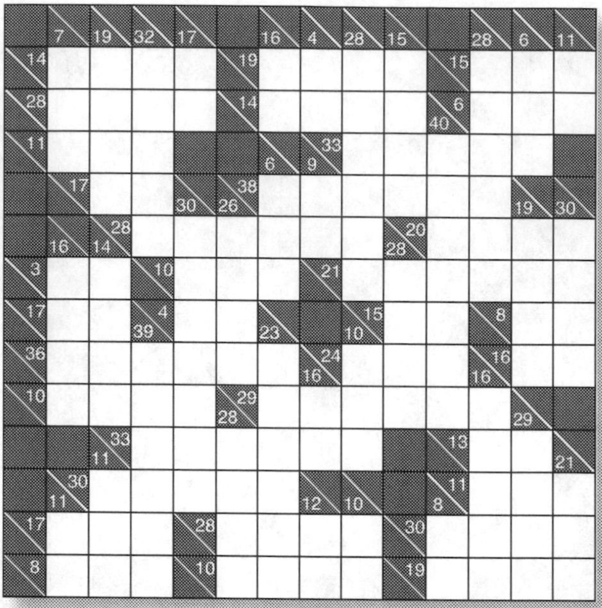

58

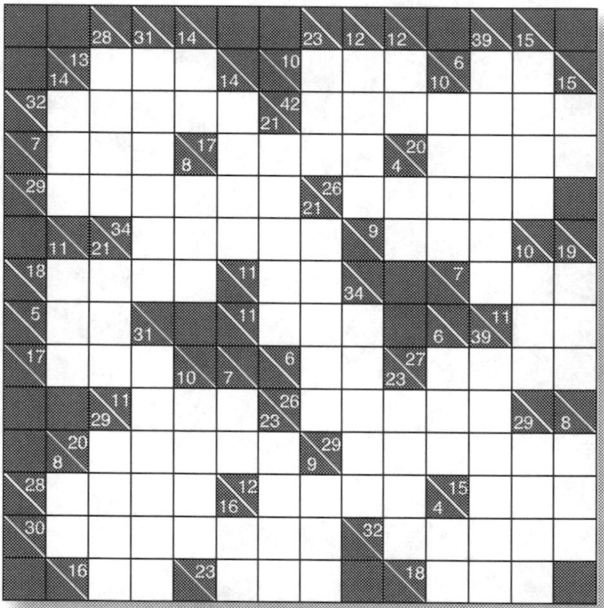

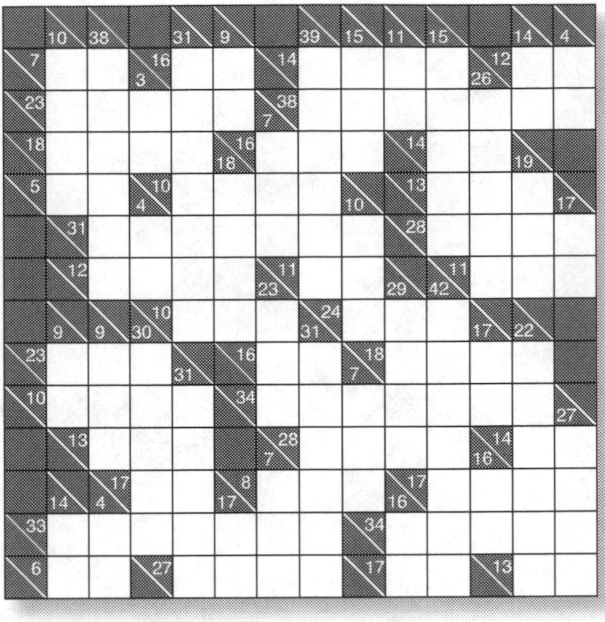

59

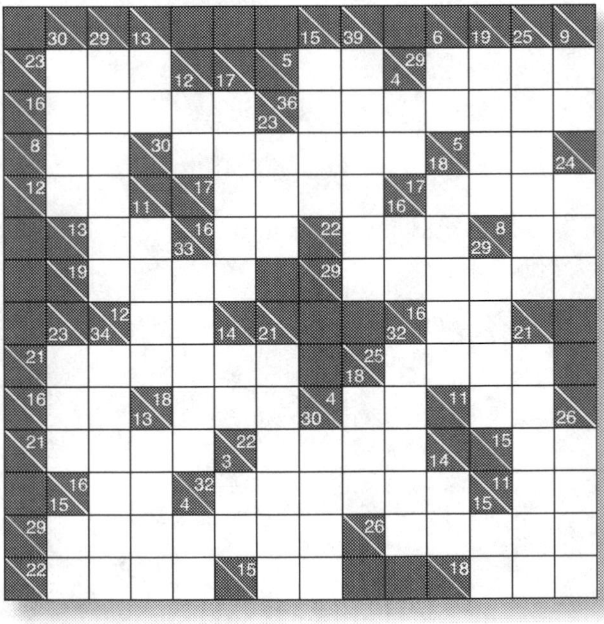

60

61

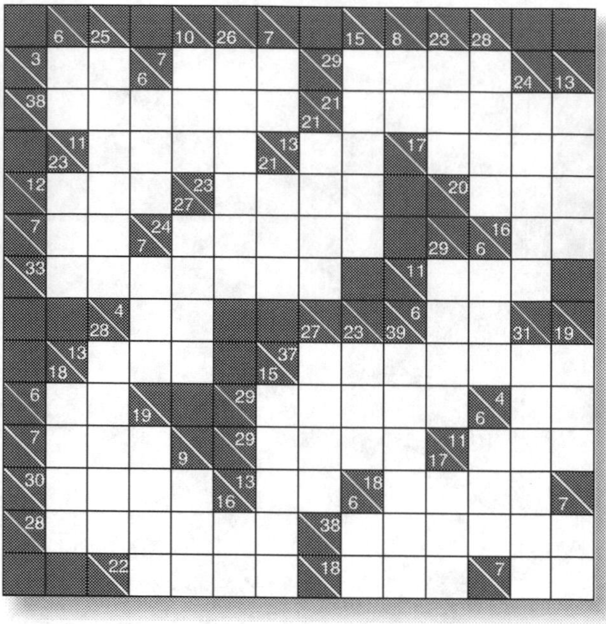

62

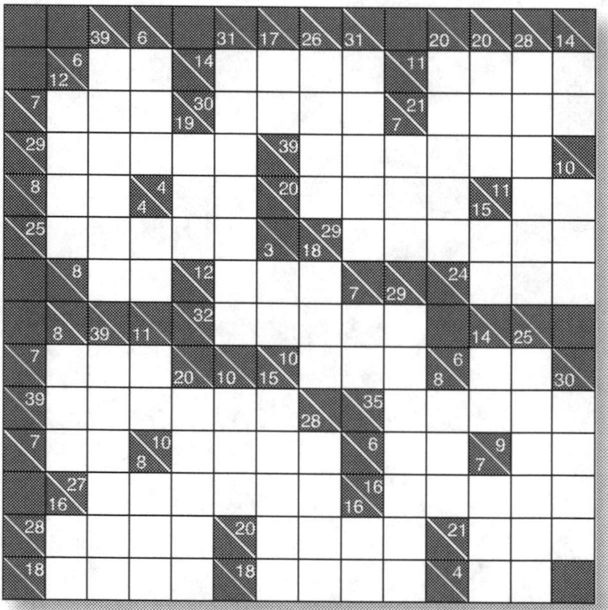

63

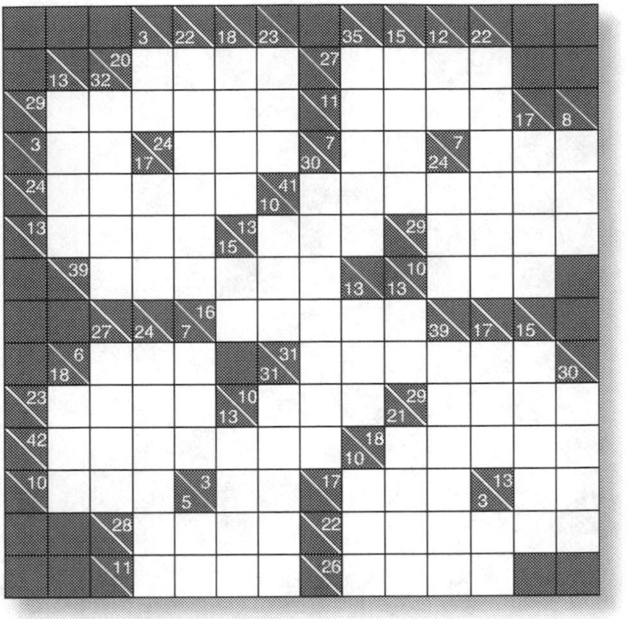

64

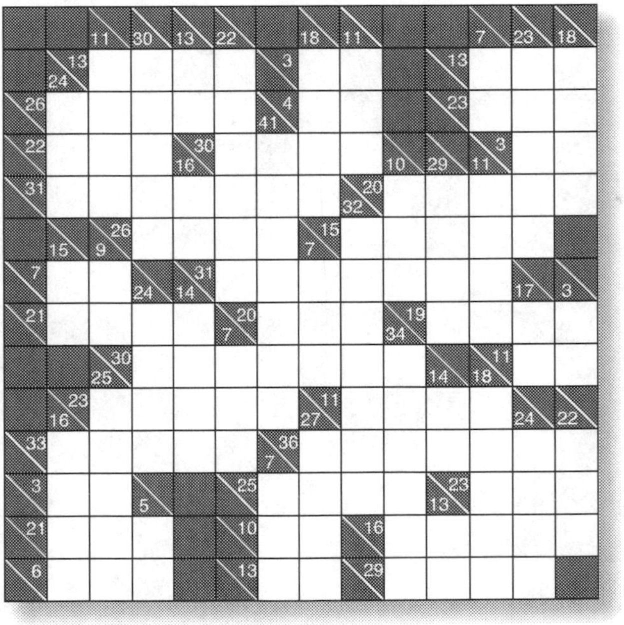

65

66

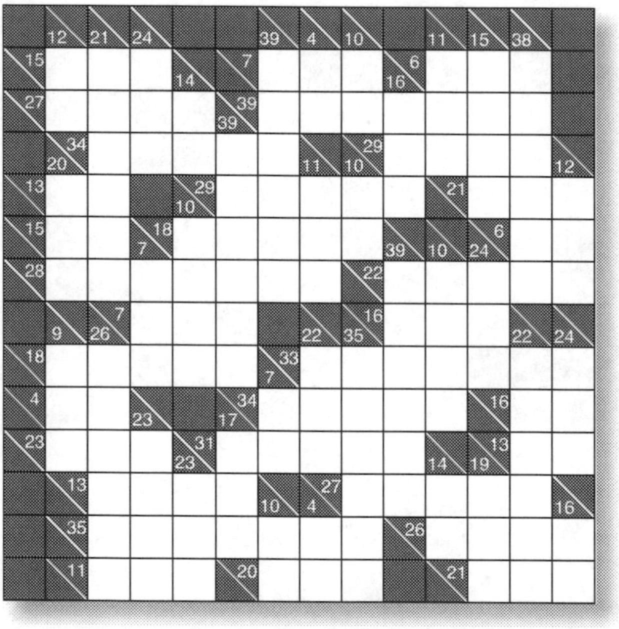

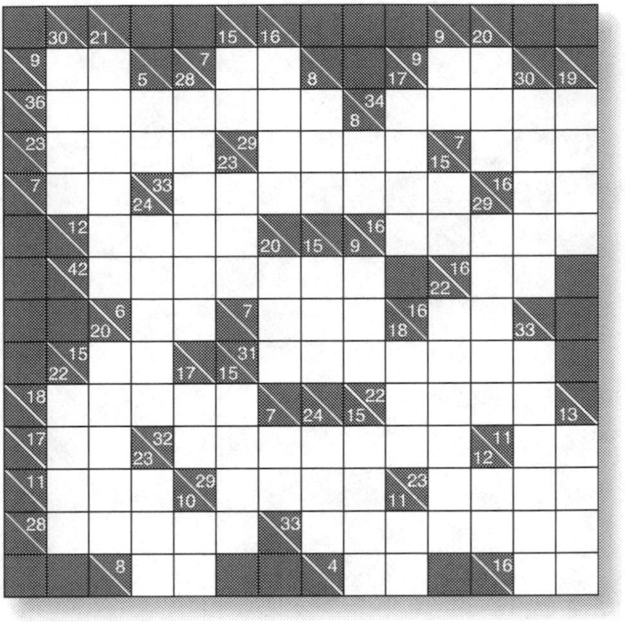

67

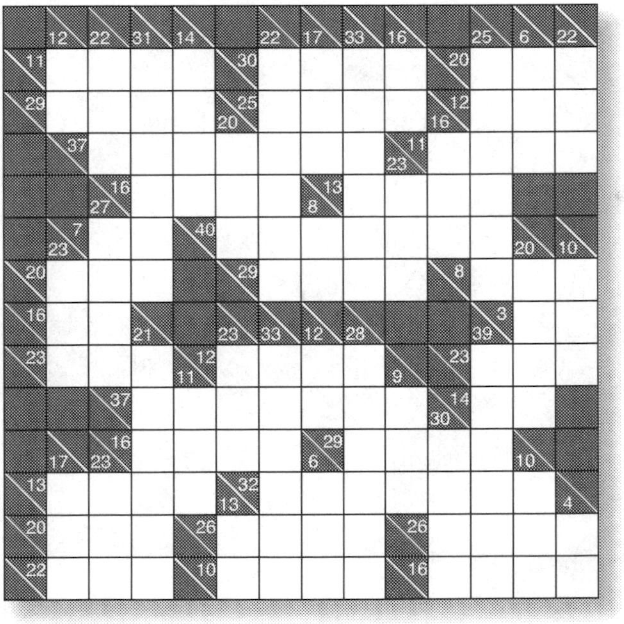

68

69

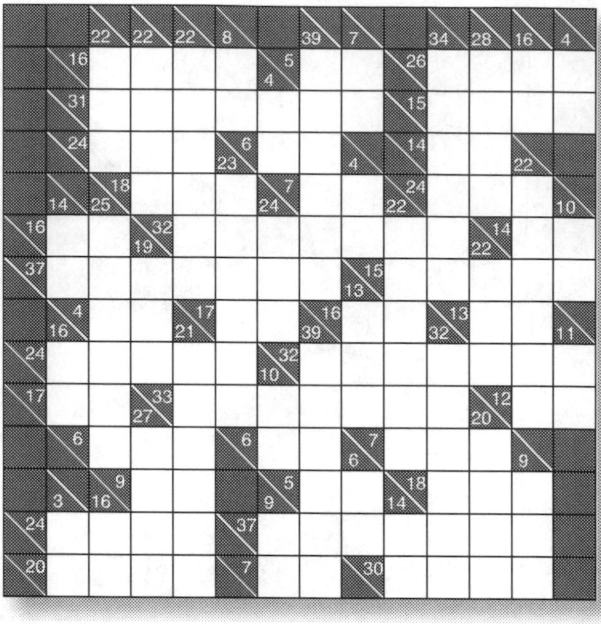

70

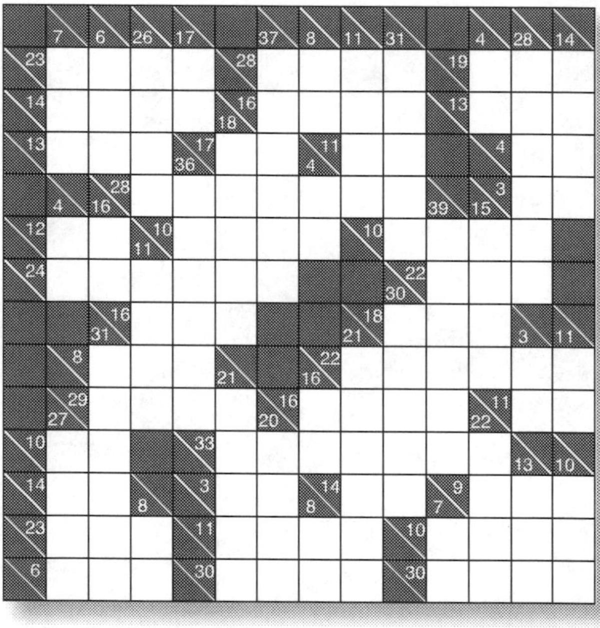

71

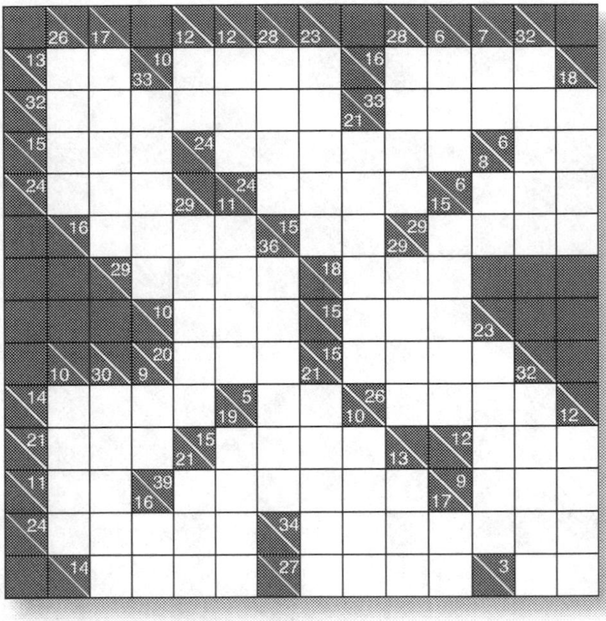

72

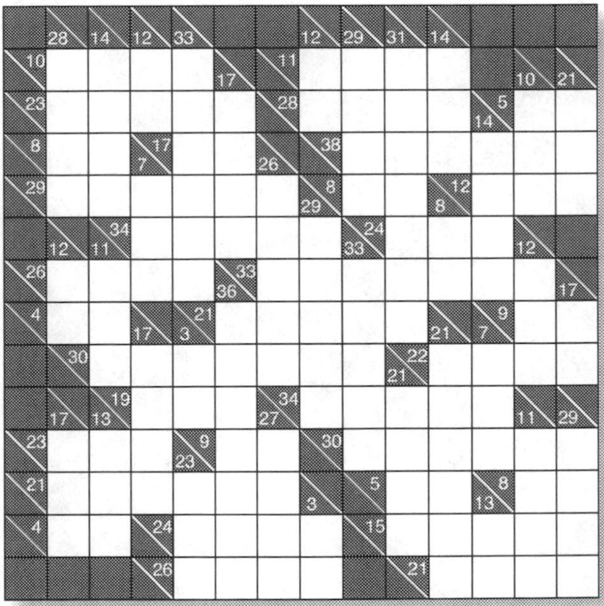

73

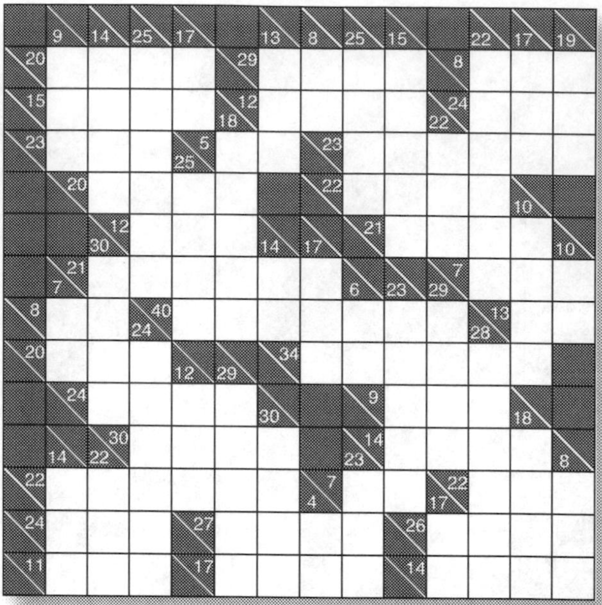

74

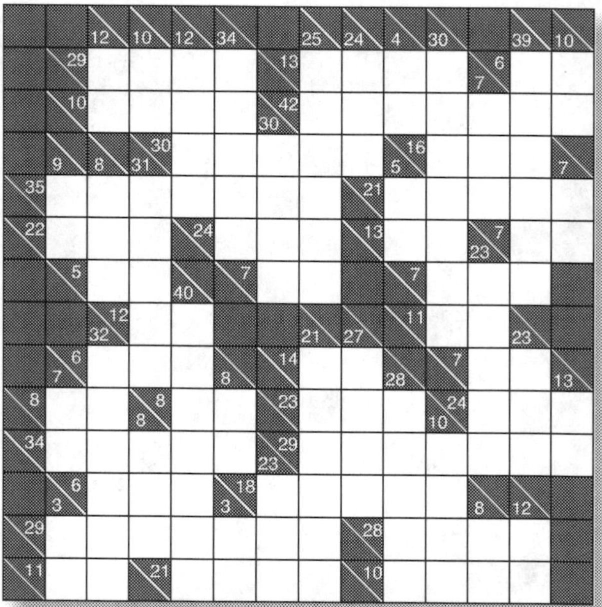

75

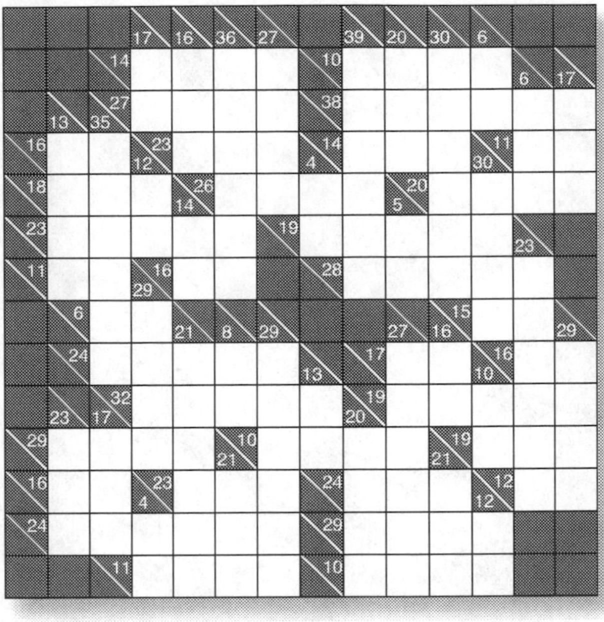

76

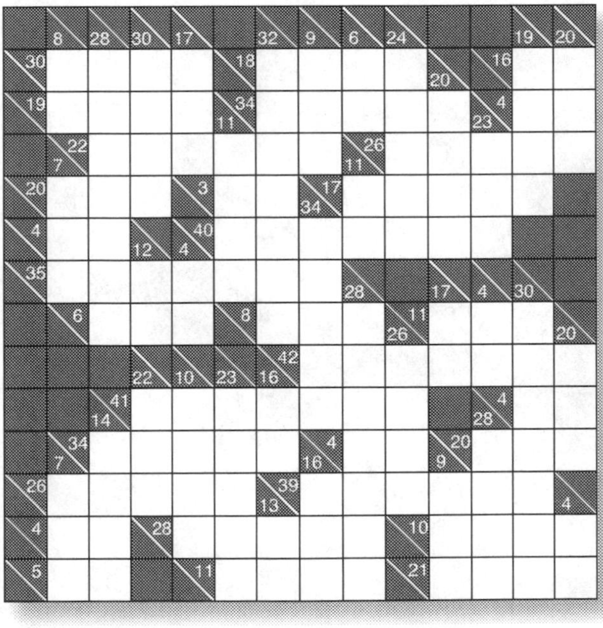

77

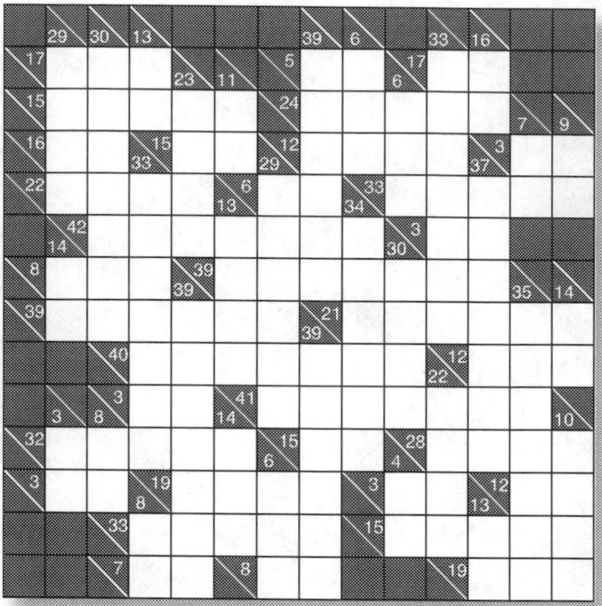

78

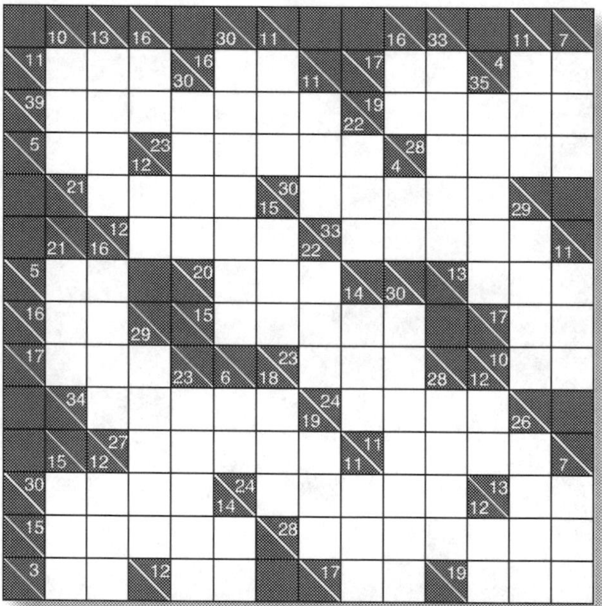

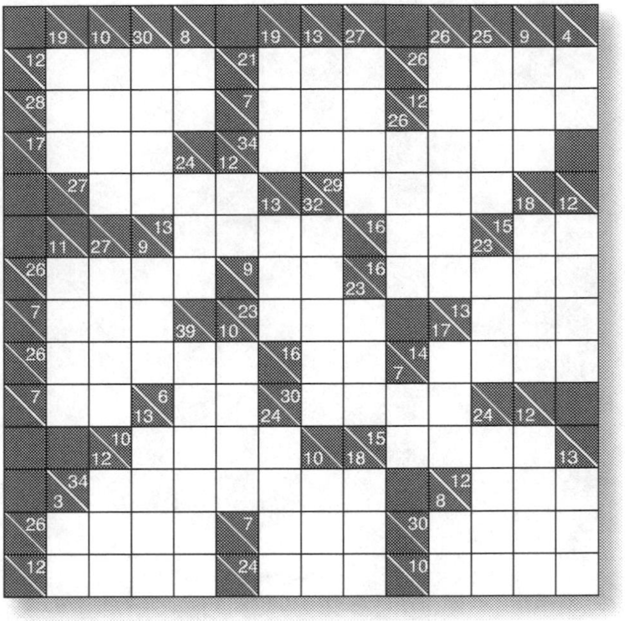

79

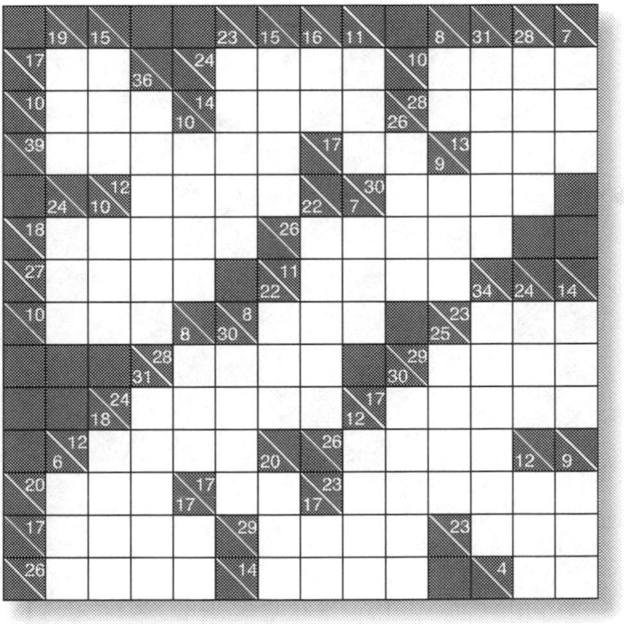

80

81

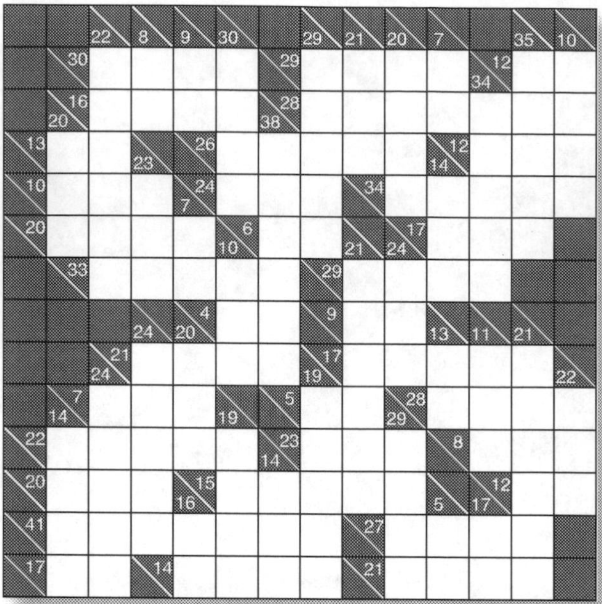

82

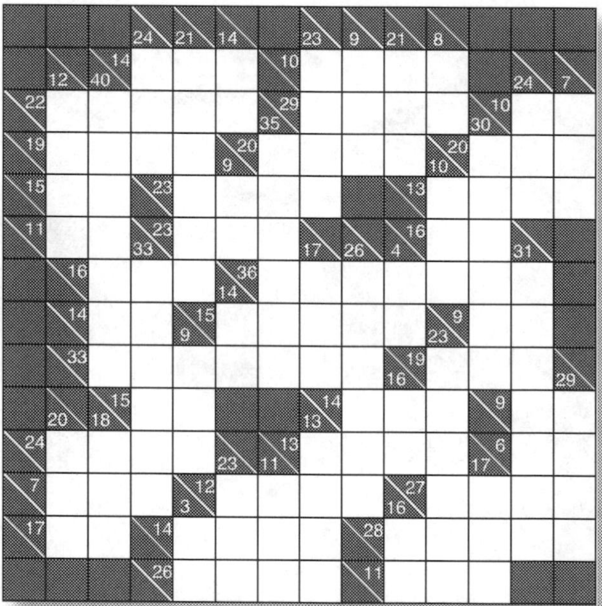

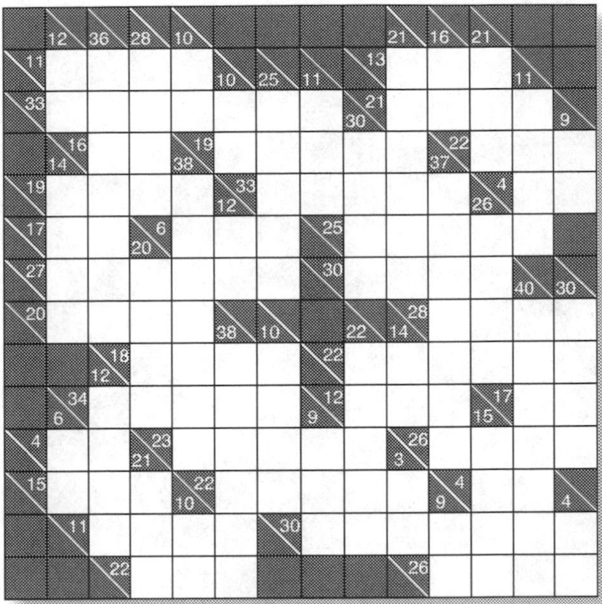

83

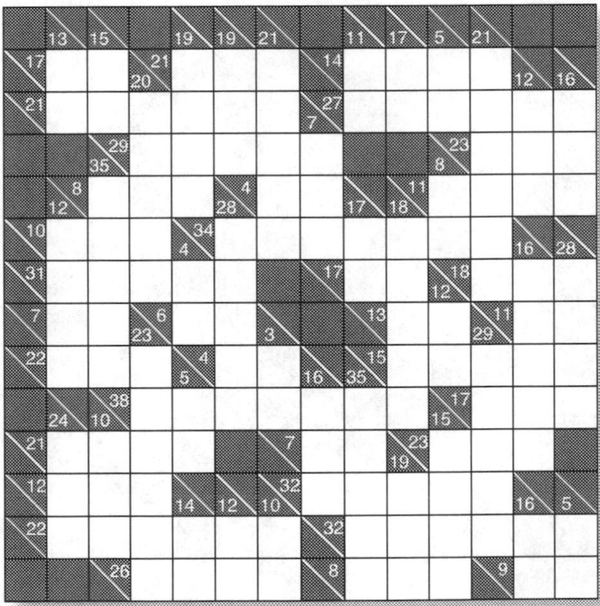

84

85

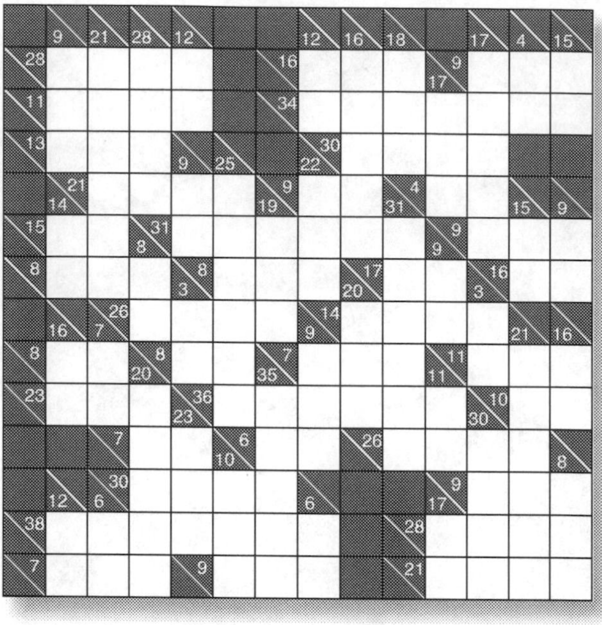

86

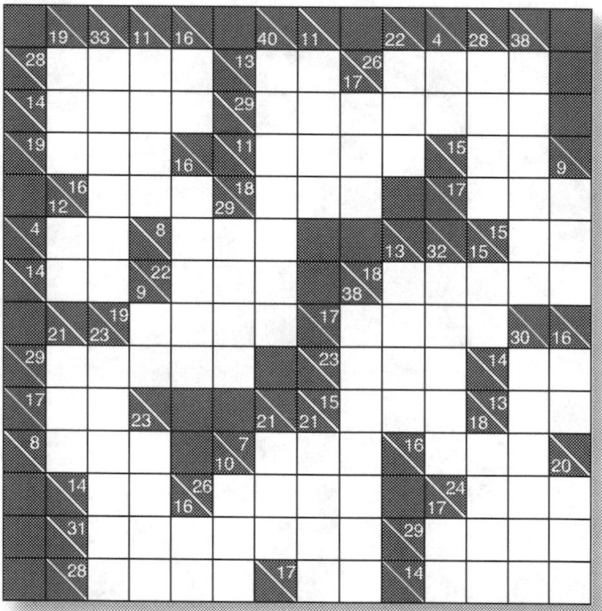

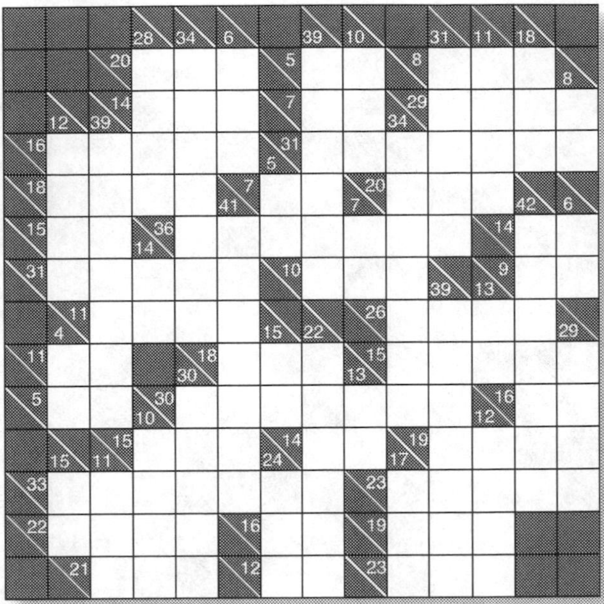

87

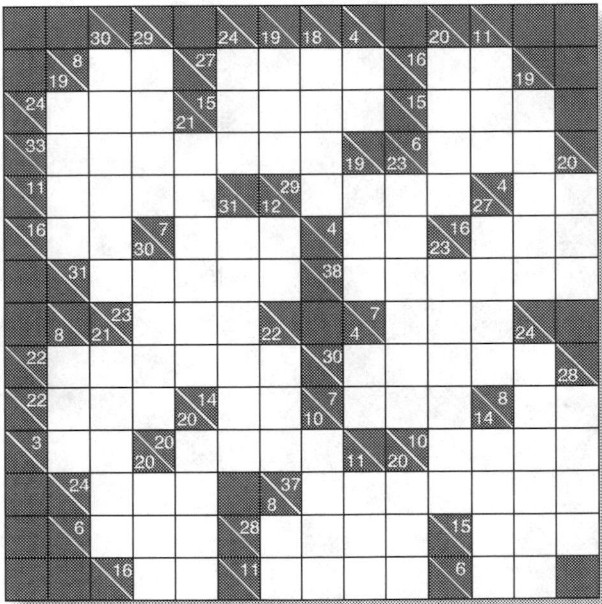

88

89

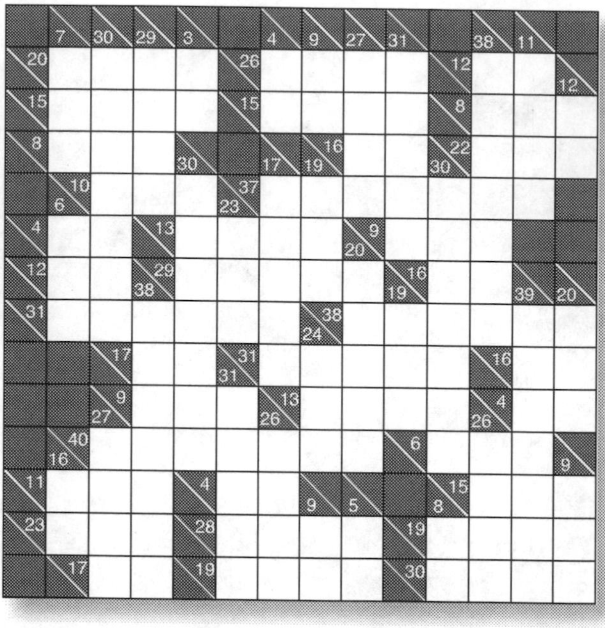

90

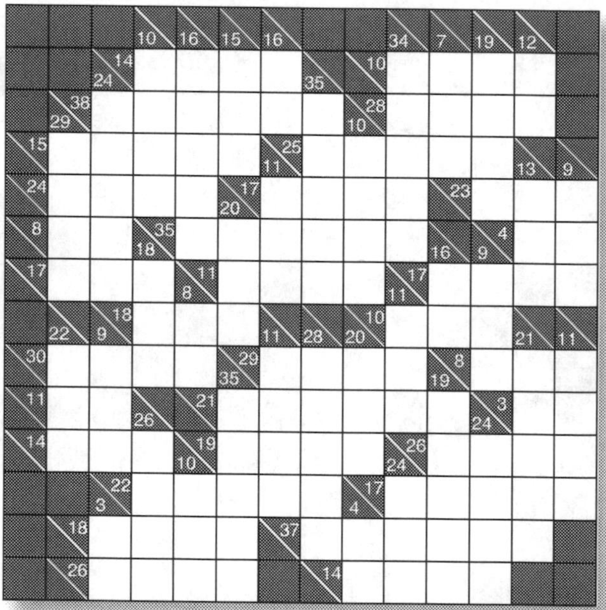

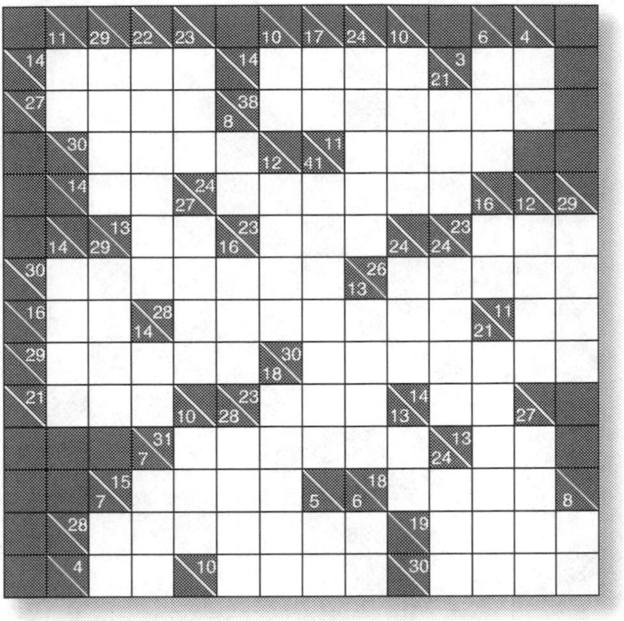

91

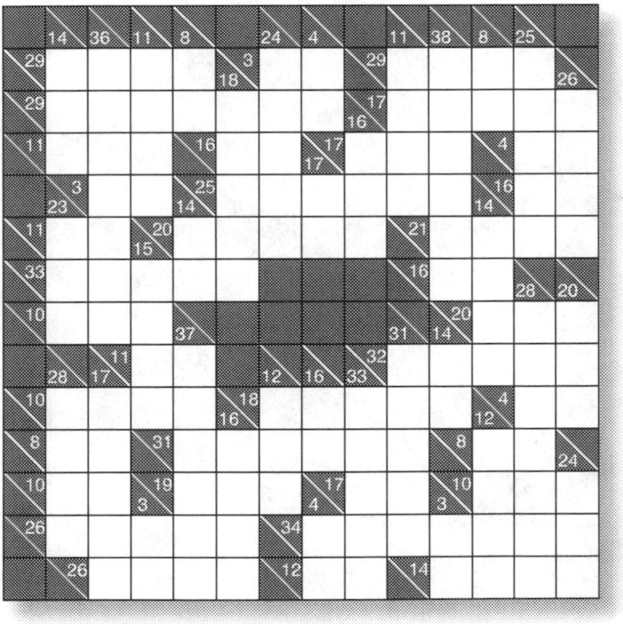

92

93

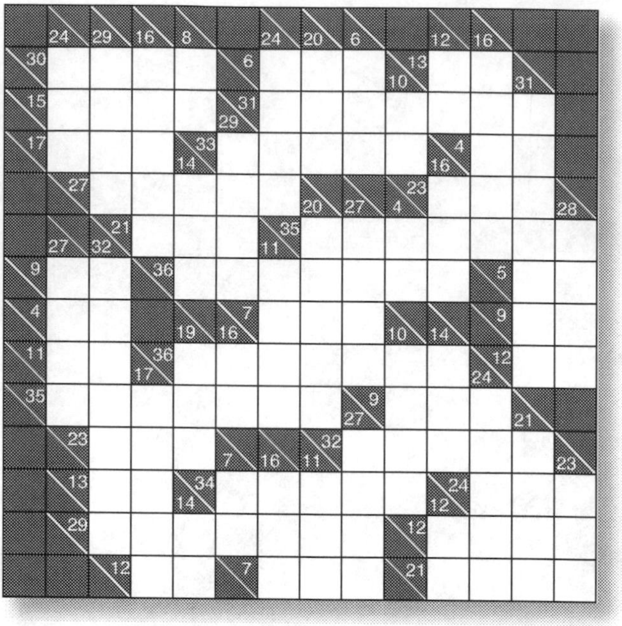

94

95

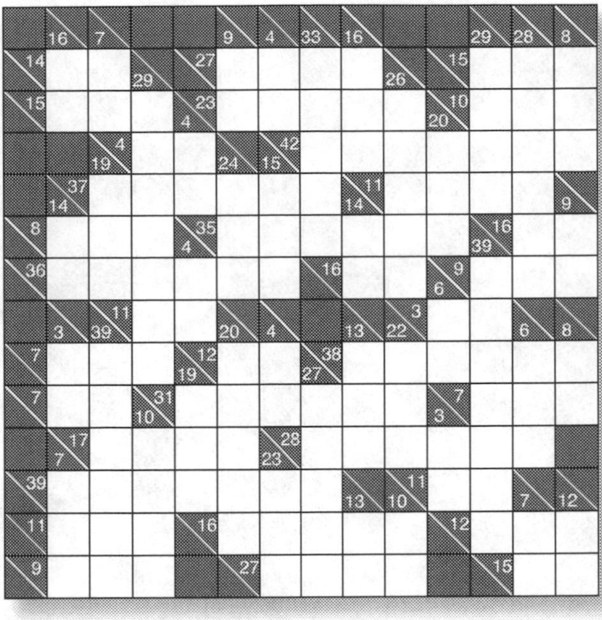

96

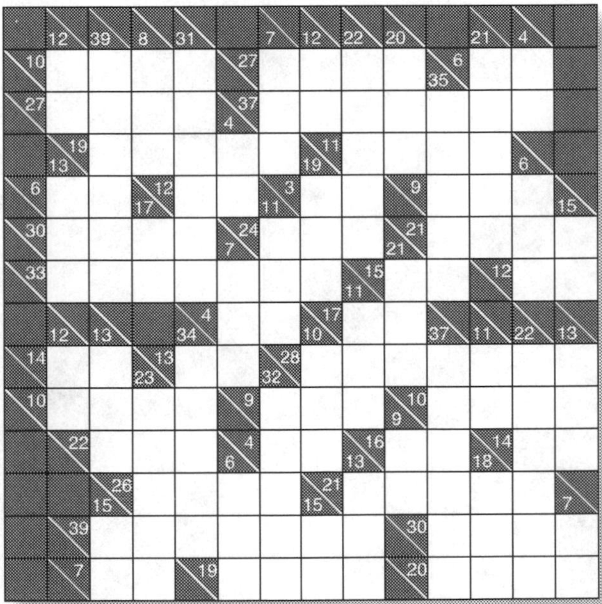

97

98

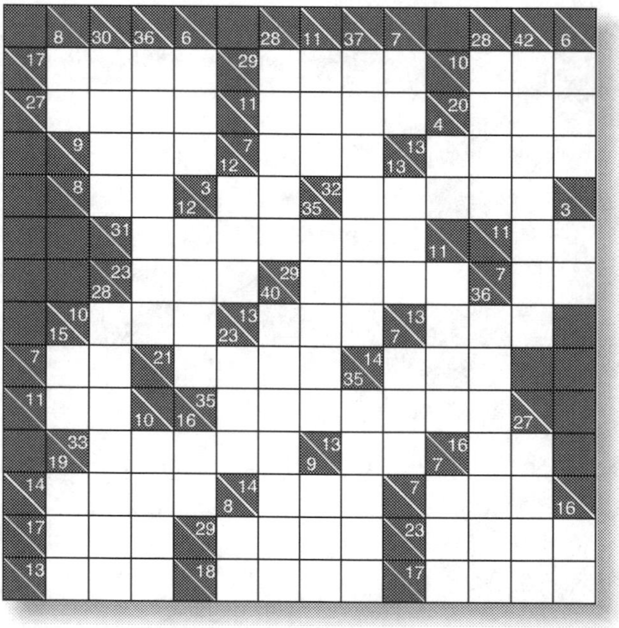

99

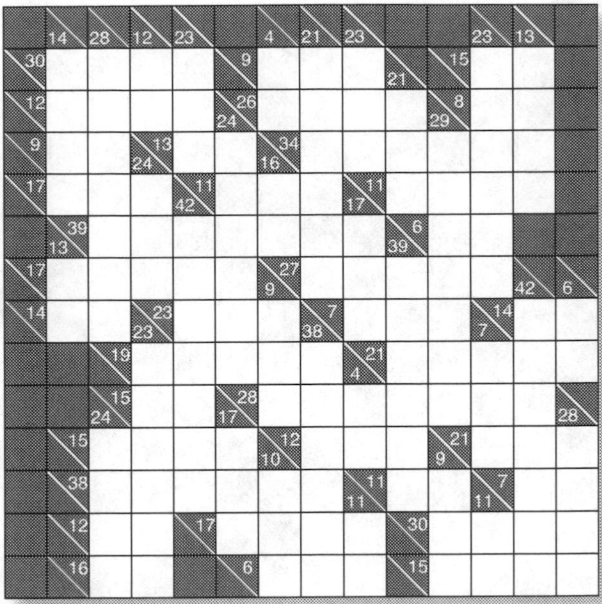
14 28 12 23 4 21 23 23 13
30 9 21 15
12 26 24 8 29
9 13 24 34 16
17 11 42 11 17
39 13 6 39
17 27 9 42 6
14 23 23 7 38 14 7
19 21 4
15 24 28 17 28
15 12 10 21 9
38 11 11 7 11
12 17 30
16 6 15

100

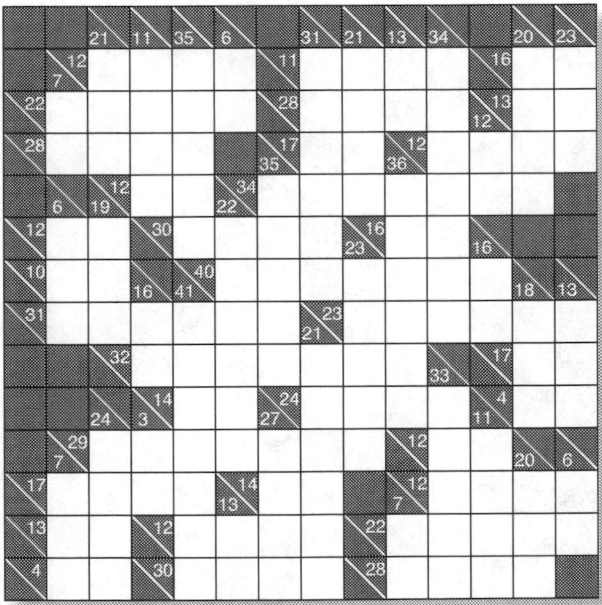
21 11 35 6 31 21 13 34 20 23
12 7 11 16
22 28 13 12
28 17 35 12 36
6 12 19 34 22
12 30 16 23 16
10 16 40 41 18 13
31 23 21
32 33 17
24 14 3 24 27 4 11
29 7 12 20 6
17 14 13 12 7
13 12 22
4 30 28

101

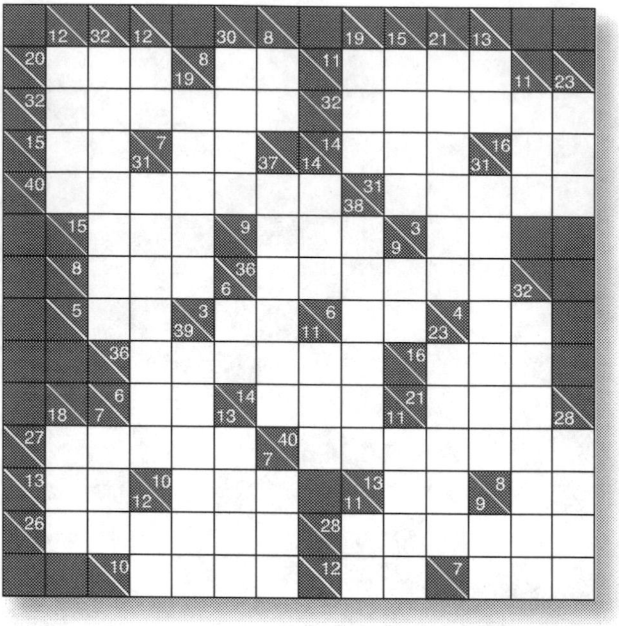

102

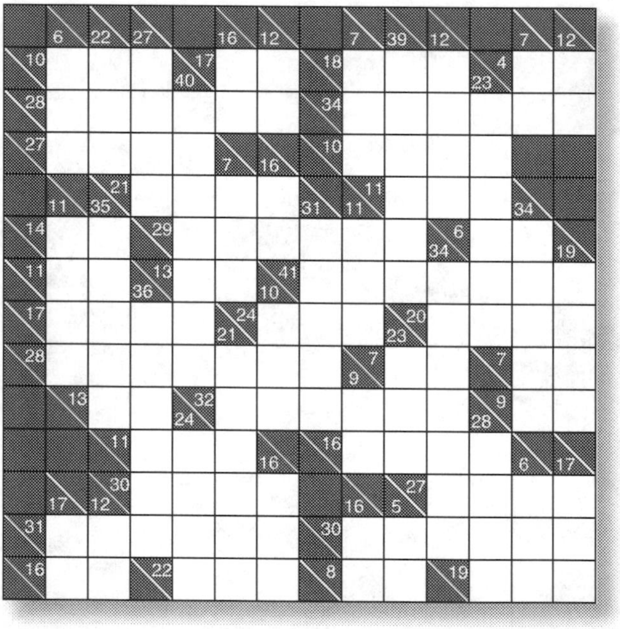

103

104

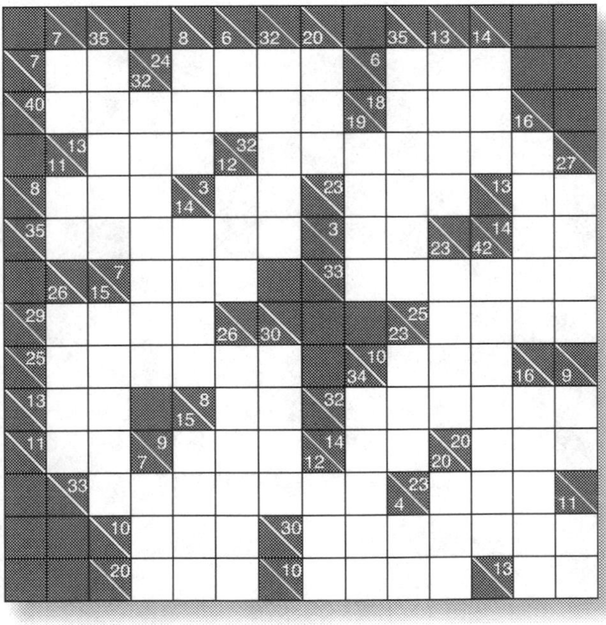

105

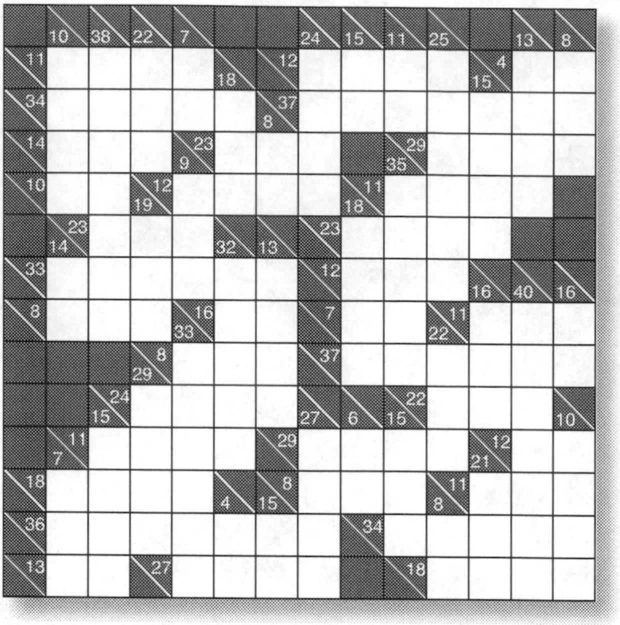

106

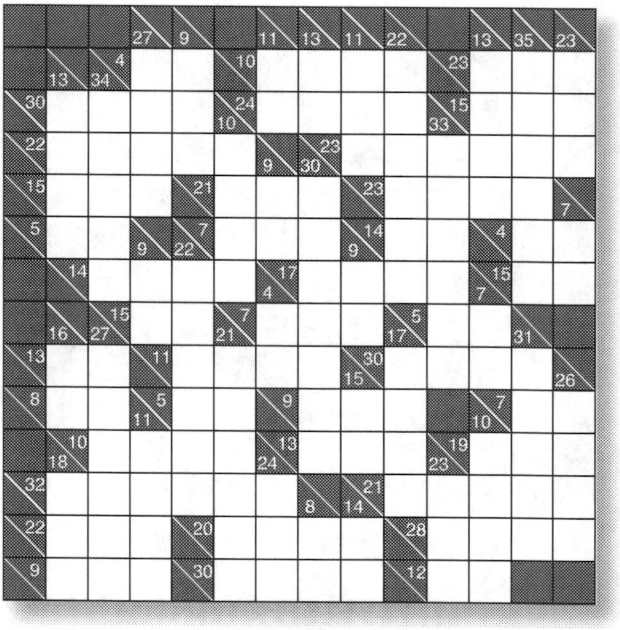

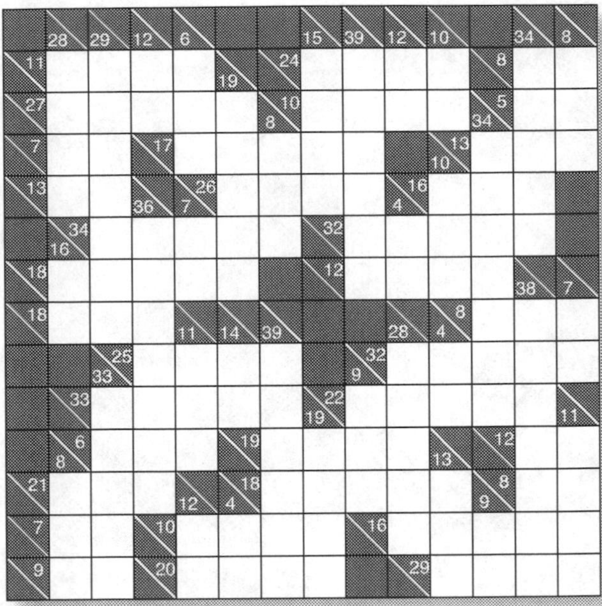
28 29 12 6 15 39 12 10 34 8
11 19 24 8
27 10 8 5 34
7 17 13 10
13 36 26 7 16 4
34 16 32
18 12 38 7
18 11 14 39 28 8 4
25 33 32 9
33 22 19 11
6 8 19 13 12
21 12 18 4 8 9
7 10 16
9 20 29

107

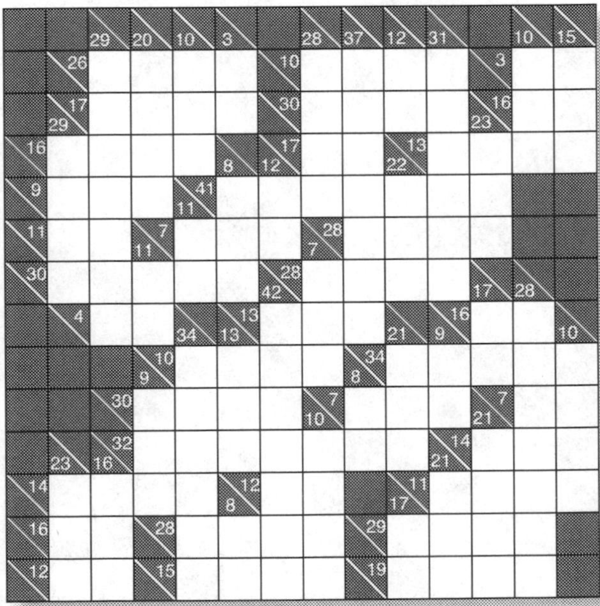
29 20 10 3 28 37 12 31 10 15
26 10 3
17 29 30 16 23
16 8 17 12 13 22
9 41 11
11 7 11 28 7
30 28 42 17 28
4 34 13 13 21 16 9 10
10 9 34 8
30 7 10 7 21
23 32 16 14 21
14 12 8 11 17
16 28 29
12 15 19

108

109

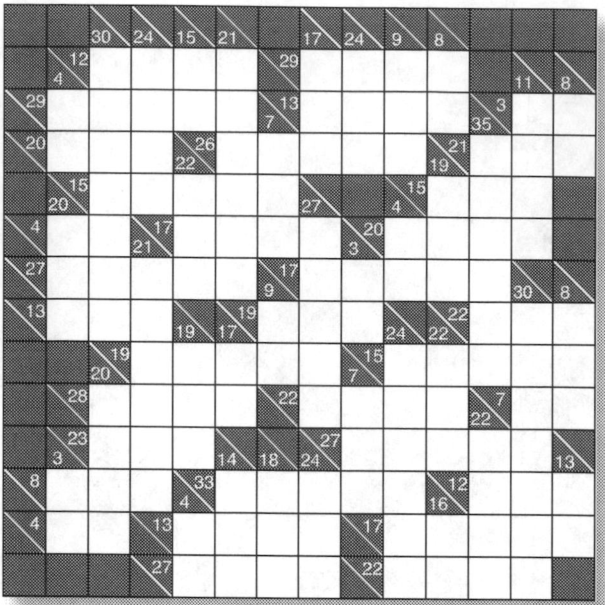

110

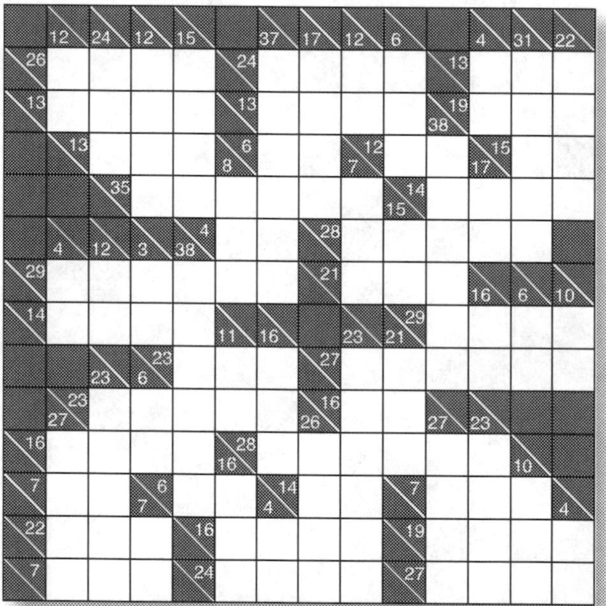

111

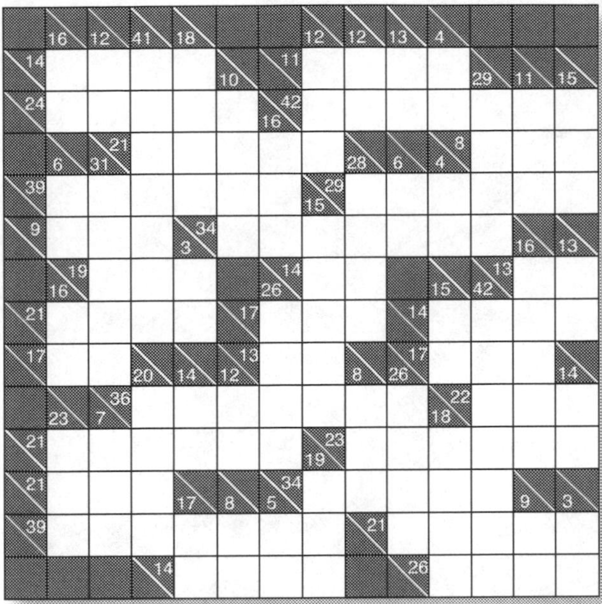

112

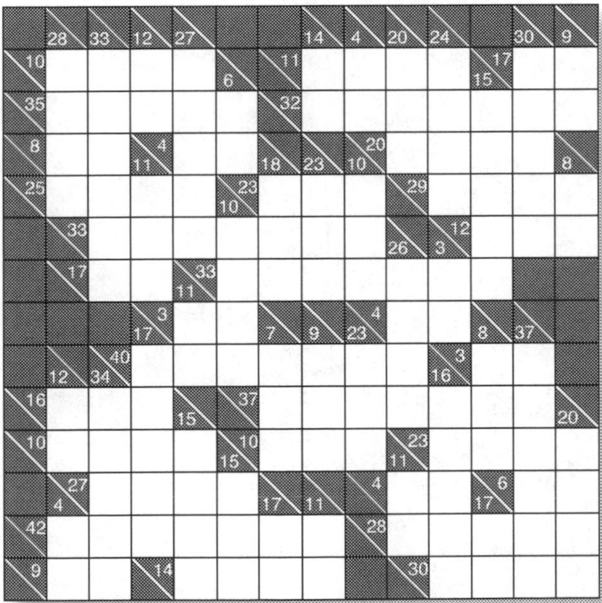

PART 3

Extremely Challenging Puzzles

1

2

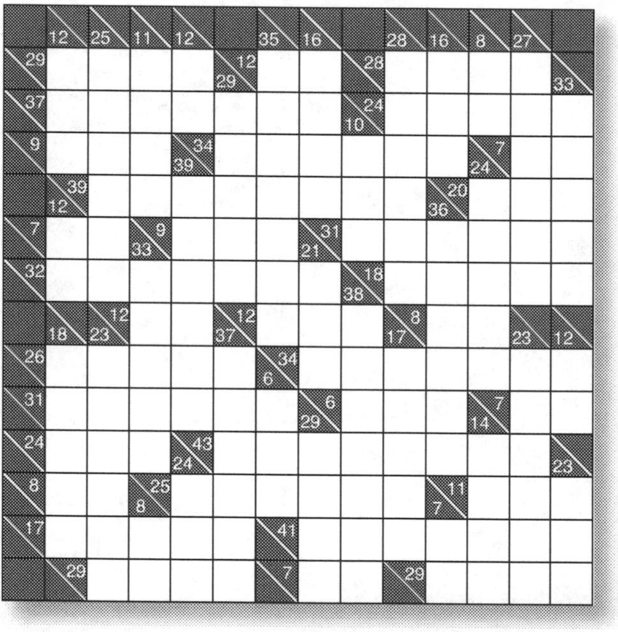

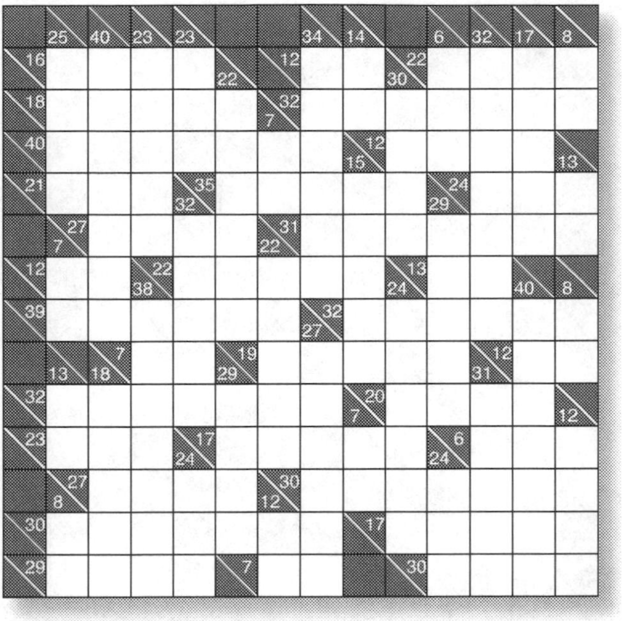
25 40 23 23 34 14 6 32 17 8
16 22 12 22 30
18 32 7
40 12 15 13
21 35 32 24 29
27 7 31 22
12 22 38 13 24 40 8
39 32 27
13 7 18 19 29 12 31
32 20 7 12
23 17 24 6 24
27 8 30 12
30 17
29 7 30

3

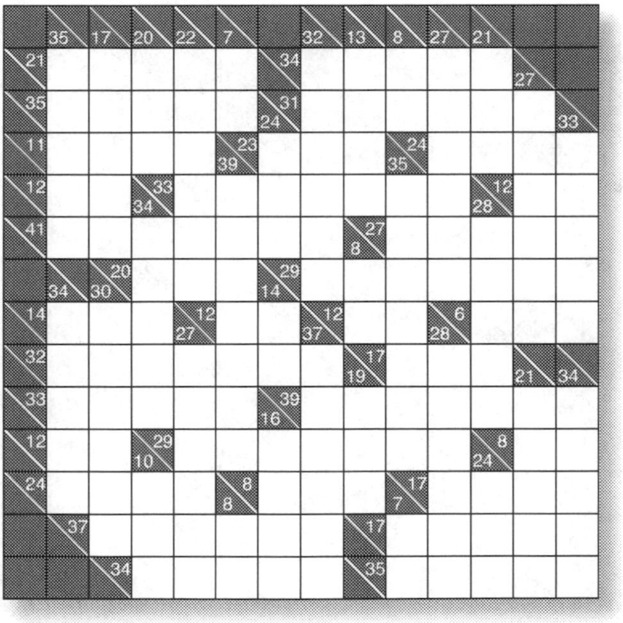
35 17 20 22 7 32 13 8 27 21
21 34 27
35 31 24 33
11 23 39 24 35
12 33 34 12 28
41 27 8
34 20 30 29 14
14 12 27 12 37 6 28
32 17 19 21 34
33 39 16
12 29 10 8 24
24 8 8 17 7
37 17
34 35

4

5

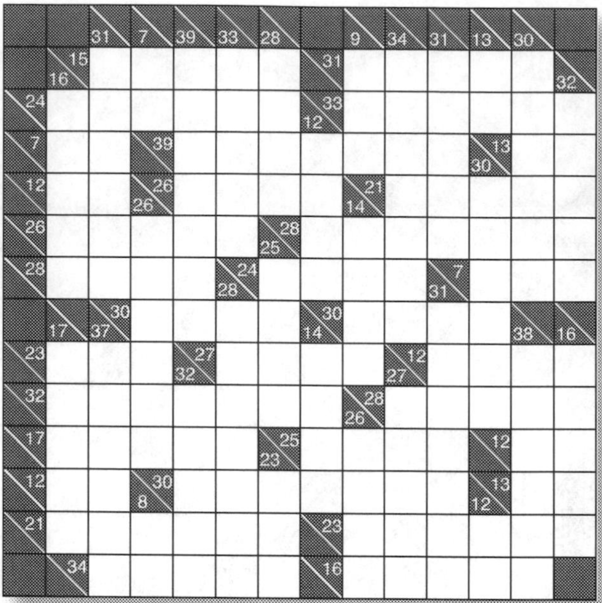
31 7 39 33 28 9 34 31 13 30
15 16 31 32
24 33 12
7 39 13 30
12 26 26 21 14
26 28 25
28 24 28 7 31
17 30 37 30 14 38 16
23 27 32 12 27
32 28 26
17 25 23 12
12 30 8 13 12
21 23
34 16

6

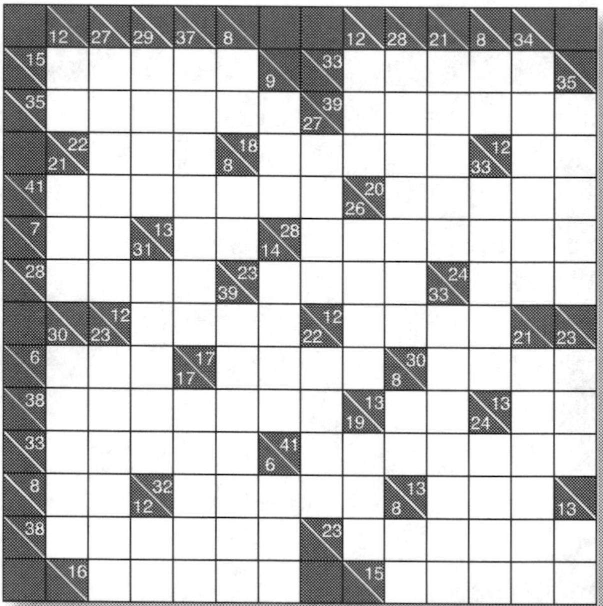
12 27 29 37 8 12 28 21 8 34
15 9 33 35
35 39 27
22 21 18 8 12 33
41 20 26
7 13 31 28 14
28 23 39 24 33
30 12 23 12 22 21 23
6 17 17 30 8
38 13 19 13 24
33 41 6
8 32 12 13 8 13
38 23
16 15

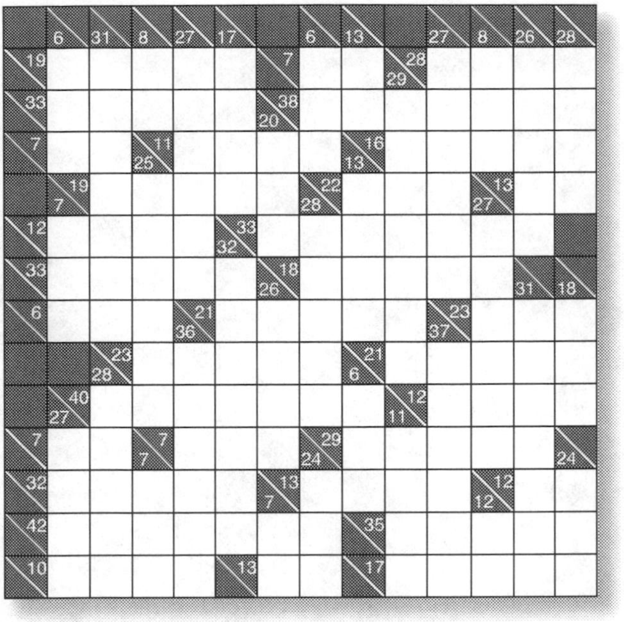

7

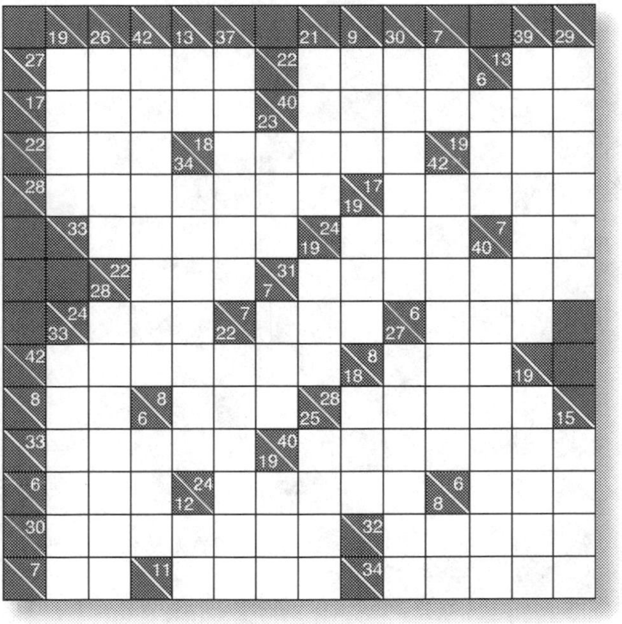

8

9

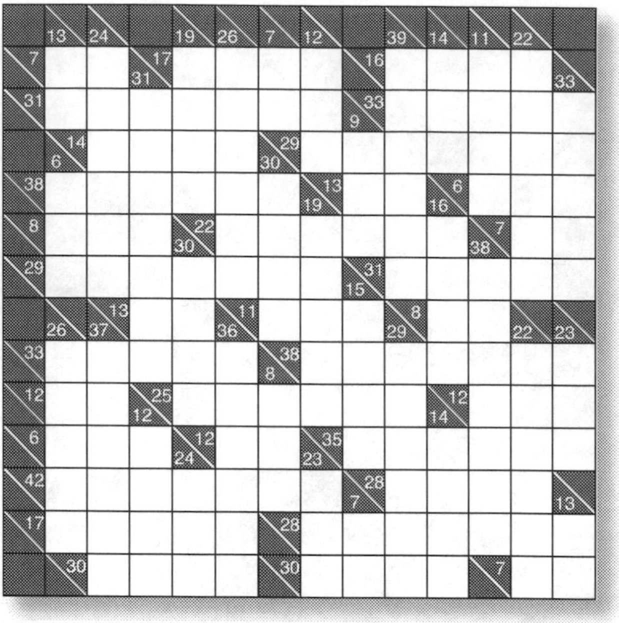

10

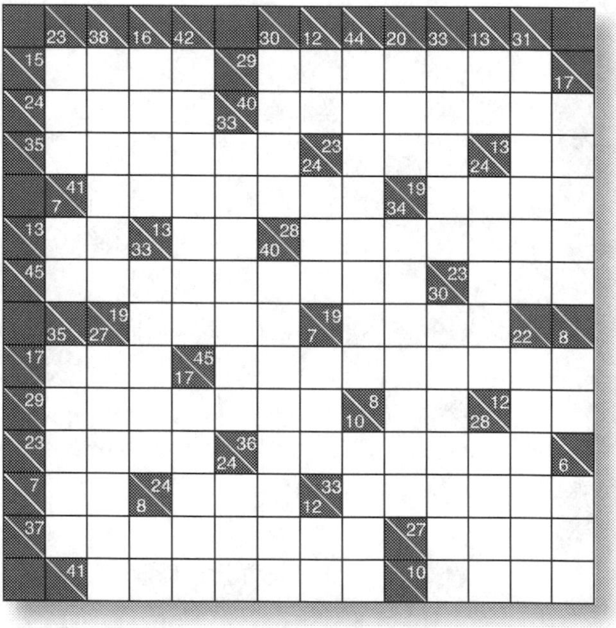

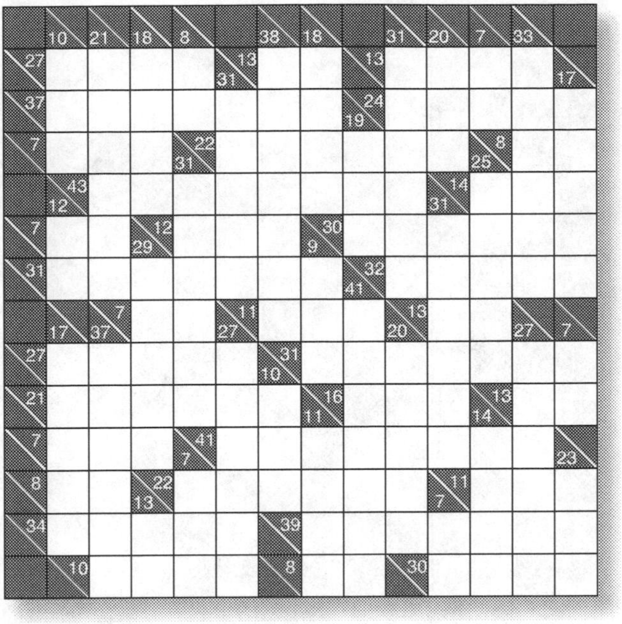

11

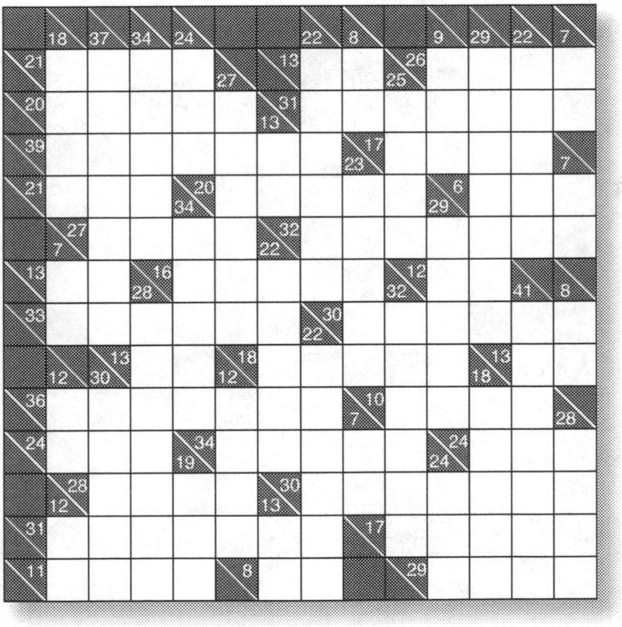

12

13

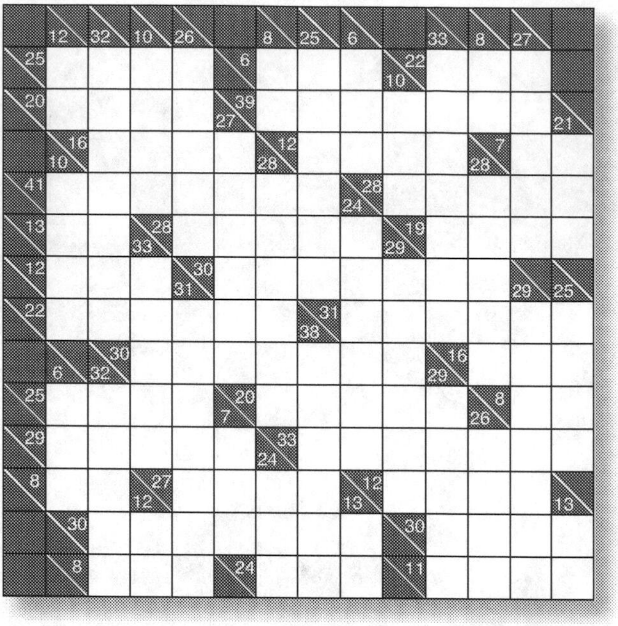

14

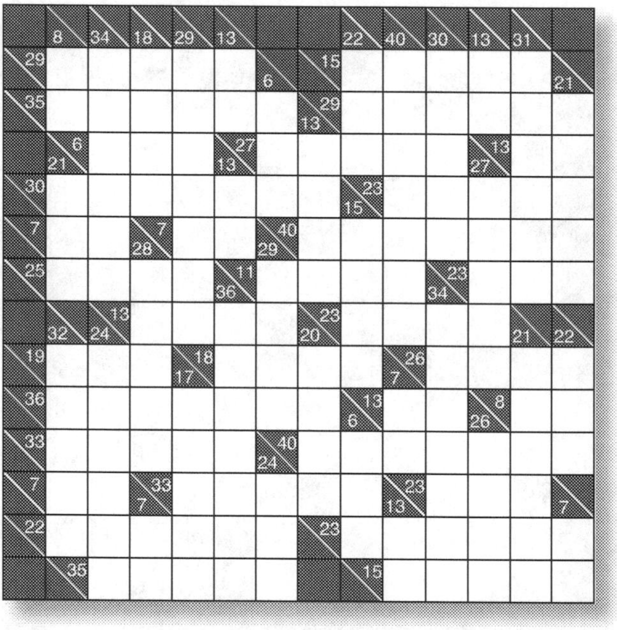

15

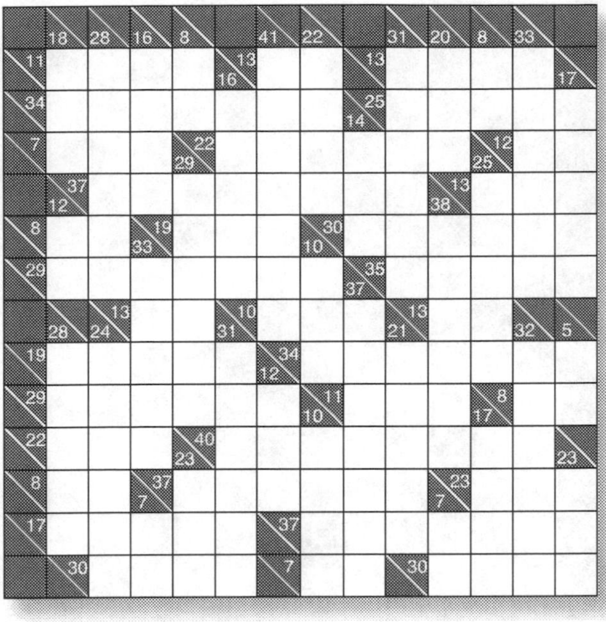

18 28 16 8 41 22 31 20 8 33
11 13 16 13 17
34 25 14
7 22 29 12 25
37 12 13 38
8 19 33 30 10
29 35 37
28 13 24 10 31 13 21 32 5
19 34 12
29 11 10 8 17
22 40 23 23
8 37 7 23 7
17 37
30 7 30

16

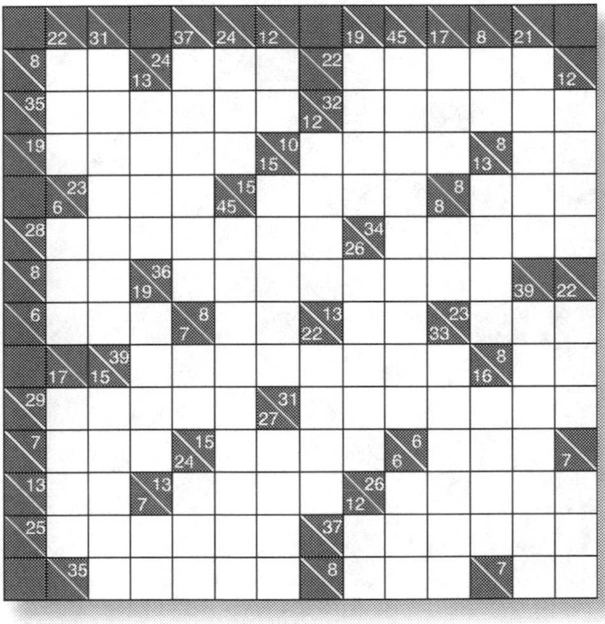

22 31 37 24 12 19 45 17 8 21
8 24 13 22 12
35 32 12
19 10 15 8 13
23 6 15 45 8 8
28 34 26
8 36 19 39 22
6 8 7 13 22 23 33
17 39 15 8 16
29 31 27
7 15 24 6 6 7
13 13 7 26 12
25 37
35 8 7

17

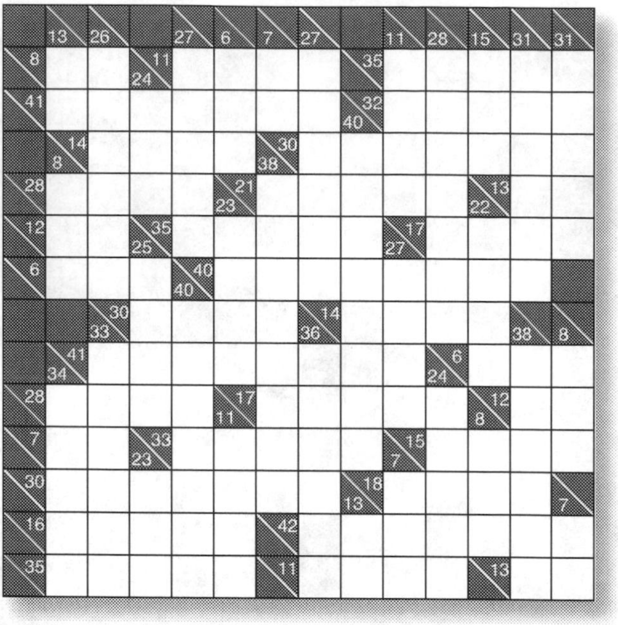

18

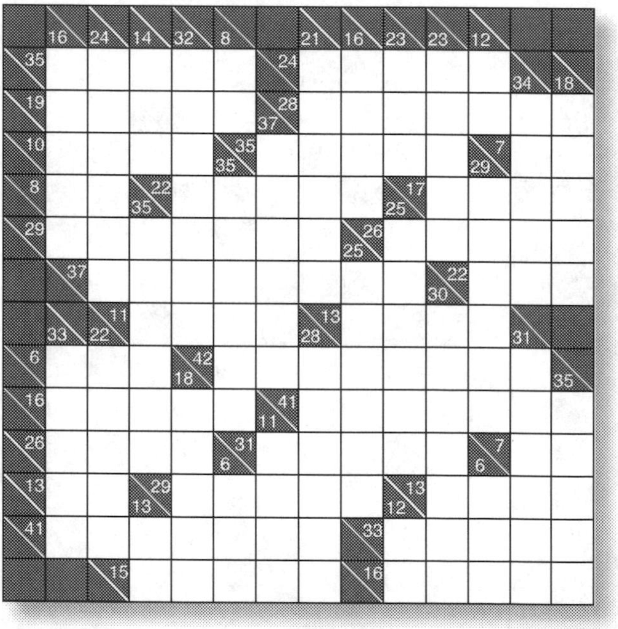

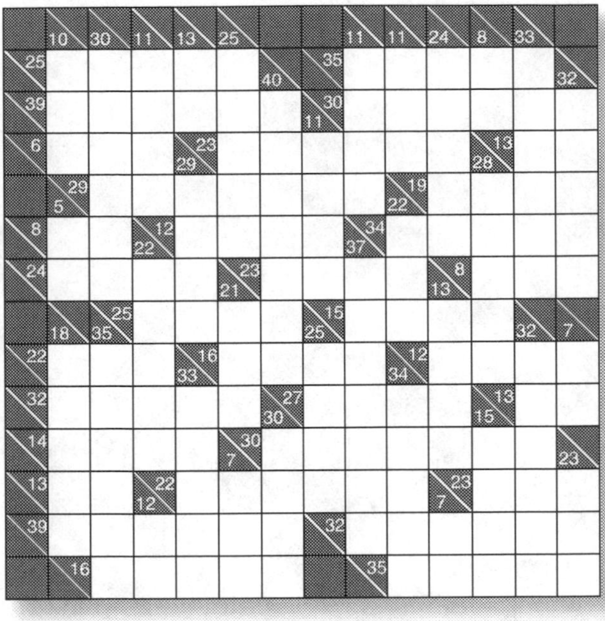

19

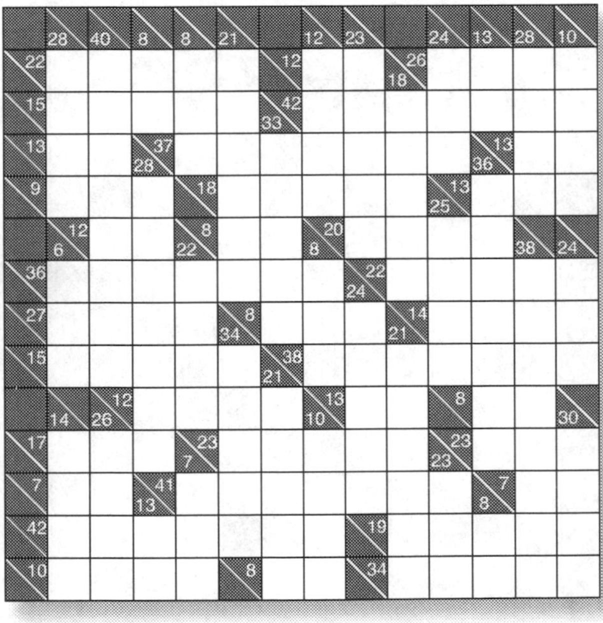

20

21

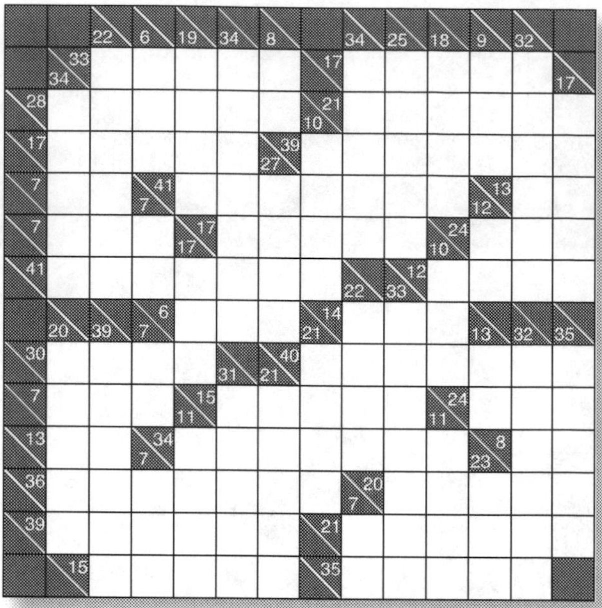

22

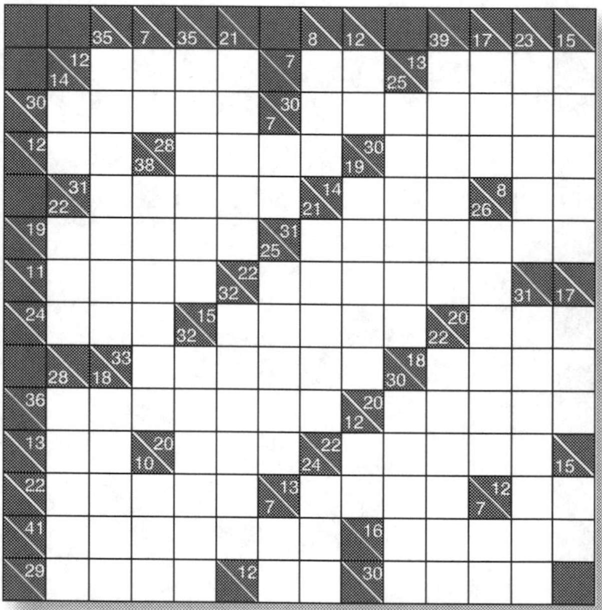

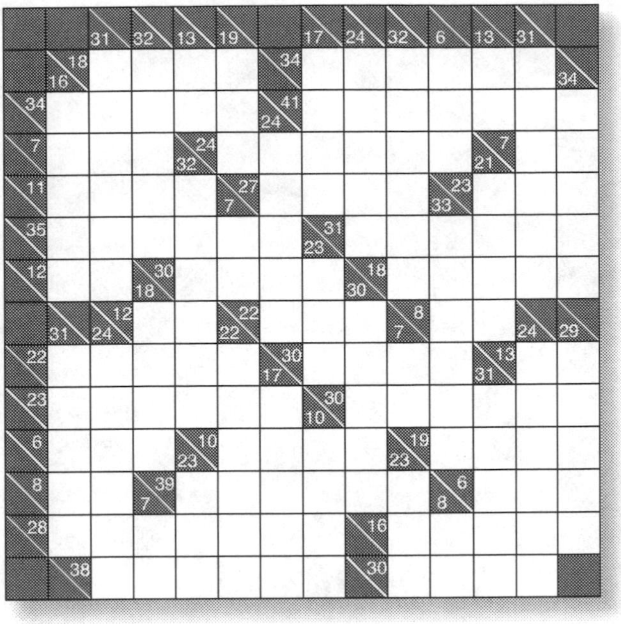
31 32 13 19 17 24 32 6 13 31
18 16 34 34
34 41 24
7 24 32 7 21
11 27 7 23 33
35 31 23
12 30 18 18 30
31 12 24 22 22 8 7 24 29
22 30 17 13 31
23 30 10
6 10 23 19 23
8 39 7 6 8
28 16
38 30

23

29 40 13 19 32 27 25 6 7 13 29
33 7 14 20
17 36 22
7 34 35 8 29
14 31 8 16
8 23 12 16 10 8 39 24
36 35 25
22 10 24 13 21
31 38 23
18 26 12 12 12 7 30
14 15 23 23 24
12 41 8 7 8
38 21
30 12 34

24

25

16 36 26 13 23 8 23 32 12 17 12
27 12 27 18
32 16 25
8 30 24 8 16
25 39 28
12 12 34 32 22 41 13
37 12 13 26
24 15 30 9 8
17 39 33 33
11 27 30 12 11 13 14
29 36 21
8 23 12 7 7
35 28
16 7 30

26

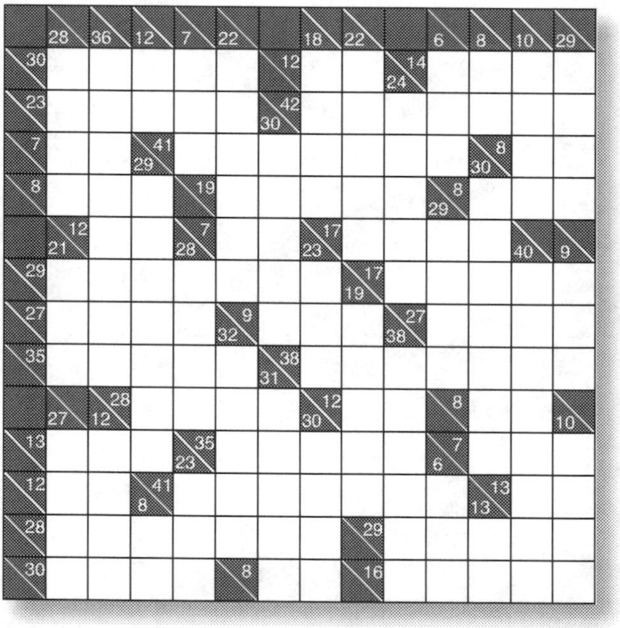
28 36 12 7 22 18 22 6 8 10 29
30 12 14 24
23 42 30
7 41 29 8 30
8 19 8 29
12 21 7 28 17 23 40 9
29 17 19
27 9 32 27 38
35 38 31
27 28 12 12 30 8 10
13 35 23 7 6
12 41 8 13 13
28 29
30 8 16

27

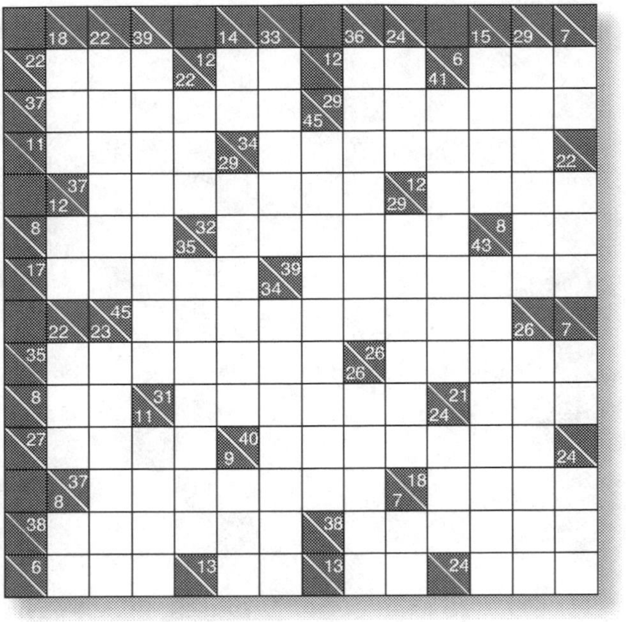
18 22 39 14 33 36 24 15 29 7
22 12 22 12 6 41
37 29 45
11 34 29 22
37 12 12 29
8 32 35 8 43
17 39 34
22 45 23 26 7
35 26 26
8 31 11 21 24
27 40 9 24
37 8 18 7
38 38
6 13 13 24

28

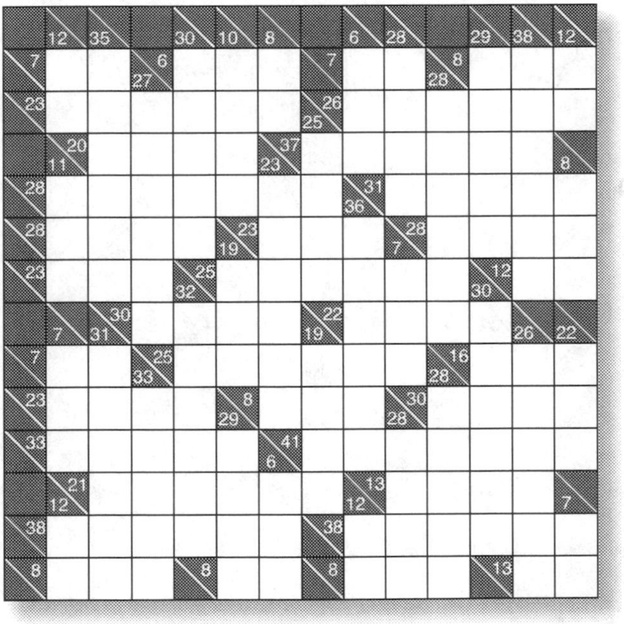
12 35 30 10 8 6 28 29 38 12
7 6 27 7 8 28
23 26 25
20 11 37 23 8
28 31 36
28 23 19 28 7
23 25 32 12 30
7 30 31 22 19 26 22
7 25 33 16 28
23 8 29 30 28
33 41 6
21 12 13 12 7
38 38
8 8 8 13

29

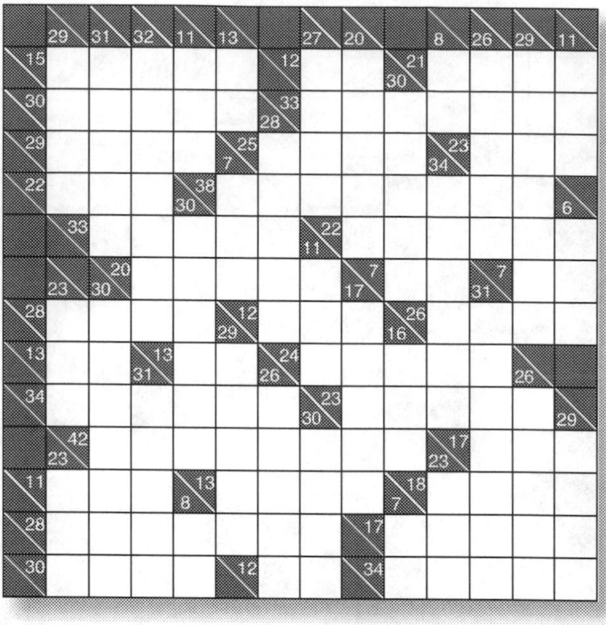

30

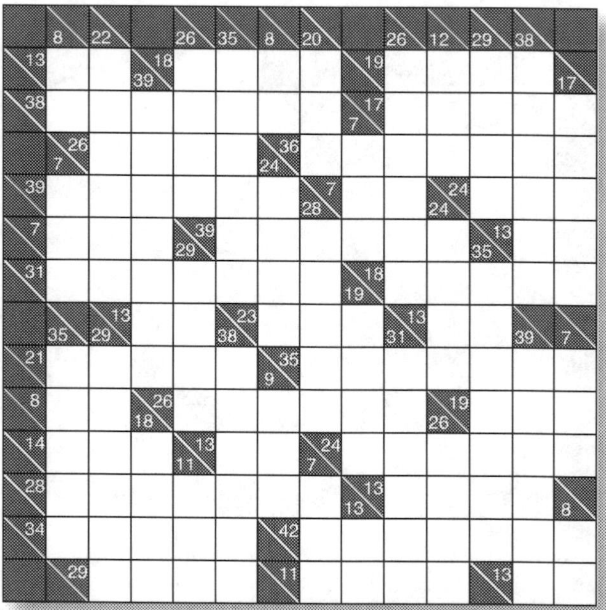

31

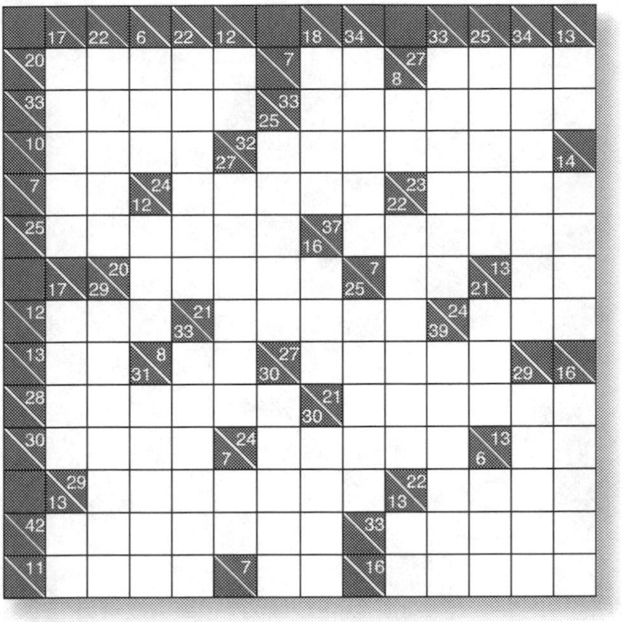

32

33

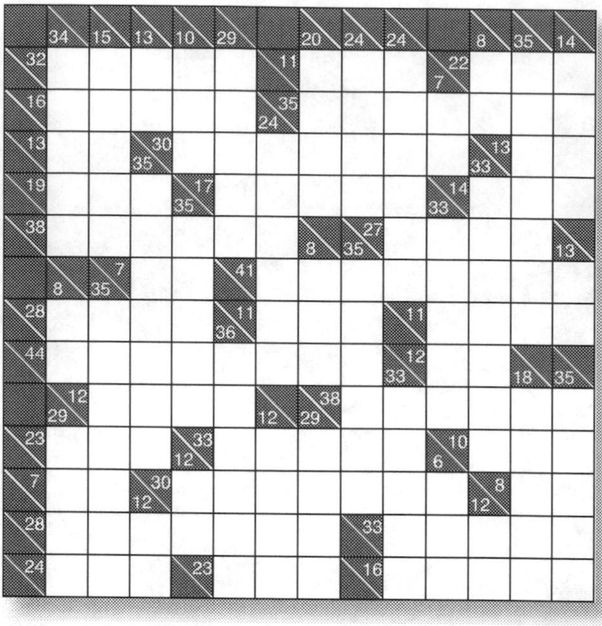

34

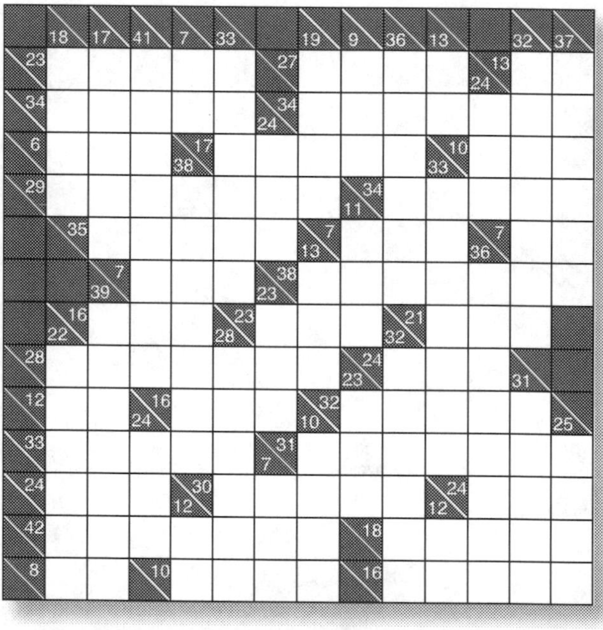

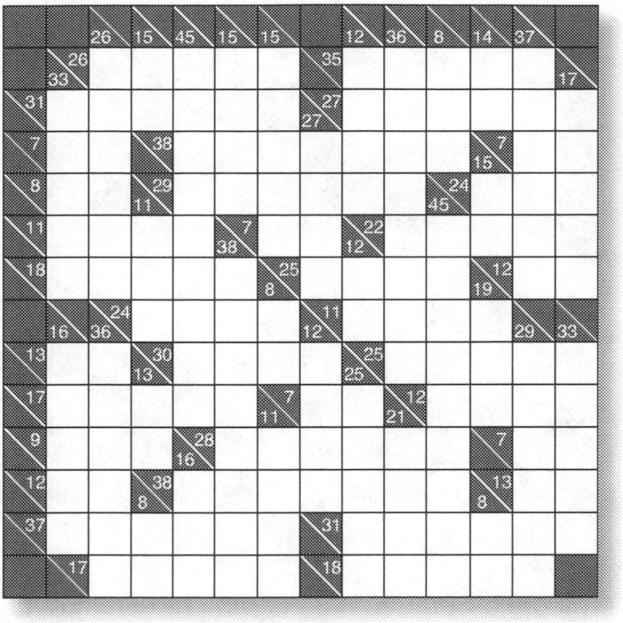

35

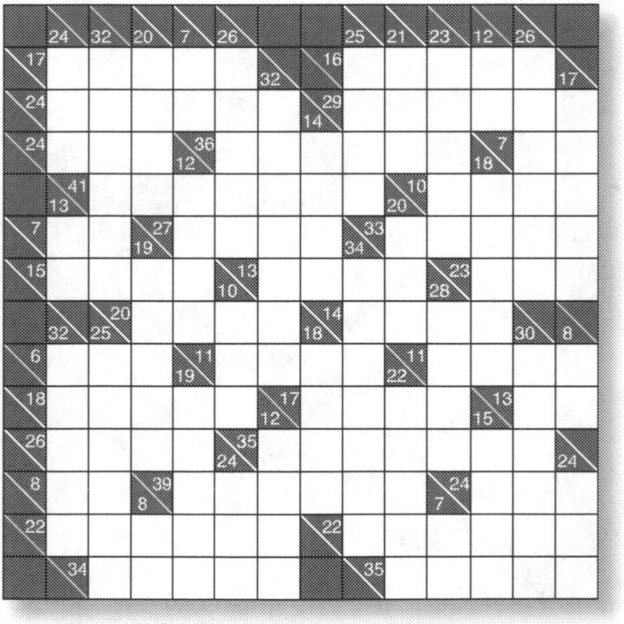

36

37

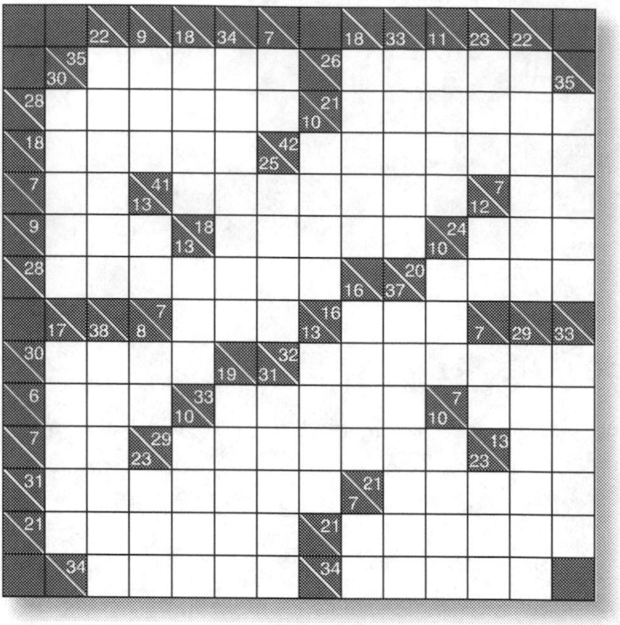

38

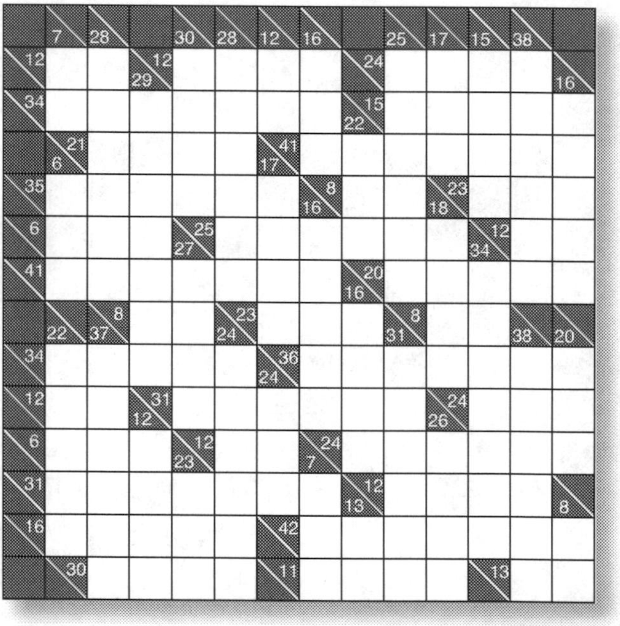

39

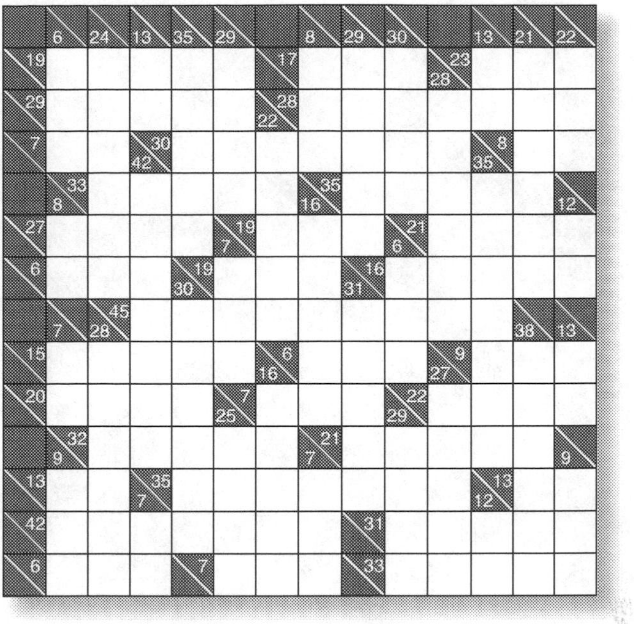

40

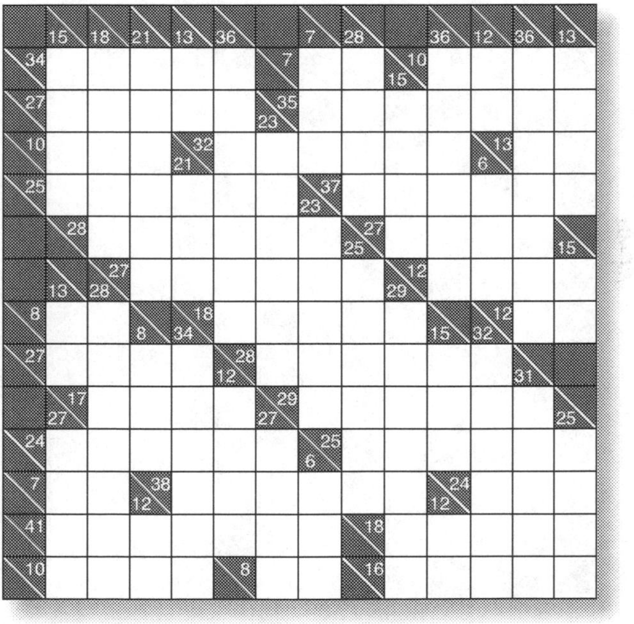

41

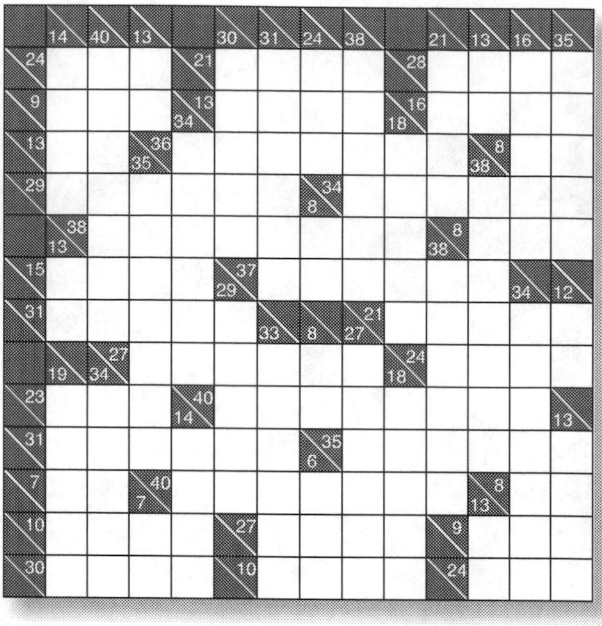

42

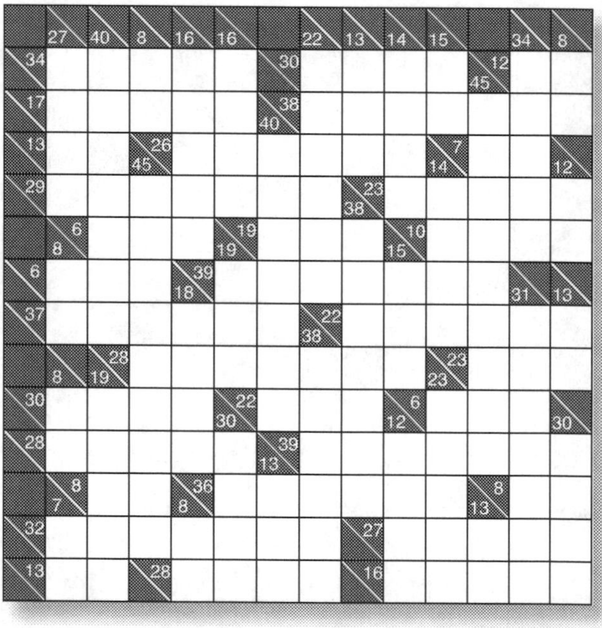

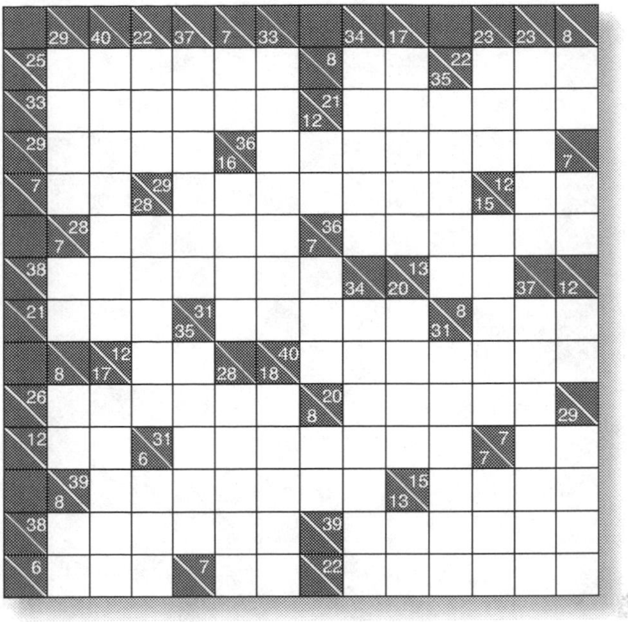

43

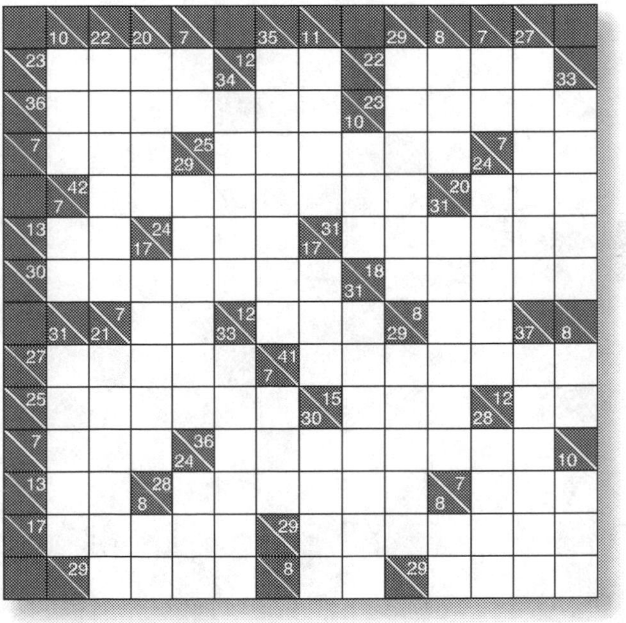

44

45

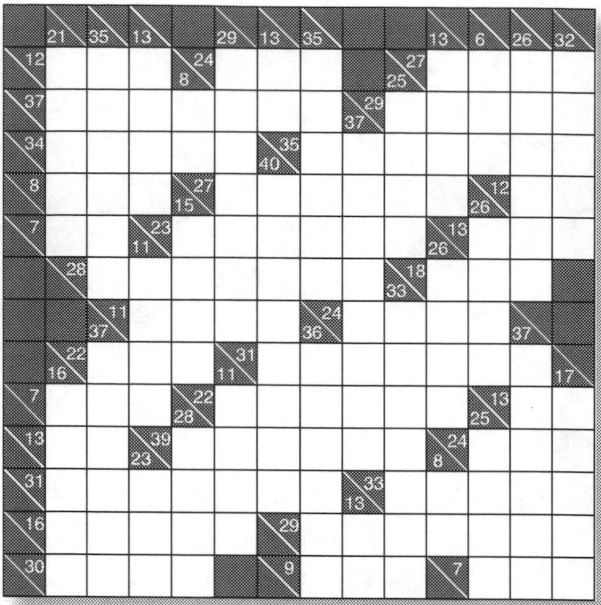

46

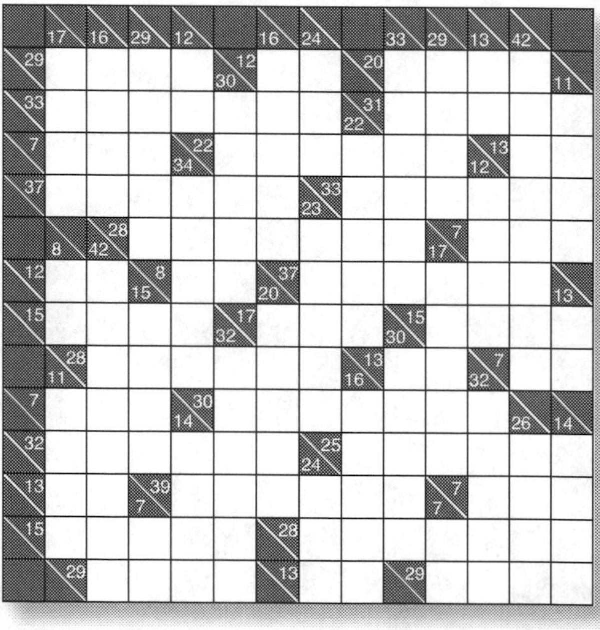

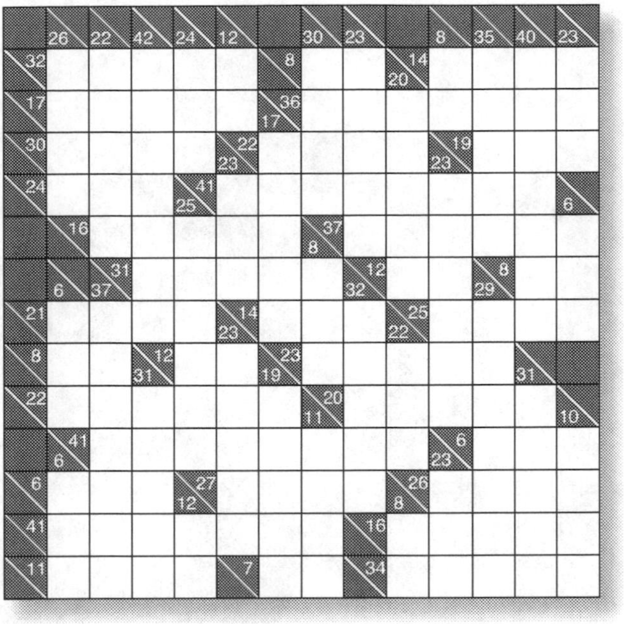
26 22 42 24 12 30 23 8 35 40 23
32 8 14 20
17 36 17
30 22 23 19 23
24 41 25 6
16 37 8
6 31 37 12 32 8 29
21 14 23 25 22
8 12 31 23 19 31
22 20 11 10
41 6 6 23
6 27 12 26 8
41 16
11 7 34

47

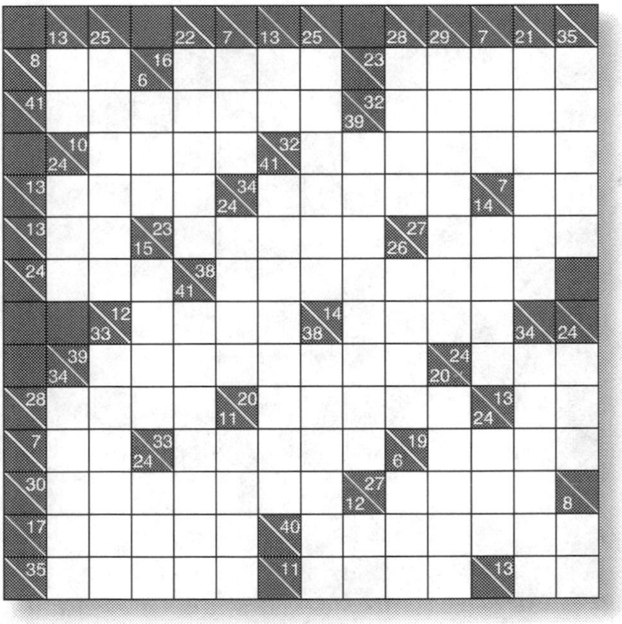
13 25 22 7 13 25 28 29 7 21 35
8 16 6 23
41 32 39
10 24 32 41
13 34 24 7 14
13 23 15 27 26
24 38 41
12 33 14 38 34 24
39 34 24 20
28 20 11 13 24
7 33 24 19 6
30 27 12 8
17 40
35 11 13

48

49

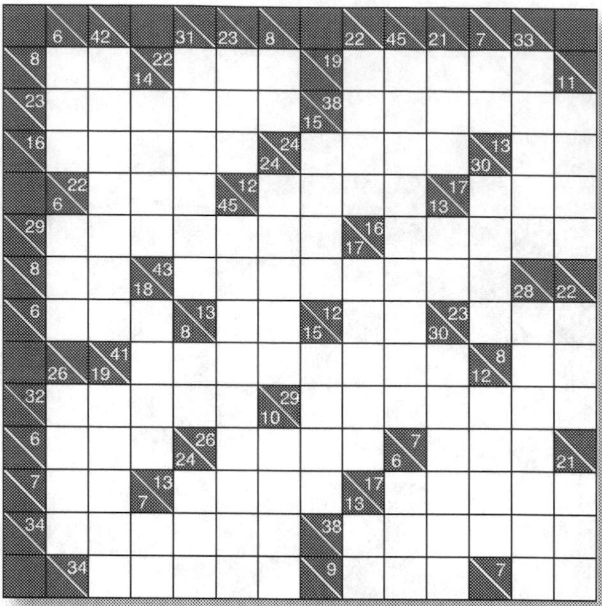

50

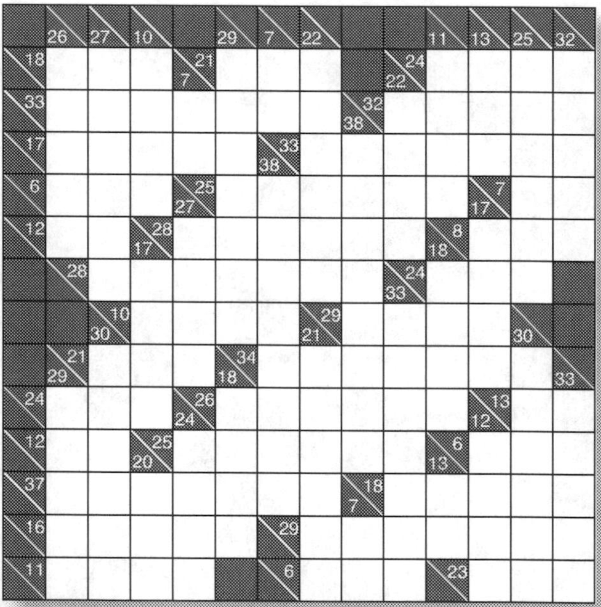

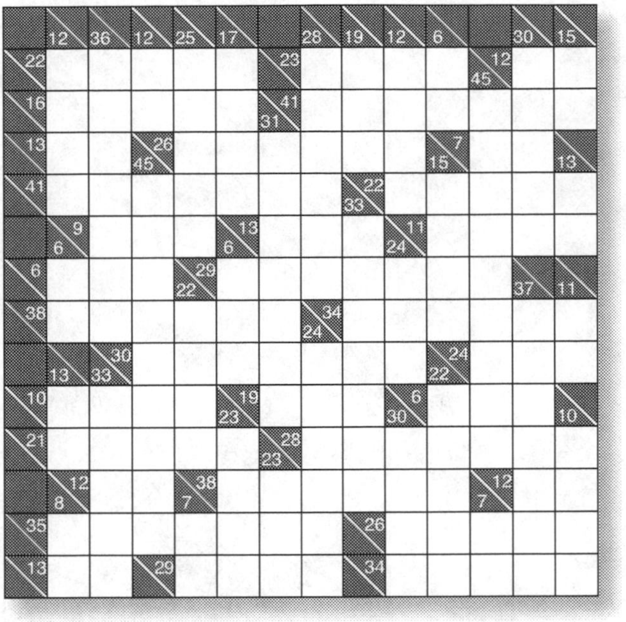

51

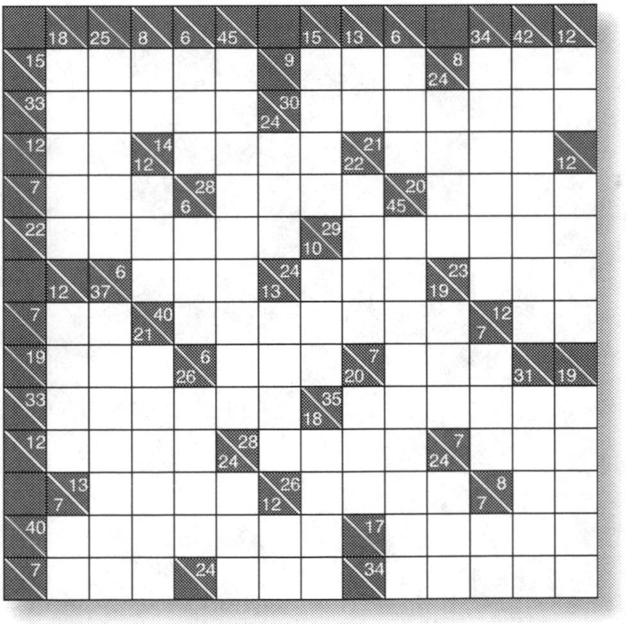

52

53

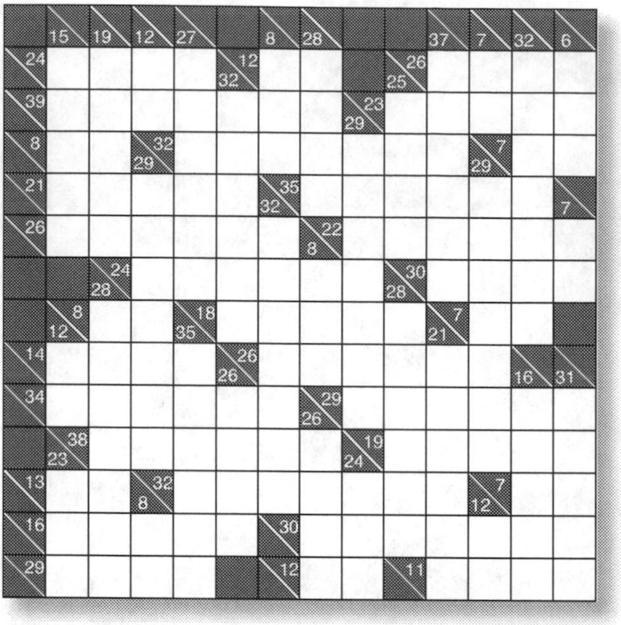

54

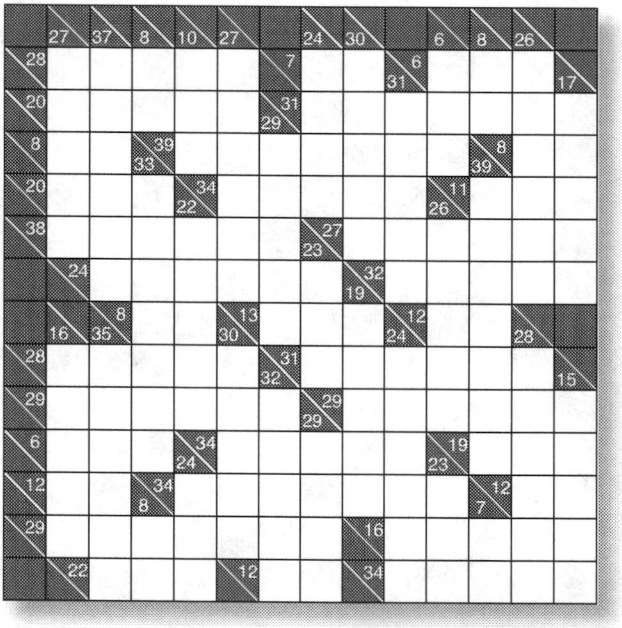

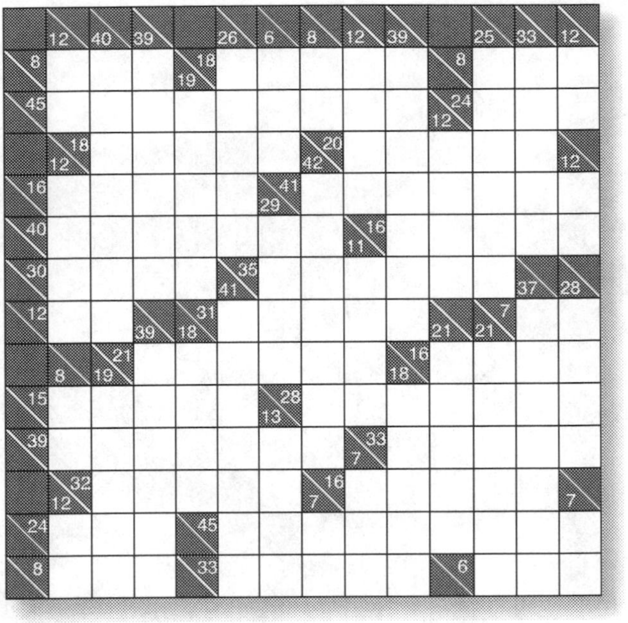
12 40 39 26 6 8 12 39 25 33 12
8 18 19 8
45 24 12
18 12 20 42 12
16 41 29
40 16 11
30 35 41 37 28
12 39 31 18 21 7 21
8 21 19 16 18
15 28 13
39 33 7
32 12 16 7 7
24 45
8 33 6

55

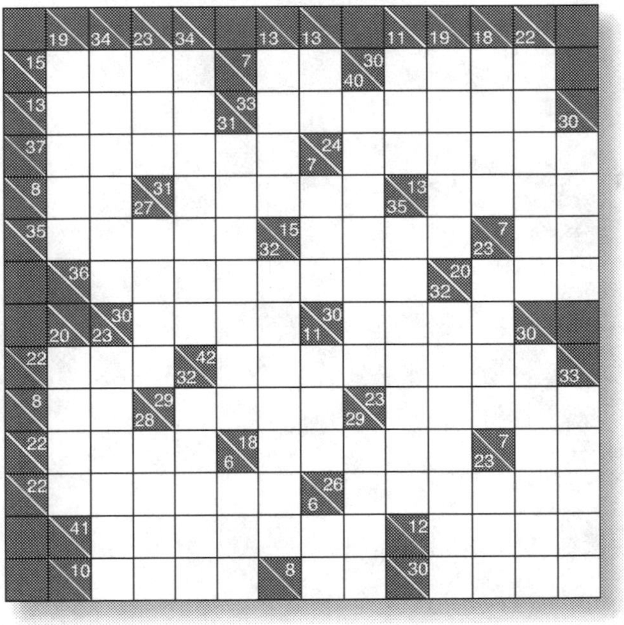
19 34 23 34 13 13 11 19 18 22
15 7 30 40
13 33 31 30
37 24 7
8 31 27 13 35
35 15 32 7 23
36 20 32
20 30 23 30 11 30
22 42 32 33
8 29 28 23 29
22 18 6 7 23
22 26 6
41 12
10 8 30

56

57

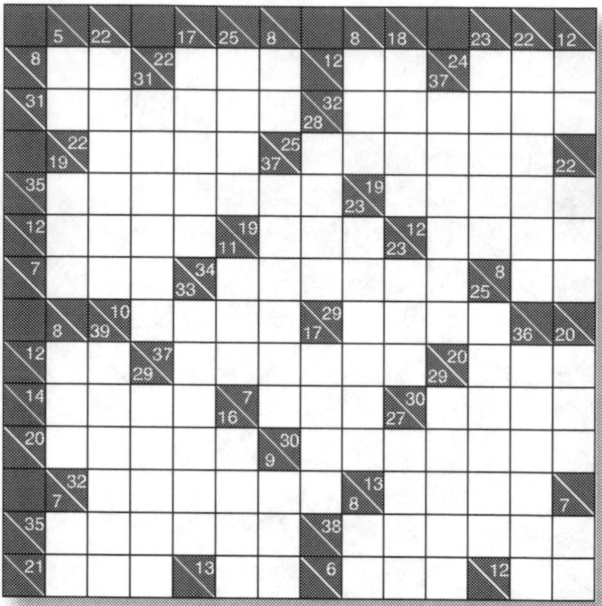

58

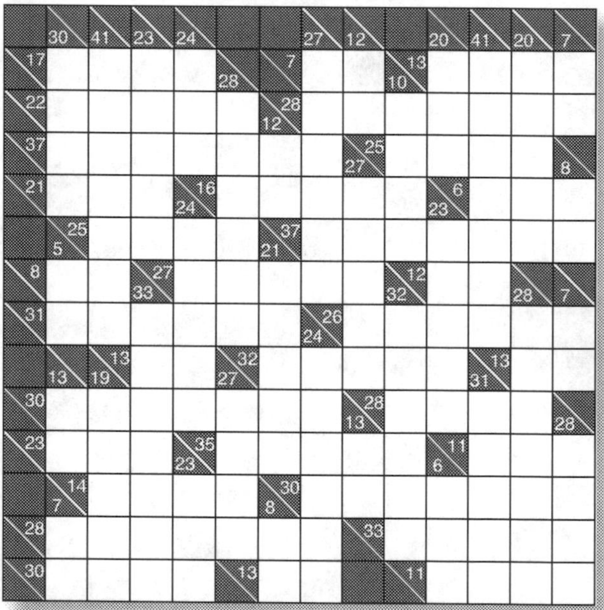

59

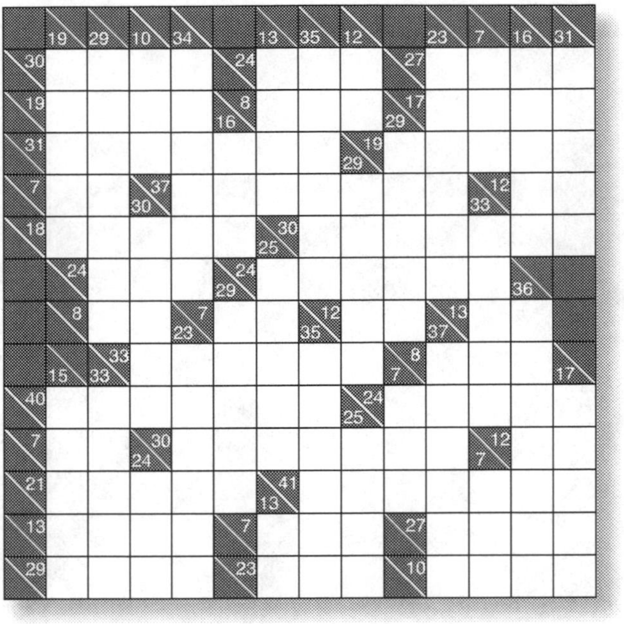

60

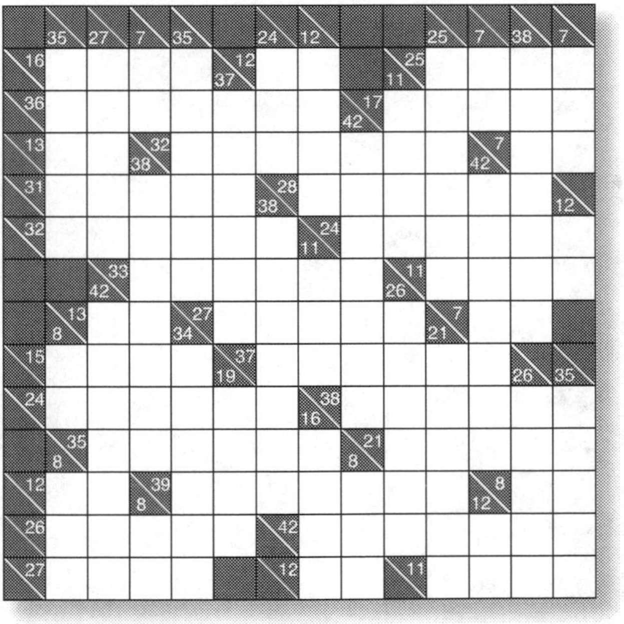

61

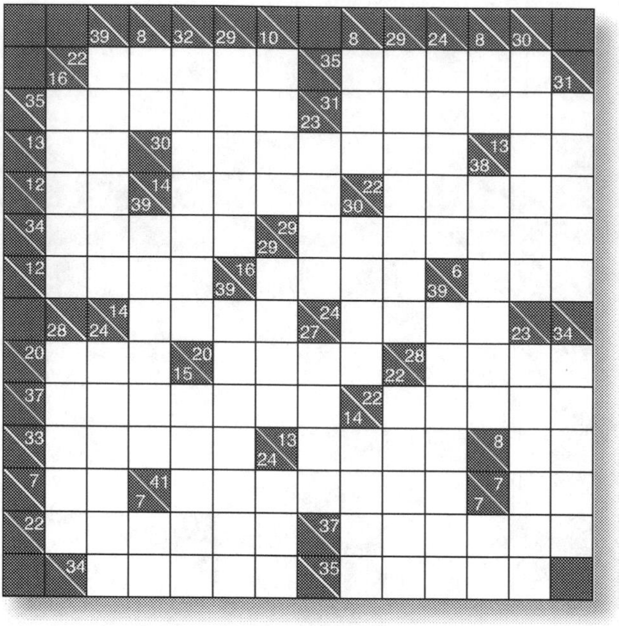

62

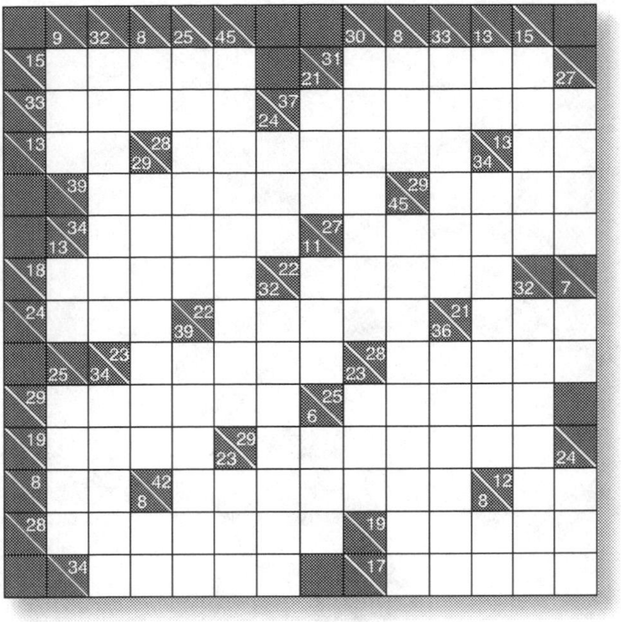
9 32 8 25 45 30 8 33 13 15
15 31 21 27
33 37 24
13 28 29 13 34
39 29 45
34 13 27 11
18 22 32 32 7
24 22 39 21 36
23 25 34 28 23
29 25 6
19 29 23 24
8 42 8 12 8
28 19
34 17

63

29 41 28 13 23 6 18 37 20 8
11 21 8 17 12
19 30 8
35 12 25 8
24 34 31 22 27
28 8 42 34
13 23 38 7 33 41 8
38 31 28
8 8 29 19 10 13 19
40 10 12 28
6 34 7 24 23
14 13 30 8
42 16
10 12 30

64

65

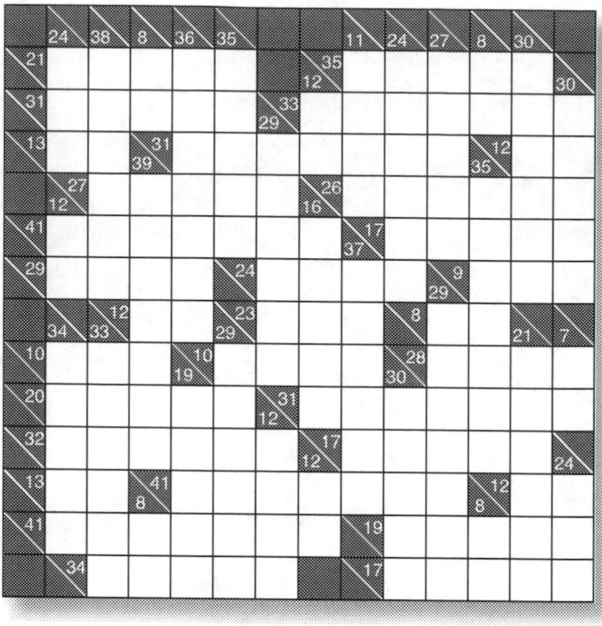

66

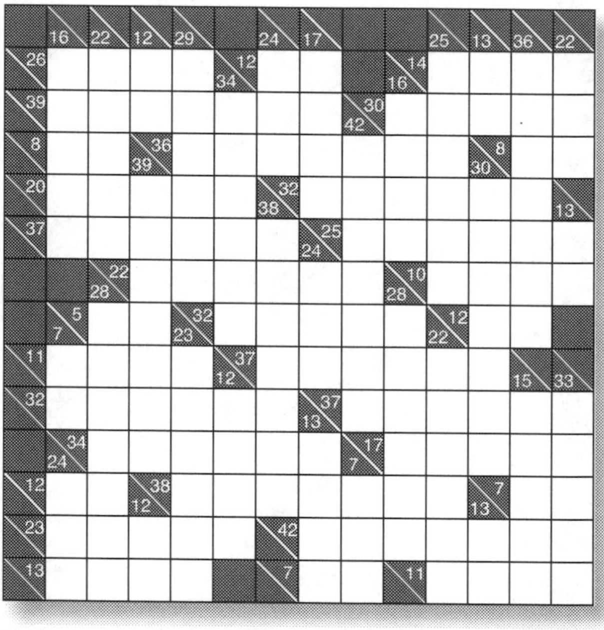

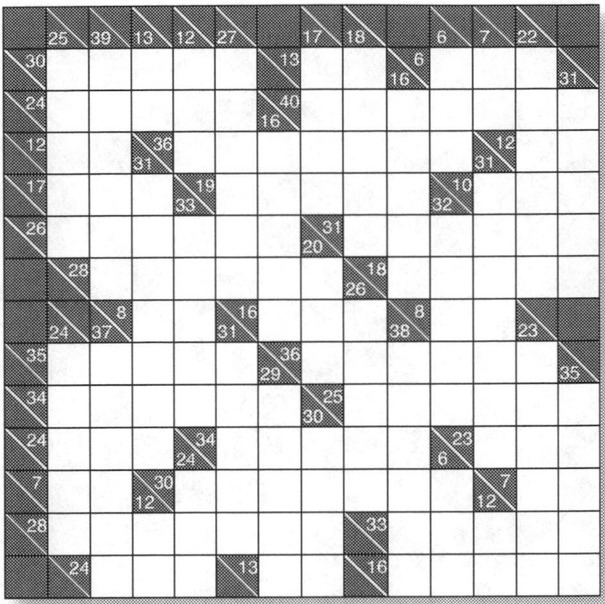
25 39 13 12 27 17 18 6 7 22
30 13 6 16 31
24 40 16
12 36 31 12 31
17 19 33 10 32
26 31 20
28 18 26
24 8 37 16 31 8 38 23
35 36 29 35
34 25 30
24 34 24 23 6
7 30 12 7 12
28 33
24 13 16

67

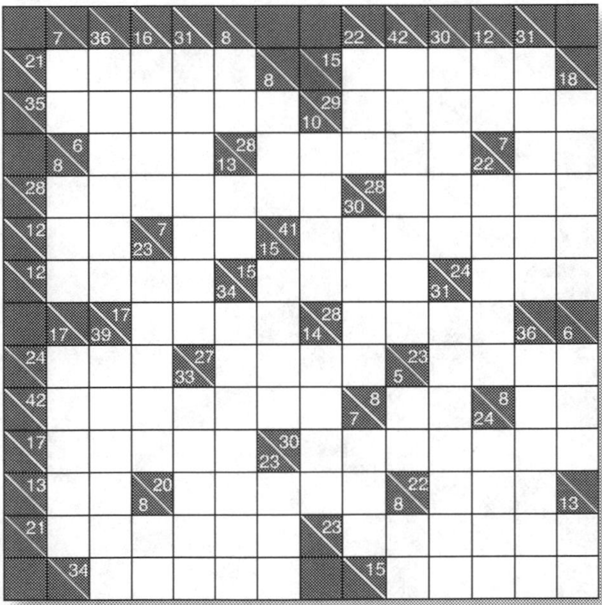
7 36 16 31 8 22 42 30 12 31
21 8 15 18
35 29 10
6 8 28 13 7 22
28 28 30
12 7 23 41 15
12 15 34 24 31
17 17 39 28 14 36 6
24 27 33 23 5
42 8 7 8 24
17 30 23
13 20 8 22 8 13
21 23
34 15

68

69

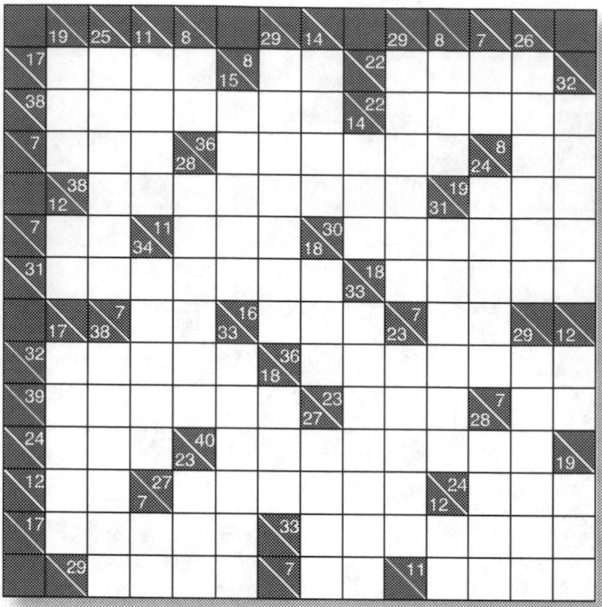

70

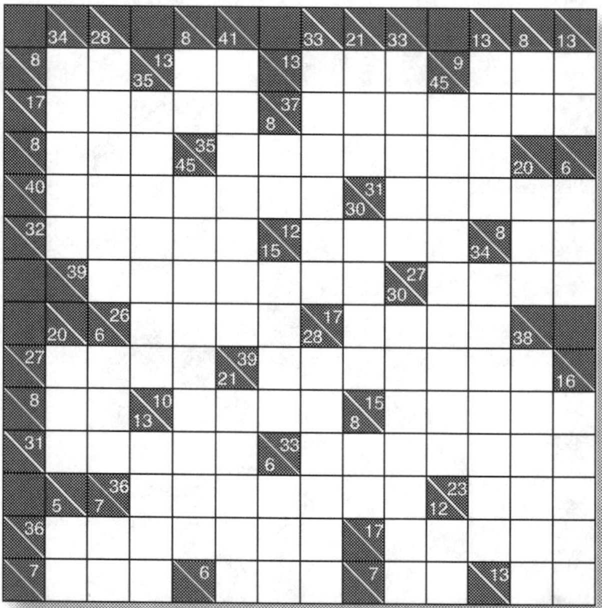

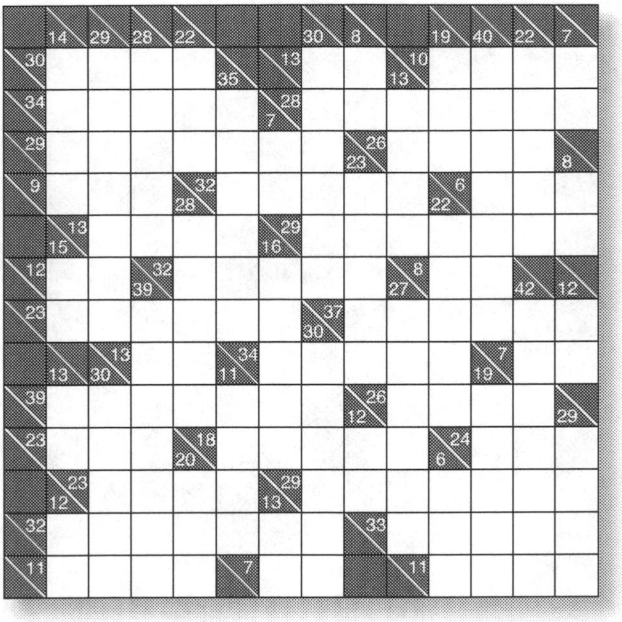

71

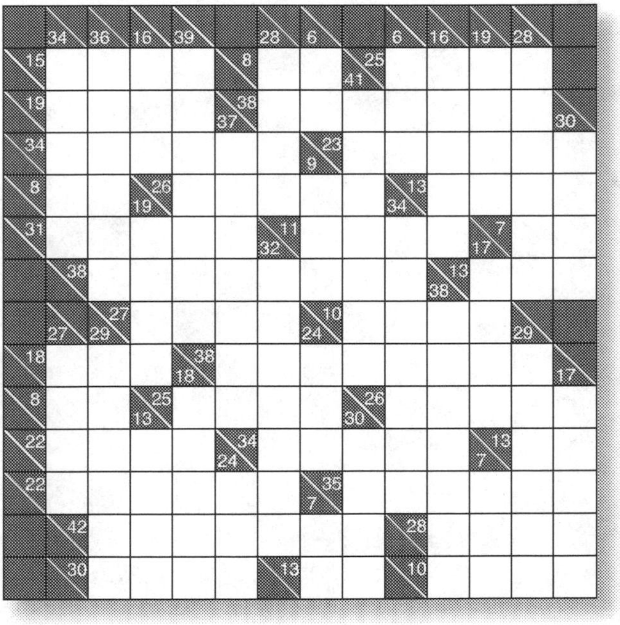

72

73

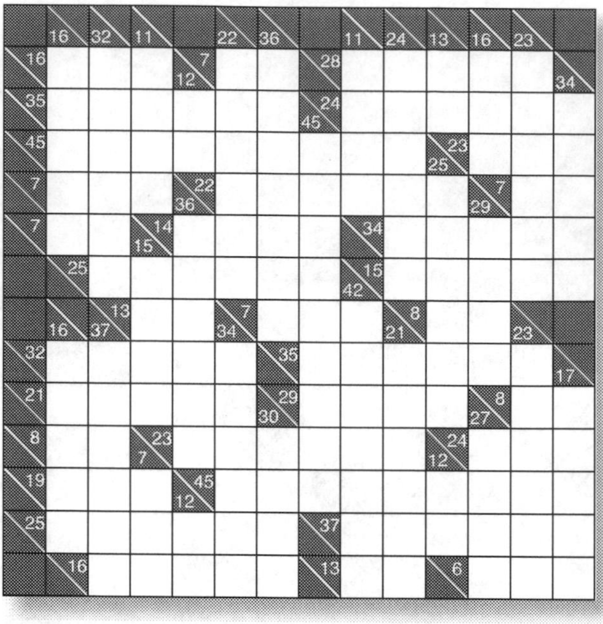
16 32 11 22 36 11 24 13 16 23
16 7 12 28 34
35 24 45
45 23 25
7 22 36 7 29
7 14 15 34
25 15 42
16 13 37 7 34 8 21 23
32 35 17
21 29 30 8 27
8 23 7 24 12
19 45 12
25 37
16 13 6

74

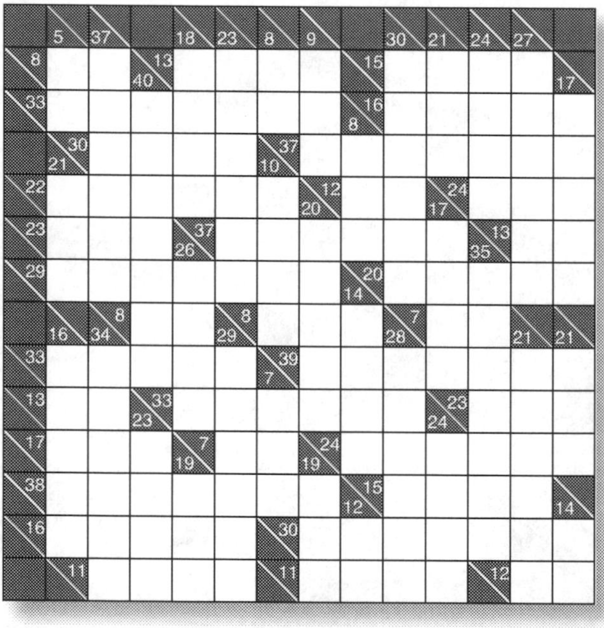
5 37 18 23 8 9 30 21 24 27
8 13 40 15 17
33 16 8
30 21 37 10
22 12 20 24 17
23 37 26 13 35
29 20 14
16 8 34 8 29 7 28 21 21
33 39 7
13 33 23 23 24
17 7 19 24 19
38 15 12 14
16 30
11 11 12

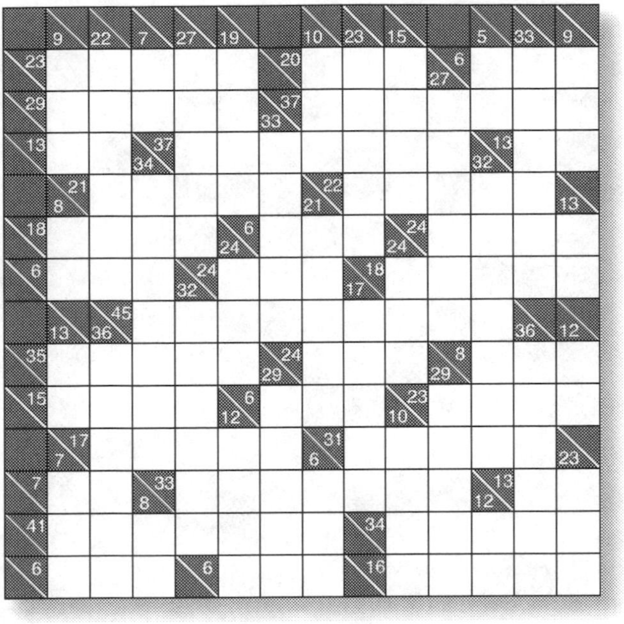

75

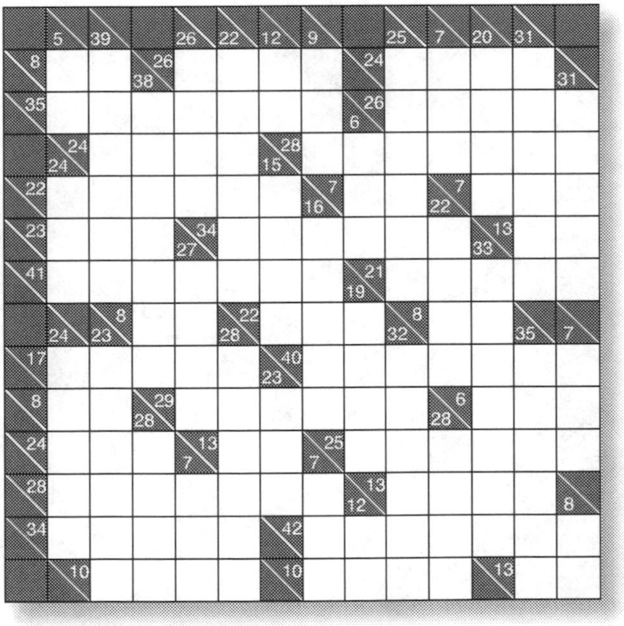

76

77

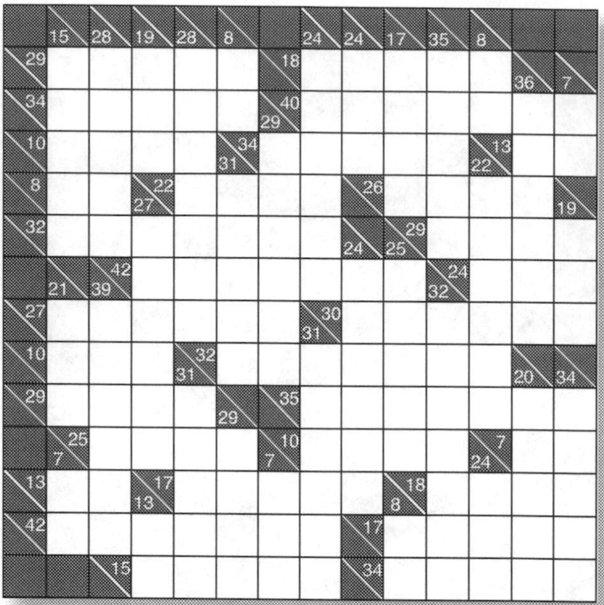

78

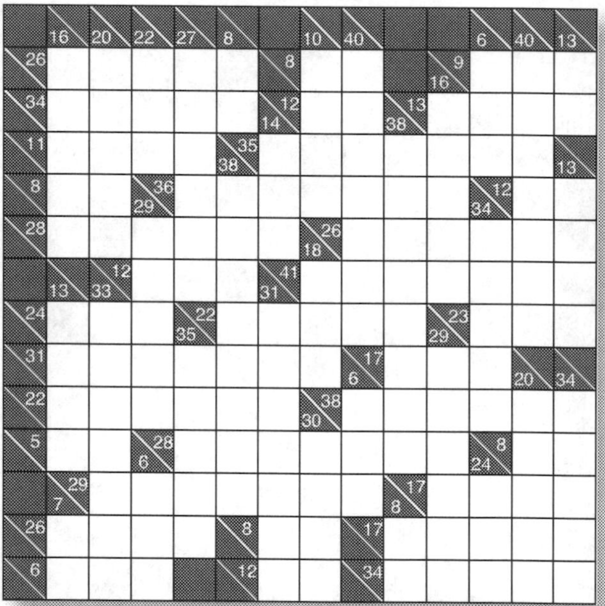

79

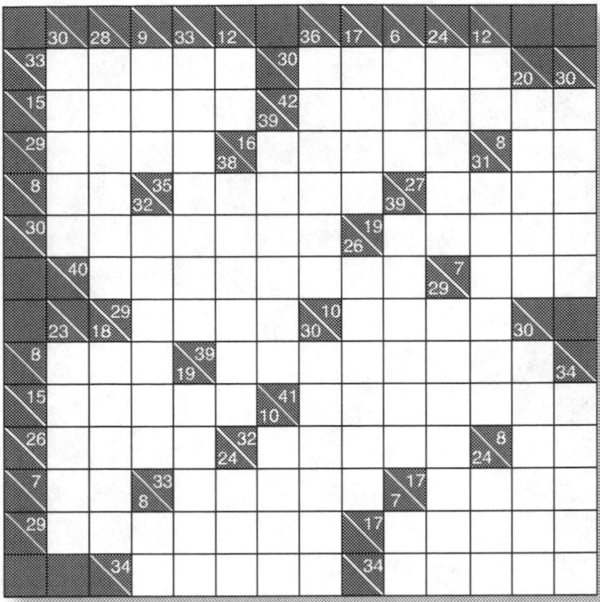
30 28 9 33 12 36 17 6 24 12
33 30 20 30
15 42 39
29 16 38 8 31
8 35 32 27 39
30 19 26
40 7 29
23 29 18 10 30 30
8 39 19 34
15 41 10
26 32 24 8 24
7 33 8 17 7
29 17
34 34

80

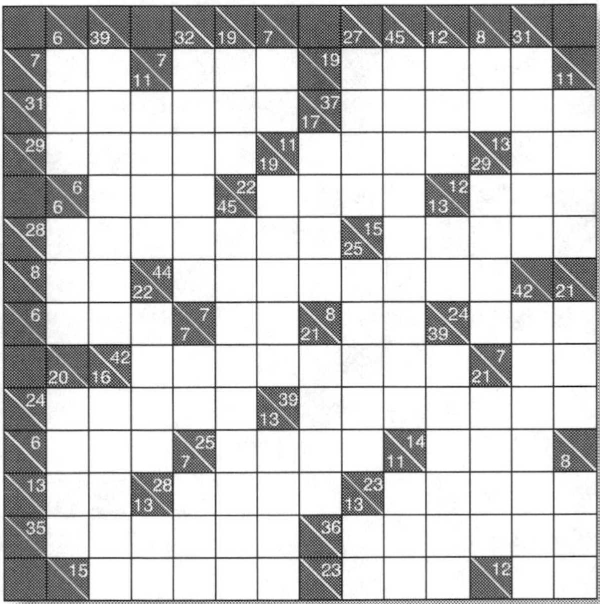
6 39 32 19 7 27 45 12 8 31
7 7 11 19 11
31 37 17
29 11 19 13 29
6 6 22 45 12 13
28 15 25
8 44 22 42 21
6 7 7 8 21 24 39
20 42 16 7 21
24 39 13
6 25 7 14 11 8
13 28 13 23 13
35 36
15 23 12

81

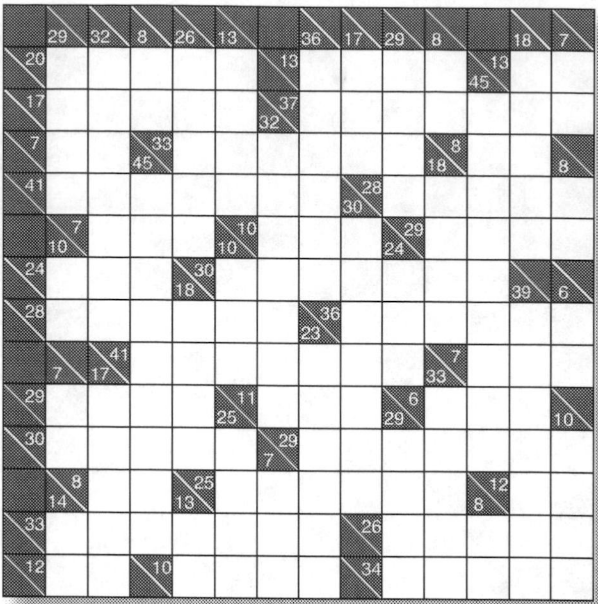
29 32 8 26 13 36 17 29 8 18 7
20 13 13 45
17 37 32
7 33 45 8 18 8
41 28 30
7 10 10 10 29 24
24 30 18 39 6
28 36 23
7 41 17 7 33
29 11 25 6 29 10
30 29 7
8 14 25 13 12 8
33 26
12 10 34

82

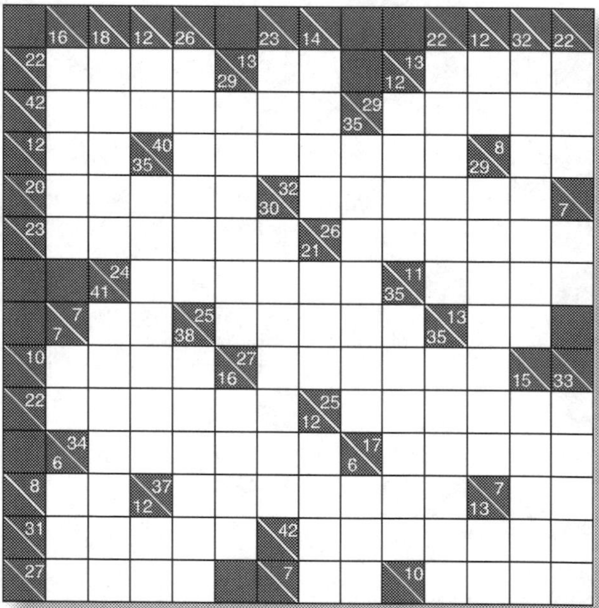
16 18 12 26 23 14 22 12 32 22
22 13 29 13 12
42 29 35
12 40 35 8 29
20 32 30 7
23 26 21
24 41 11 35
7 7 25 38 13 35
10 27 16 15 33
22 25 12
34 6 17 6
8 37 12 7 13
31 42
27 7 10

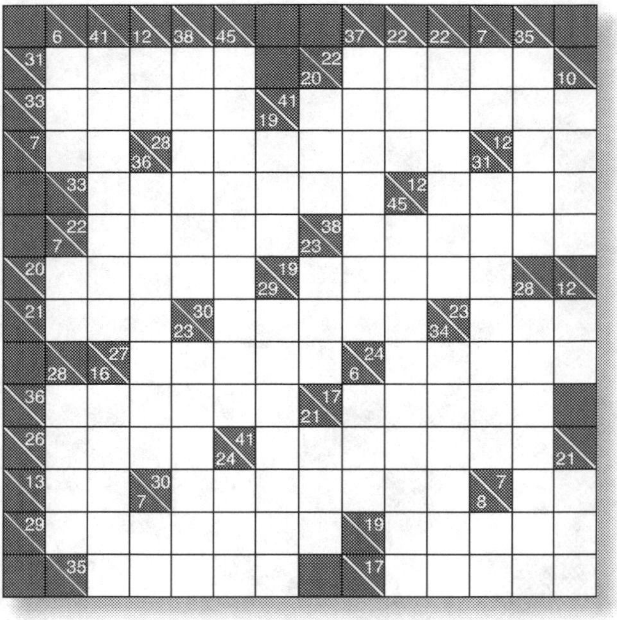

83

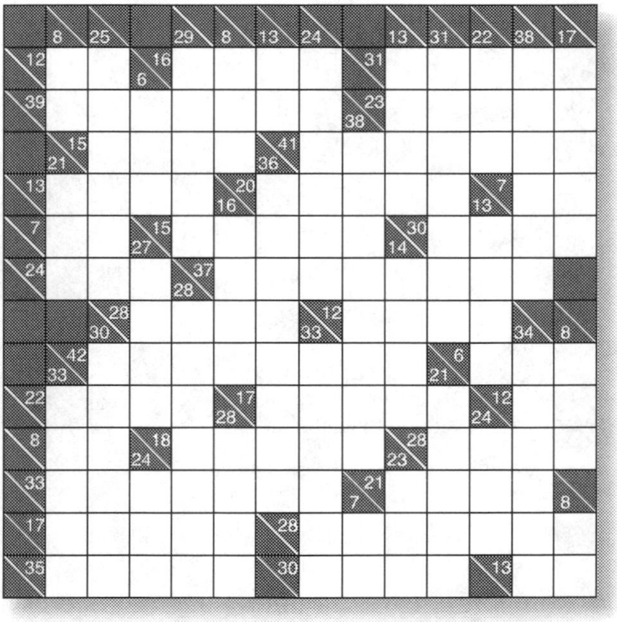

84

85

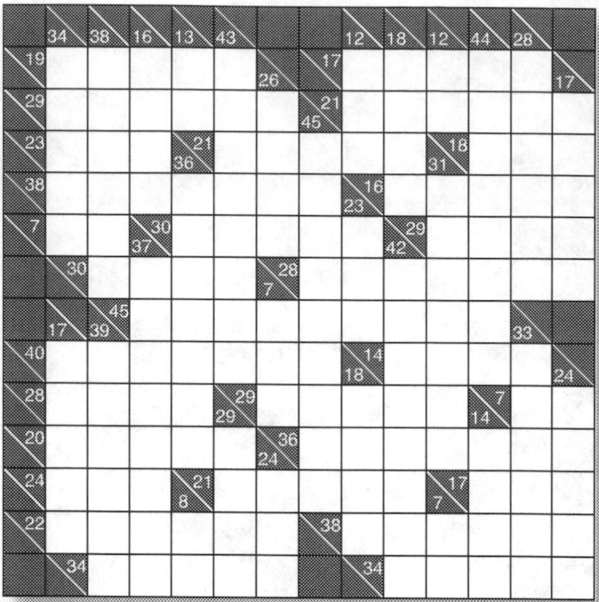
34 38 16 13 43 12 18 12 44 28
19 26 17 17
29 21 45
23 21 36 18 31
38 16 23
7 30 37 29 42
30 28 7
17 45 39 33
40 14 18 24
28 29 29 7 14
20 36 24
24 21 8 17 7
22 38
34 34

86

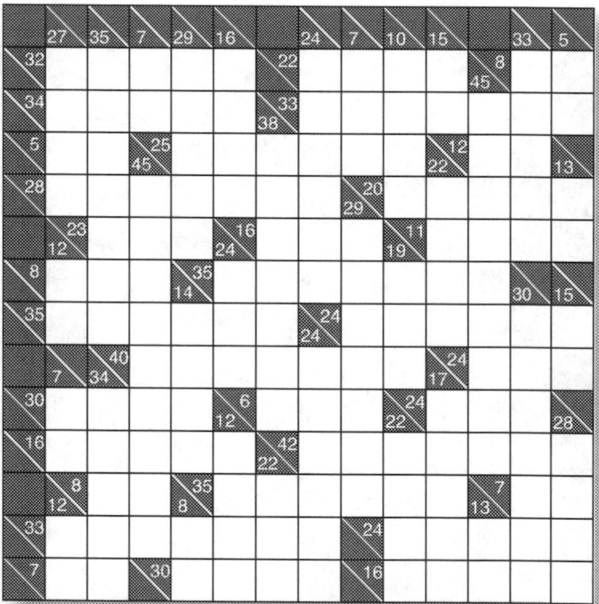
27 35 7 29 16 24 7 10 15 33 5
32 22 8 45
34 33 38
5 25 45 12 22 13
28 20 29
23 12 16 24 11 19
8 35 14 30 15
35 24 24
7 40 34 24 17
30 6 12 24 22 28
16 42 22
8 12 35 8 7 13
33 24
7 30 16

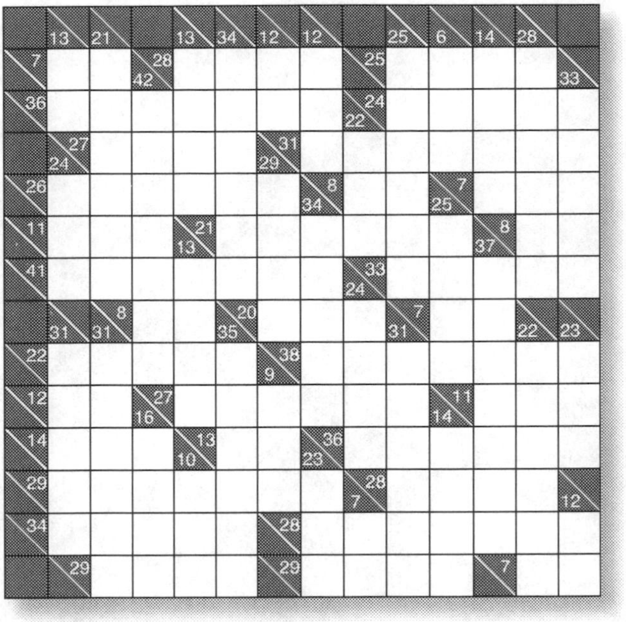

87

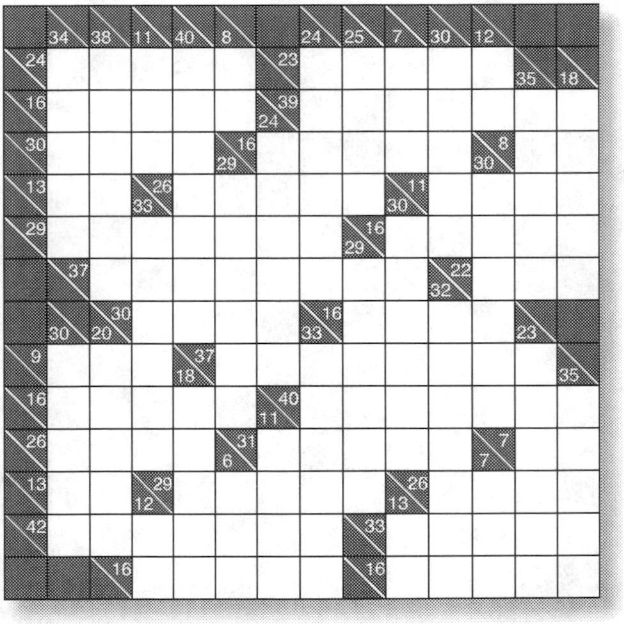

88

89

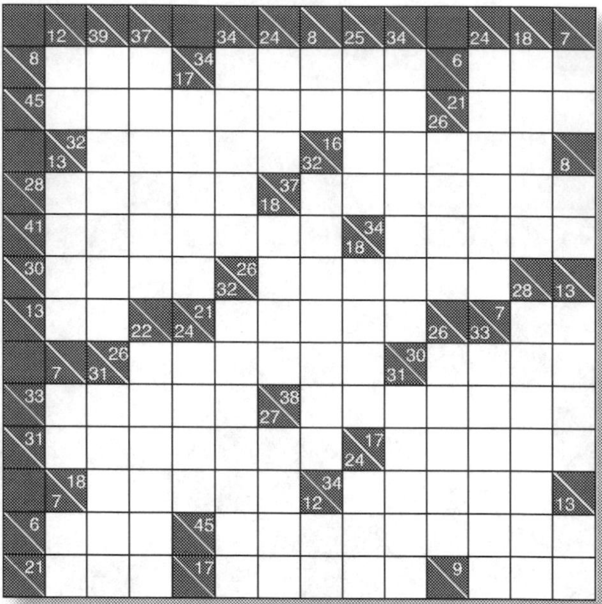

90

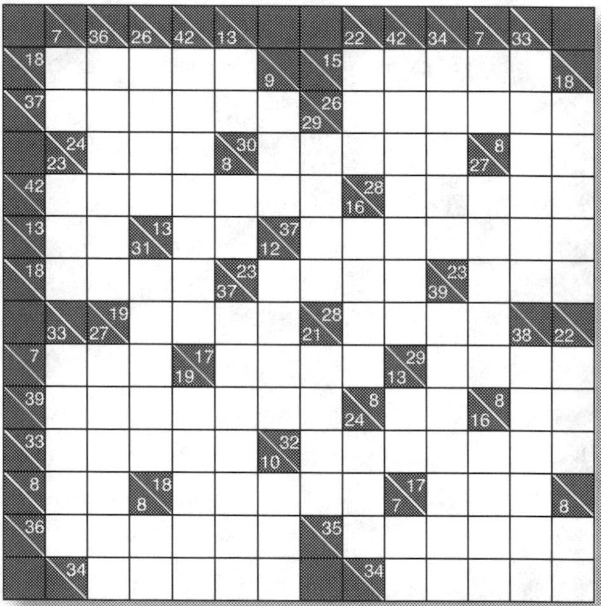

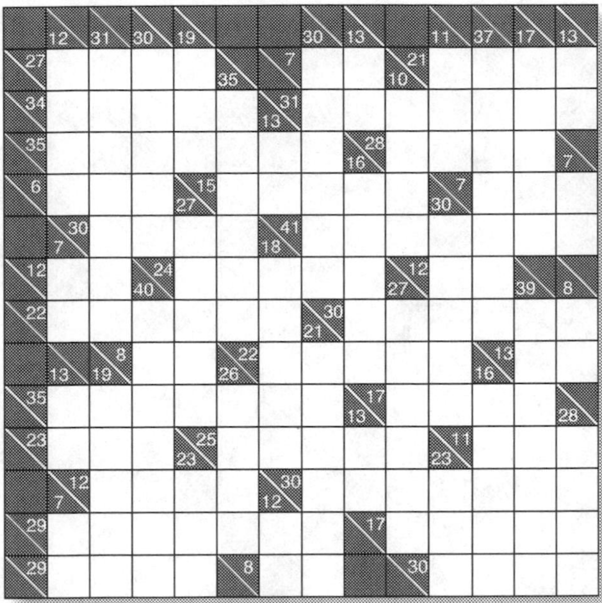
12 31 30 19 30 13 11 37 17 13
27 7 35 21 10
34 31 13
35 28 16 7
6 15 27 7 30
30 7 41 18
12 24 40 12 27 39 8
22 30 21
13 8 19 22 26 13 16
35 17 13 28
23 25 23 11 23
12 7 30 12
29 17
29 8 30

91

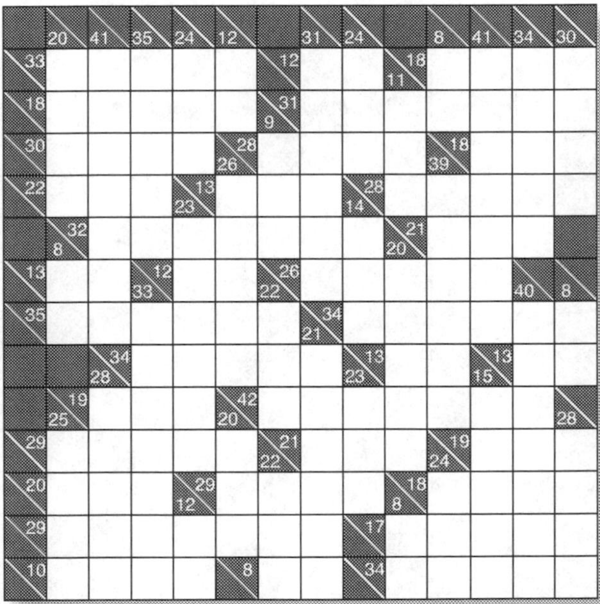
20 41 35 24 12 31 24 8 41 34 30
33 12 18 11
18 31 9
30 28 26 18 39
22 13 23 28 14
32 8 21 20
13 12 33 26 22 40 8
35 34 21
34 28 13 23 13 15
19 25 42 20 28
29 21 22 19 24
20 29 12 18 8
29 17
10 8 34

92

93

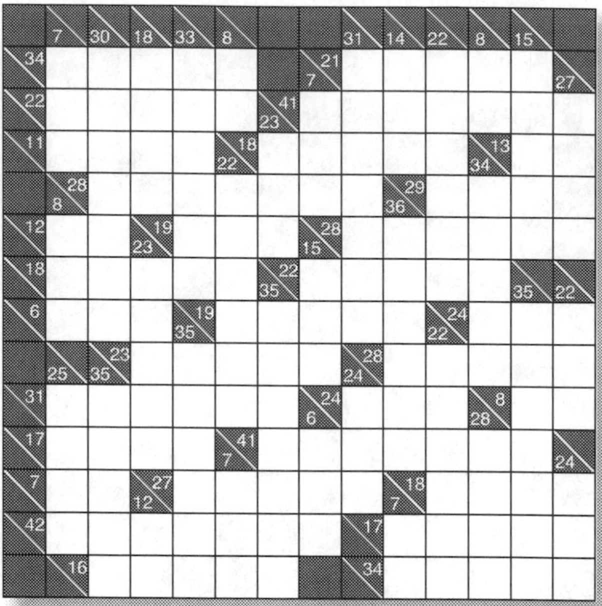

94

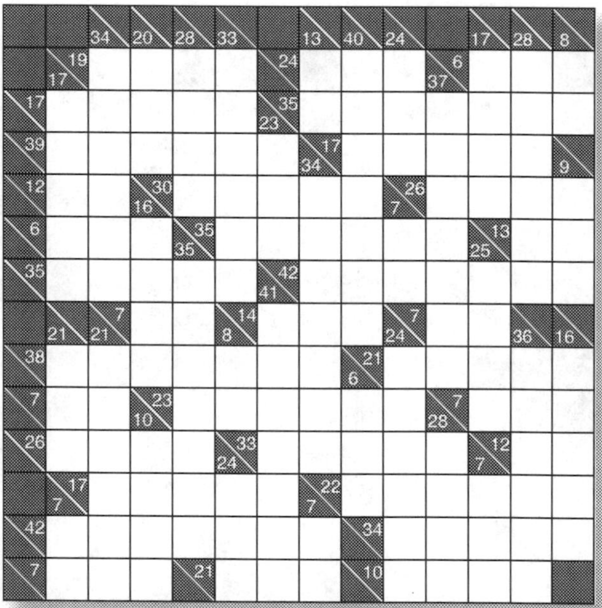

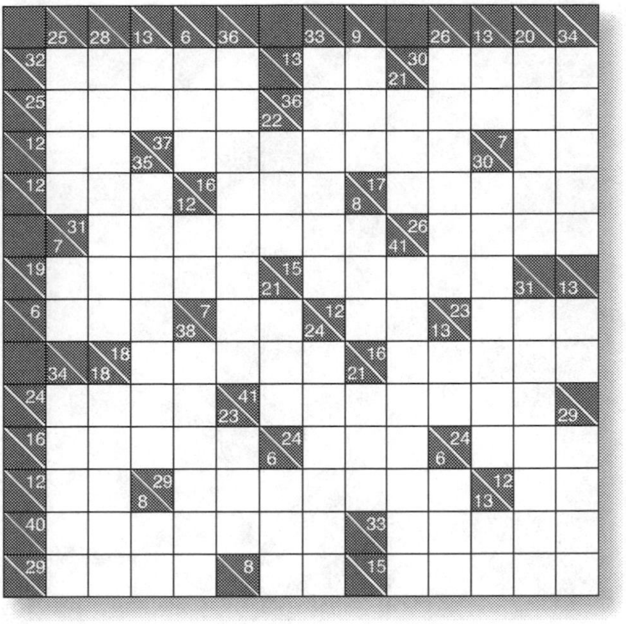

95

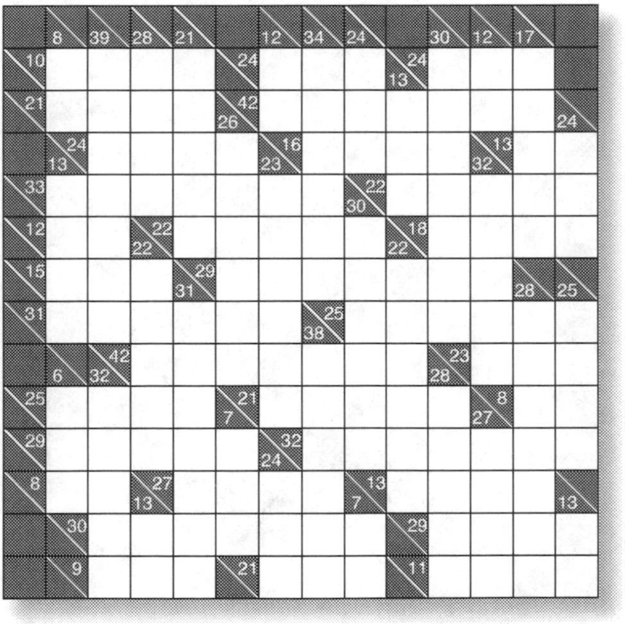

96

97

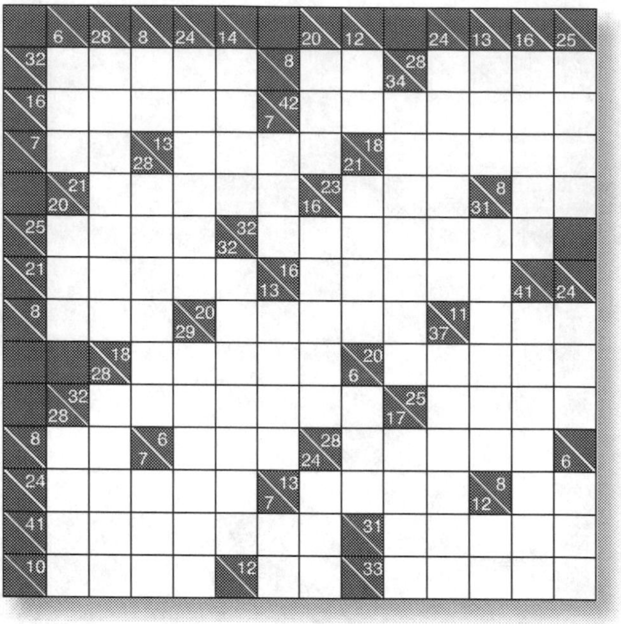

98

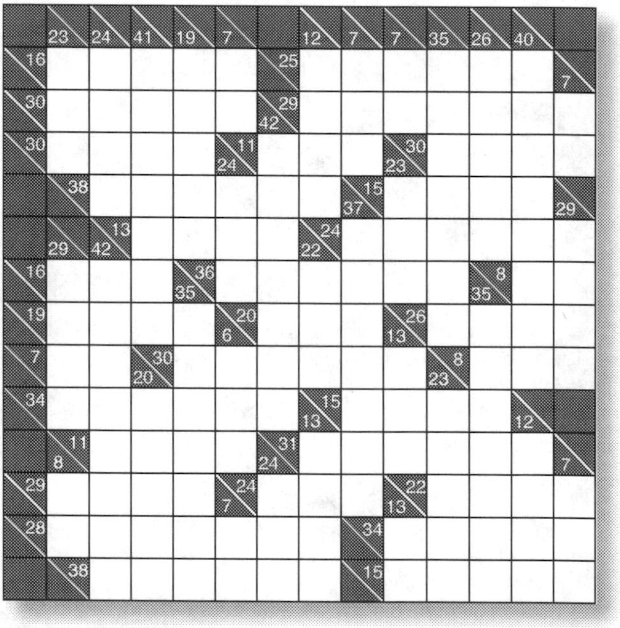

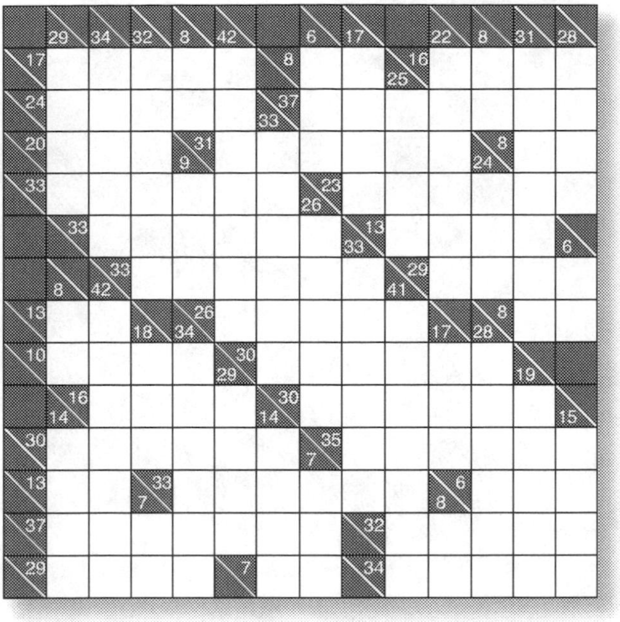
29 34 32 8 42 6 17 22 8 31 28
17 8 16 25
24 37 33
20 31 9 8 24
33 23 26
33 13 33 6
8 33 42 29 41
13 18 26 34 17 8 28
10 30 29 19
16 14 30 14 15
30 35 7
13 33 7 6 8
37 32
29 7 34

99

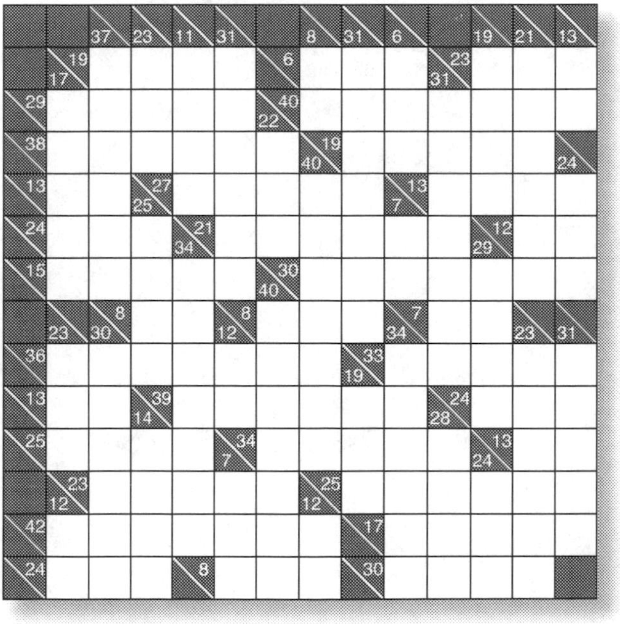
37 23 11 31 8 31 6 19 21 13
19 17 6 23 31
29 40 22
38 19 40 24
13 27 25 13 7
24 21 34 12 29
15 30 40
23 8 30 8 12 7 34 23 31
36 33 19
13 39 14 24 28
25 34 7 13 24
23 12 25 12
42 17
24 8 30

100

APPENDIX A

Answers

Part 1: Mildly Challenging Puzzles

1

2

3

4

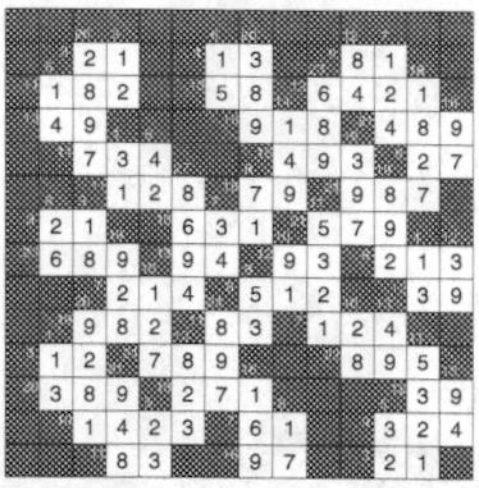

5

6

7

8

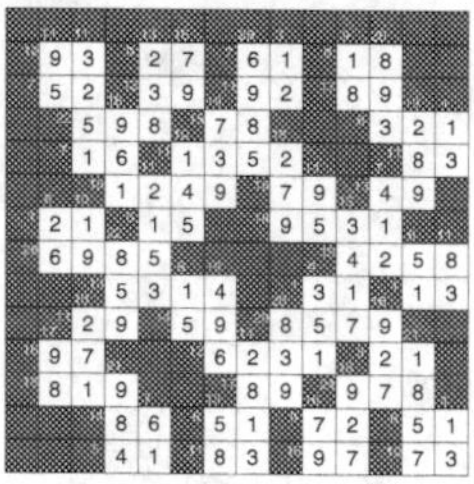

9

10

11

12

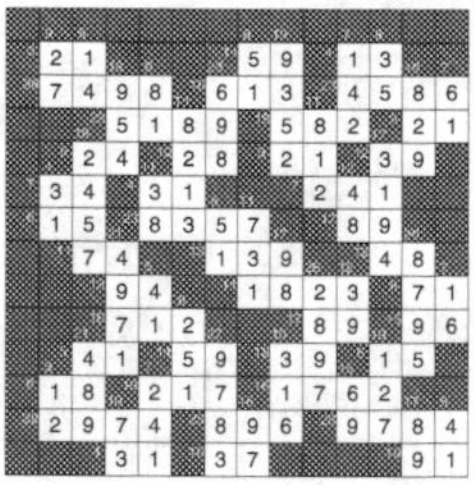

13

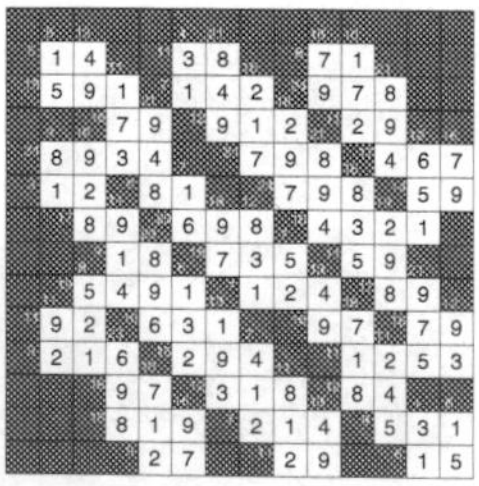

14

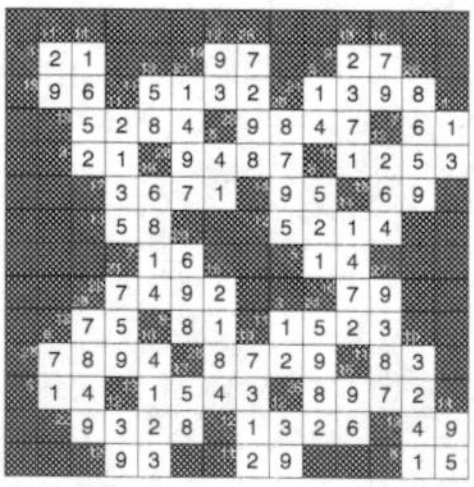

15

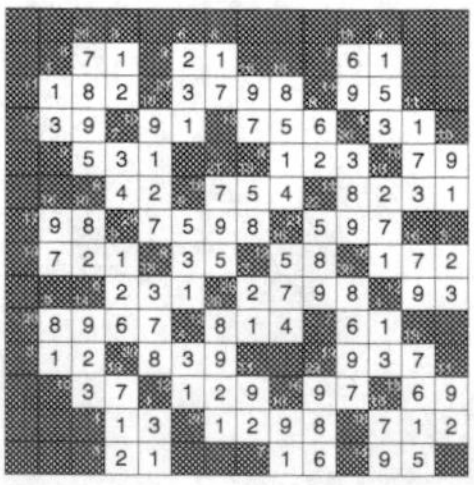

16

17

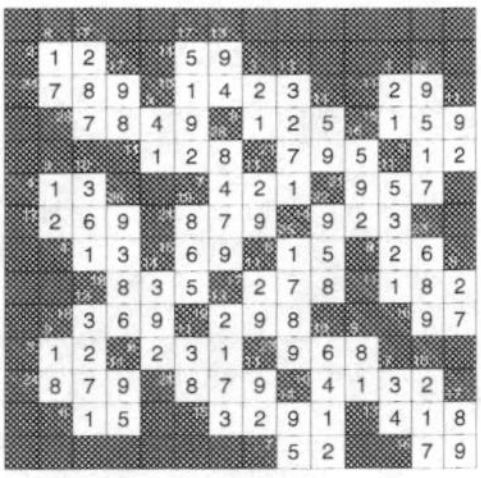

18

19

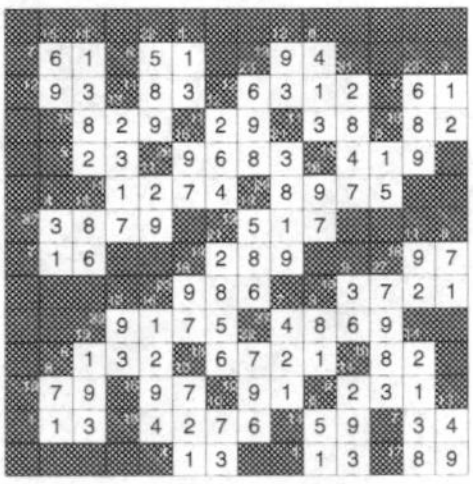

20

21

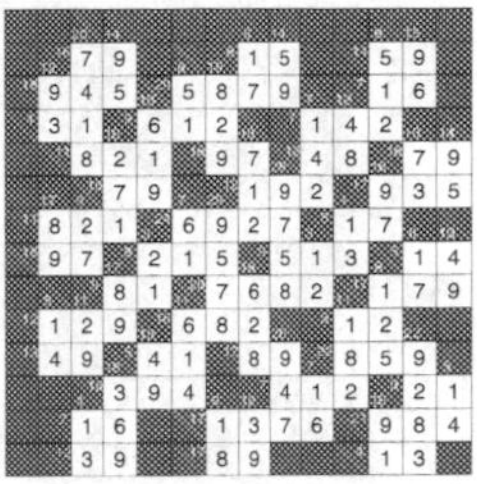

22

23

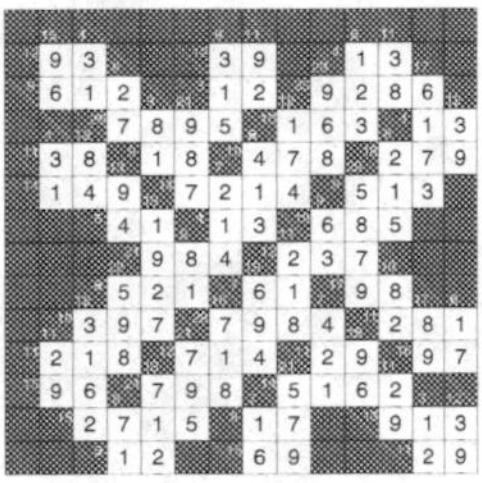

24

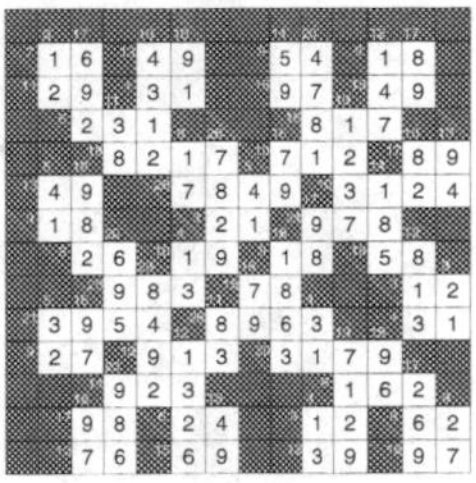

25

26

27

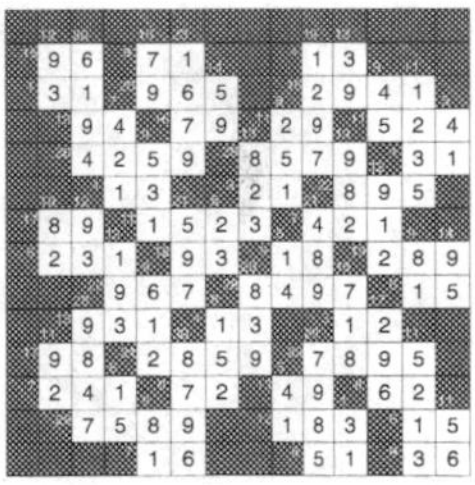

28

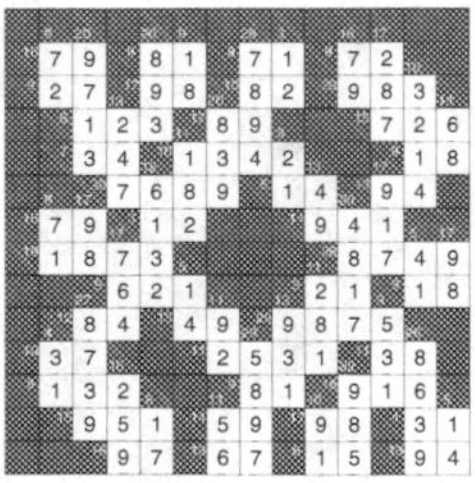

29

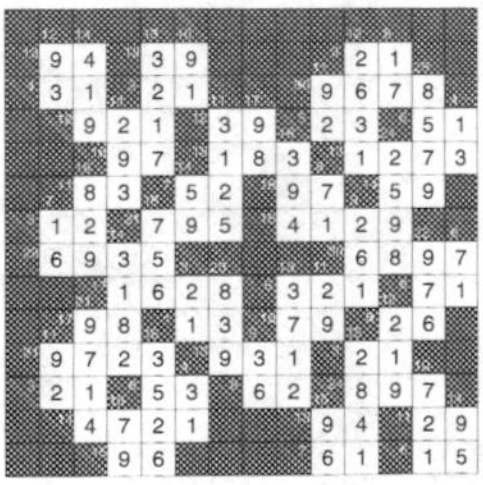

30

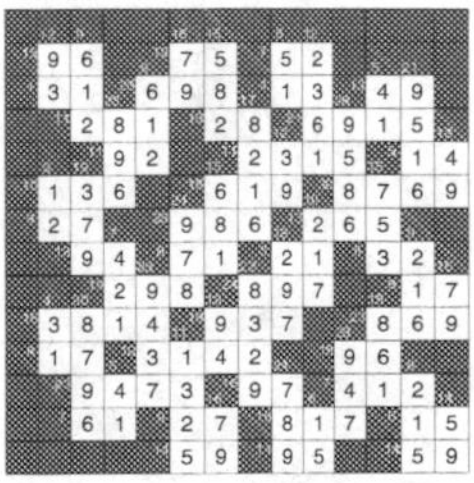

31

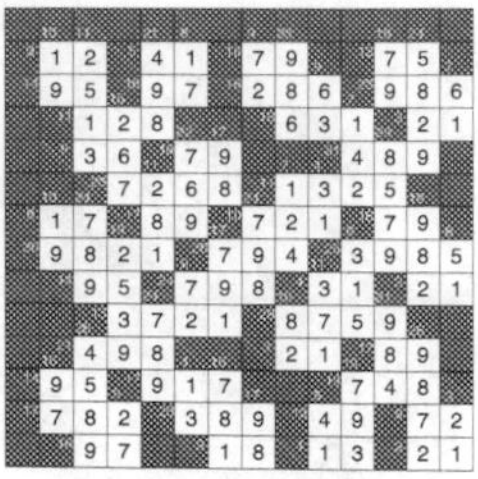

32

33

34

35

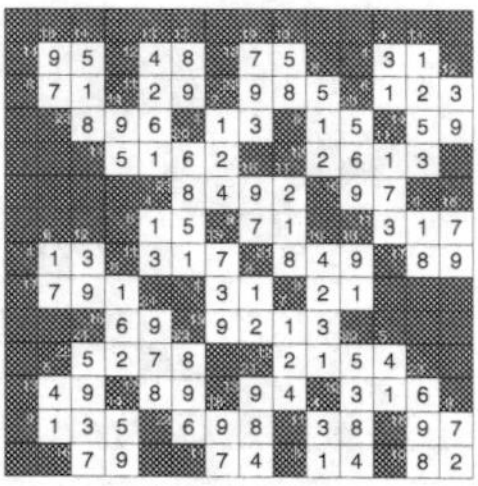

36

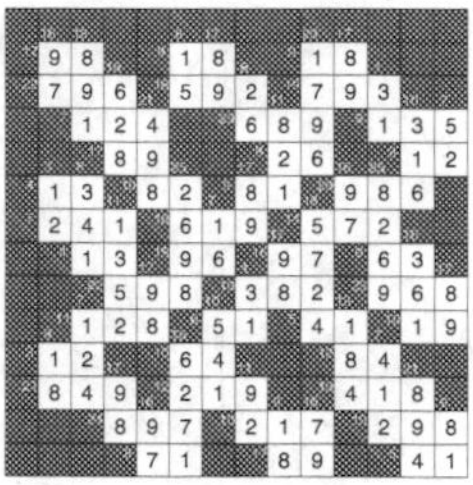

37

38

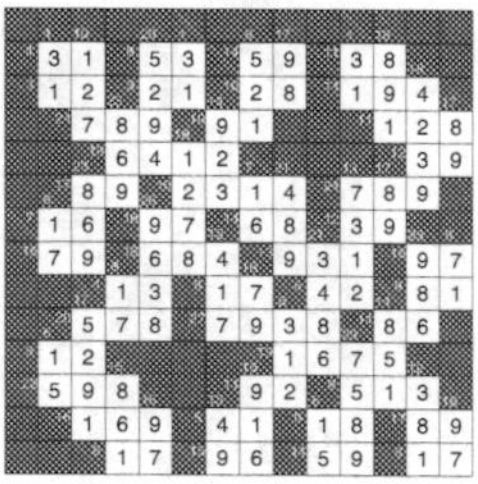

39

40

41

42

43

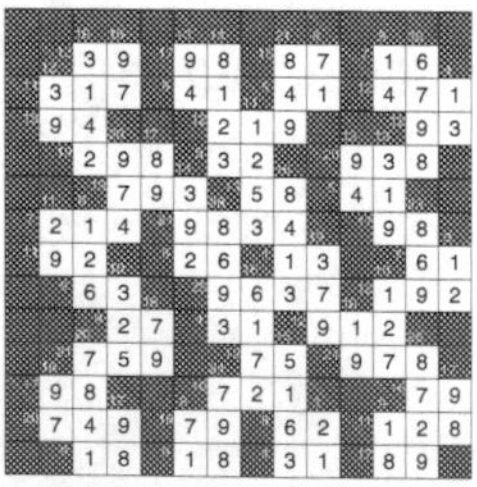

44

45

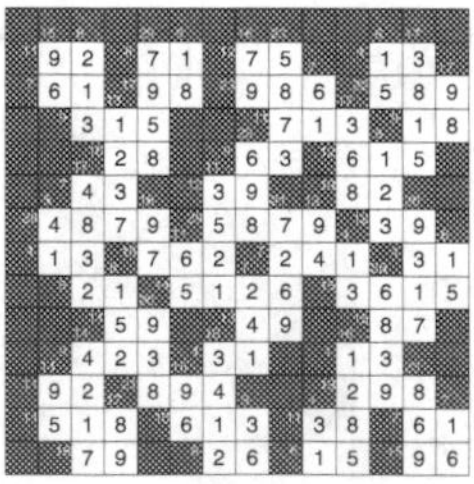

46

47

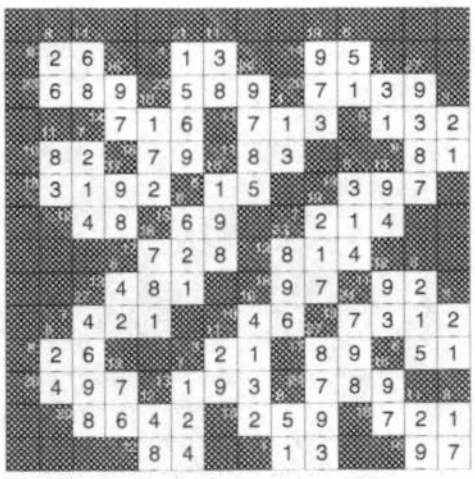

48

49

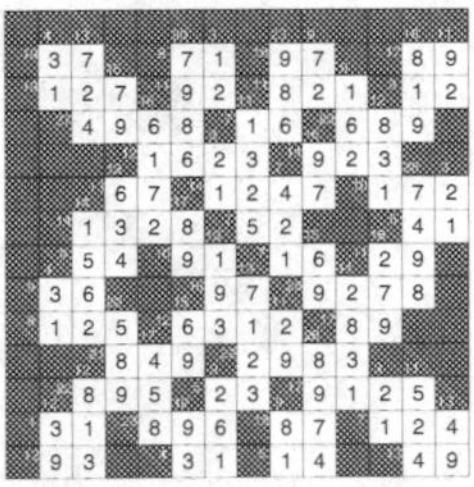

50

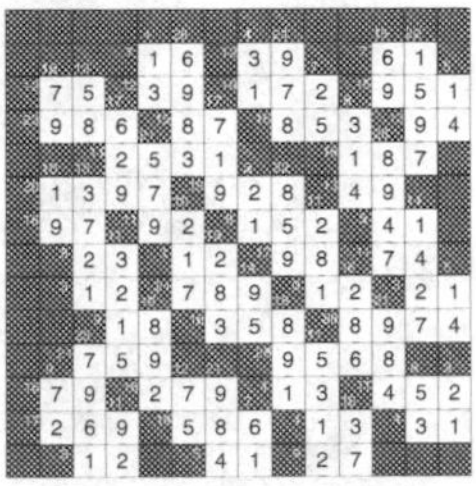

51

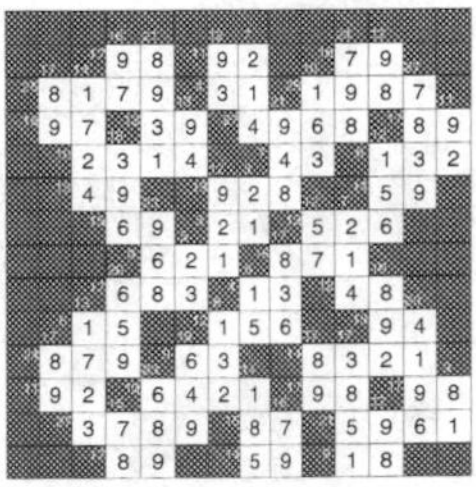

52

53

54

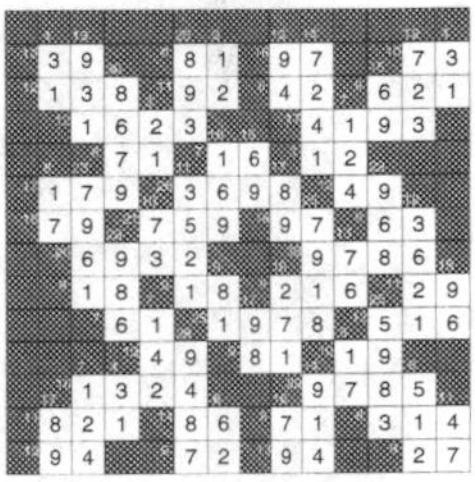

55

56

57

58

59

60

61

62

63

64

65

66

67

68

69

70

71

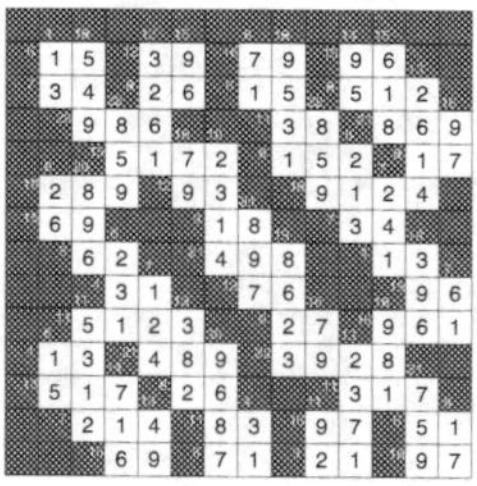

72

73

74

75

76

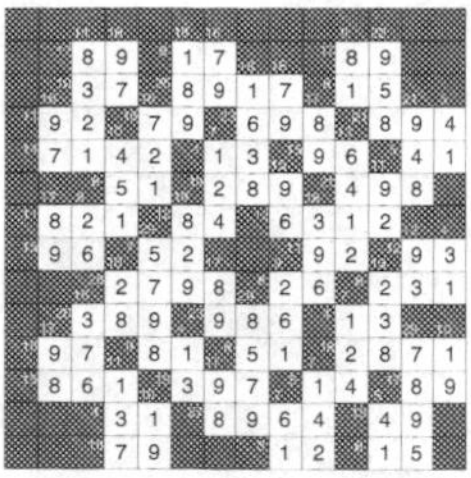

77

78

79

80

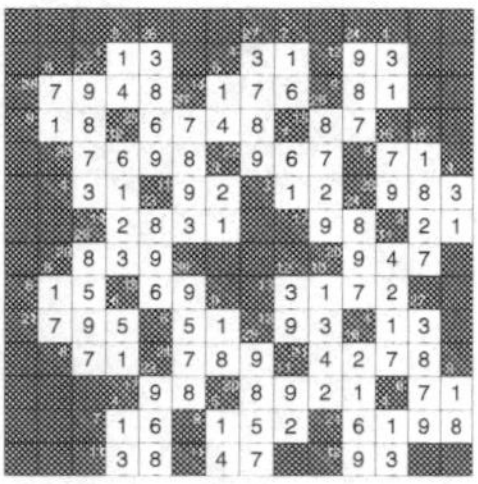

81

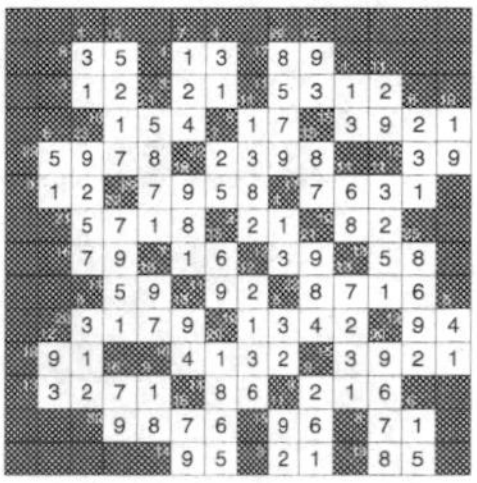

82

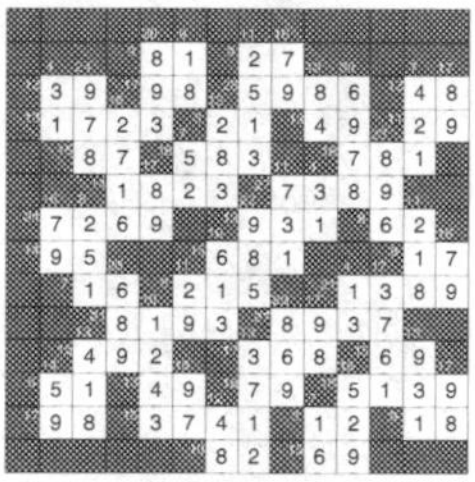

83

84

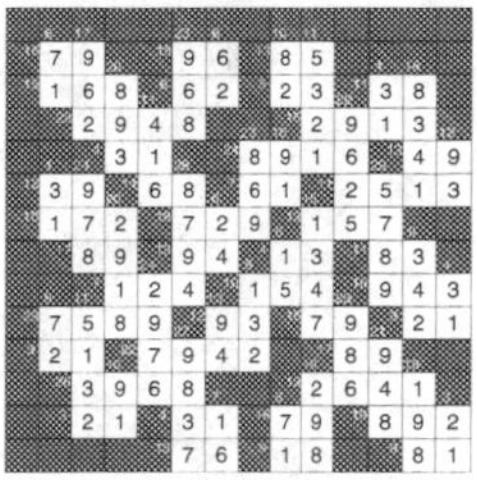

85

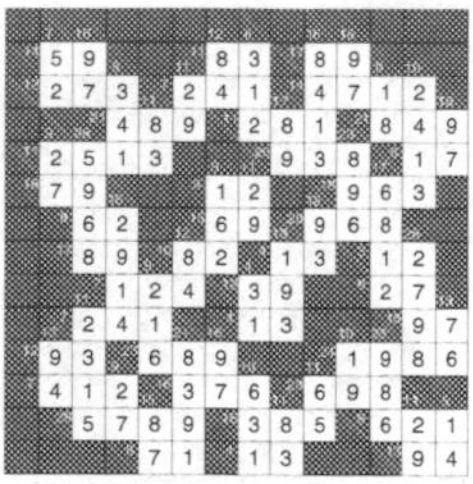

86

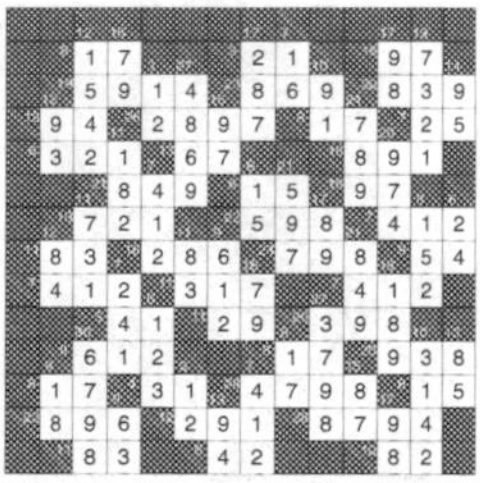

87

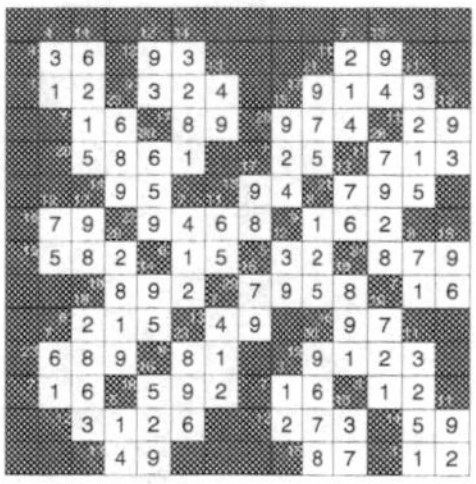

88

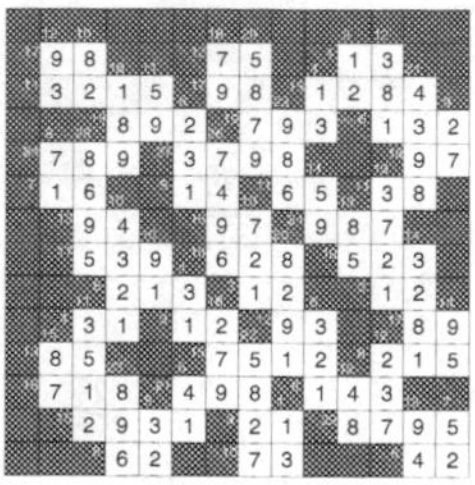

89

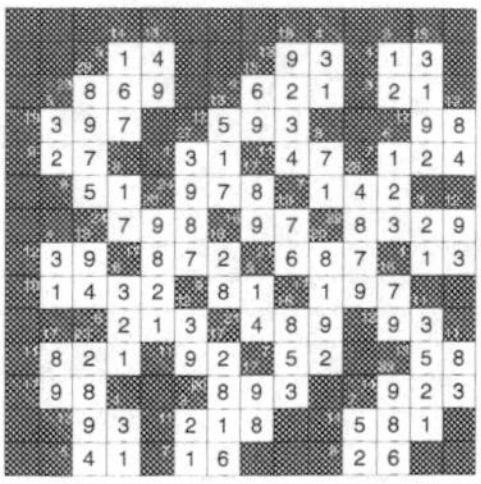

90

91

92

93

94

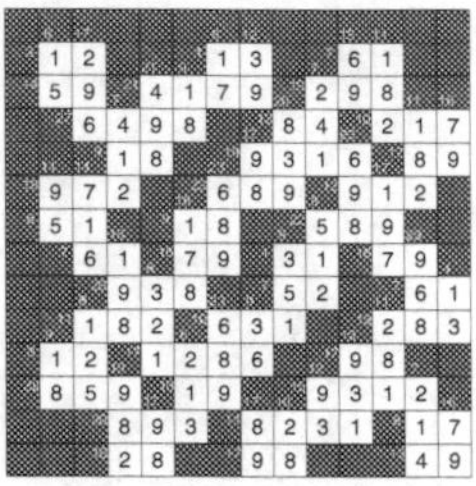

95

96

97

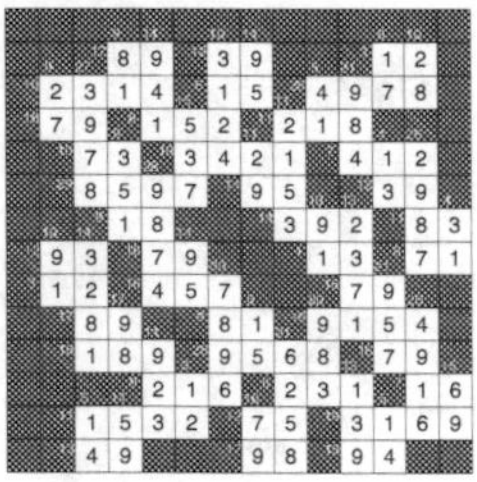

98

99

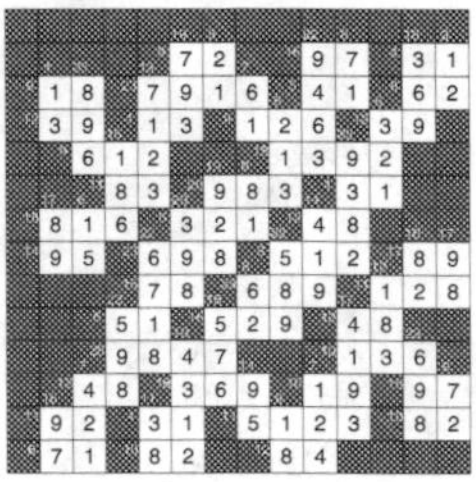

100

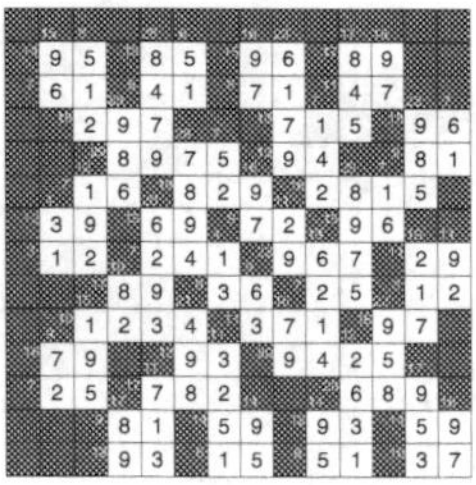

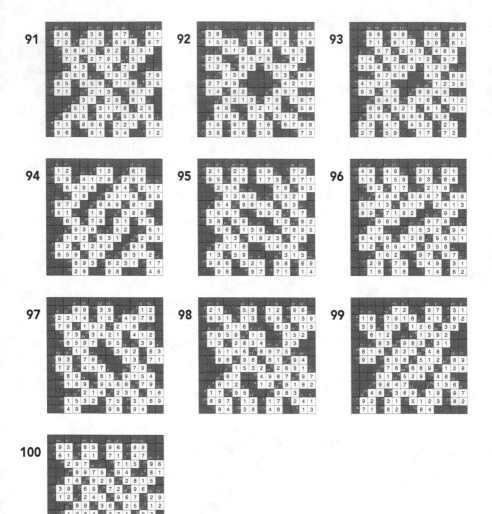

Part 2: Moderately Challenging Puzzles

1

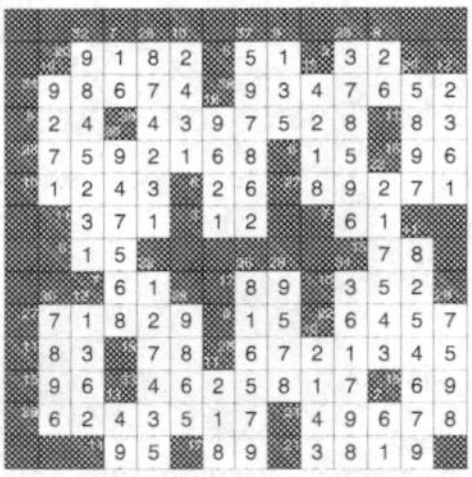

2

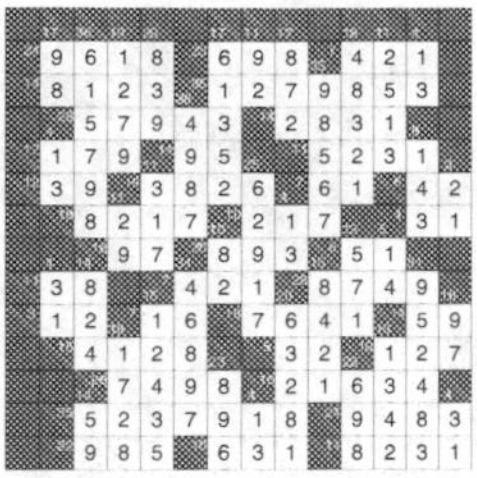

3

4

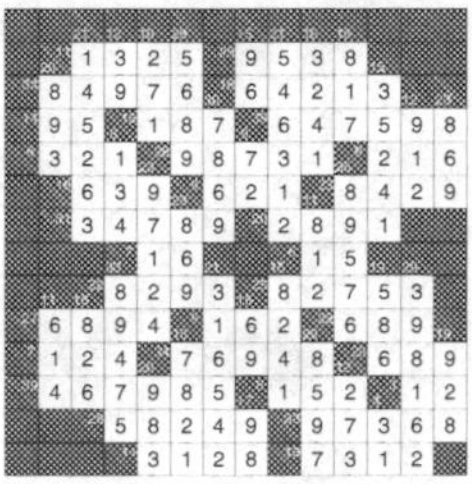

5

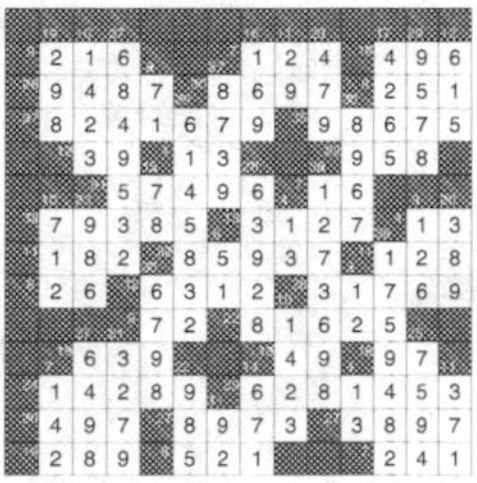

6

7

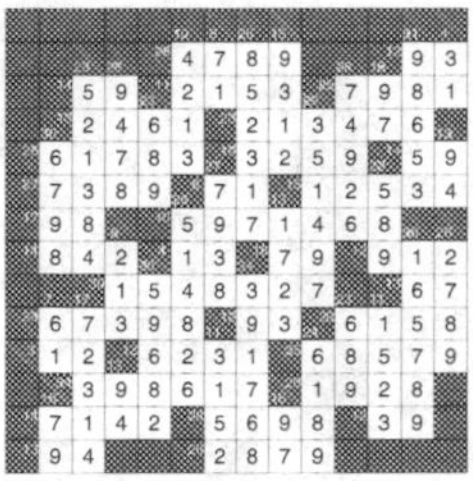

8

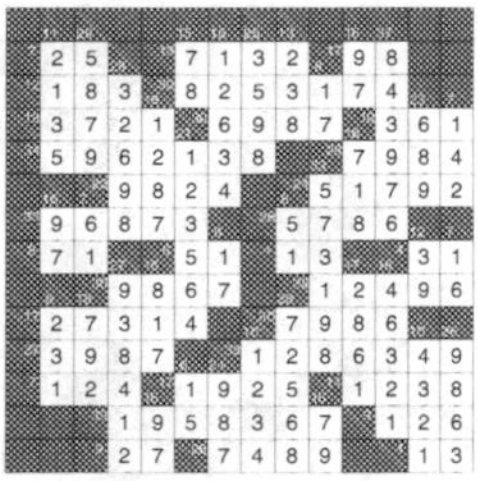

9

10

11

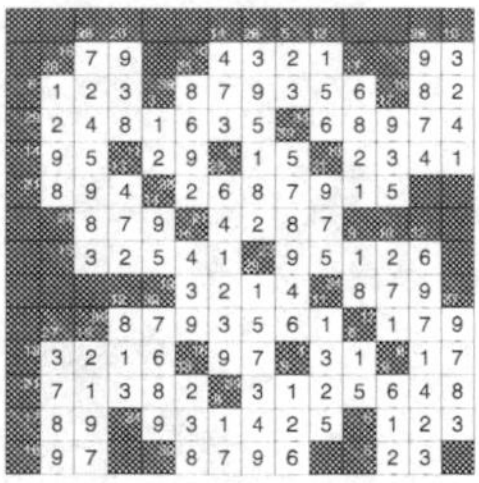

12

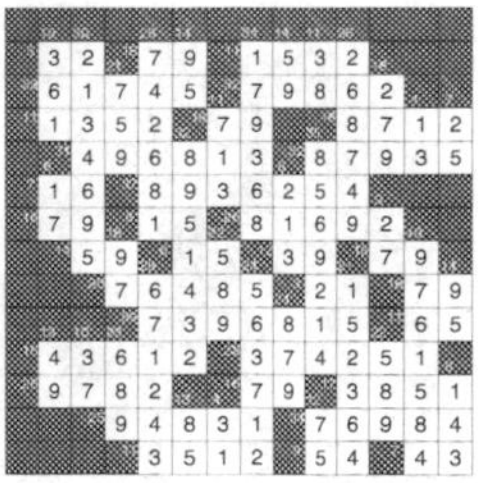

13

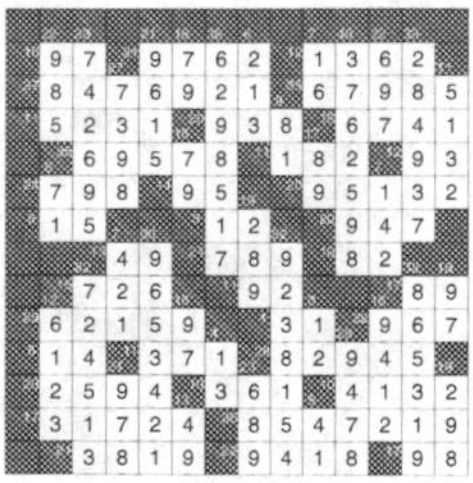

14

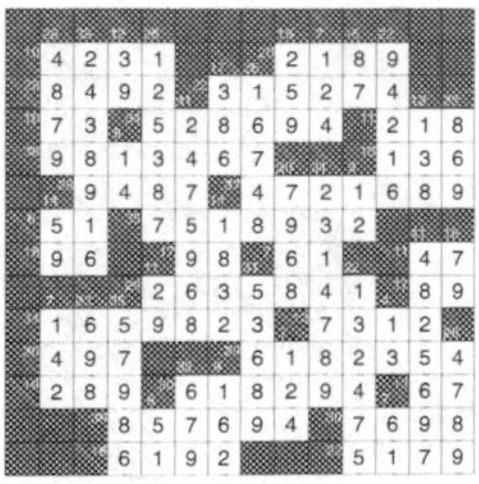

15

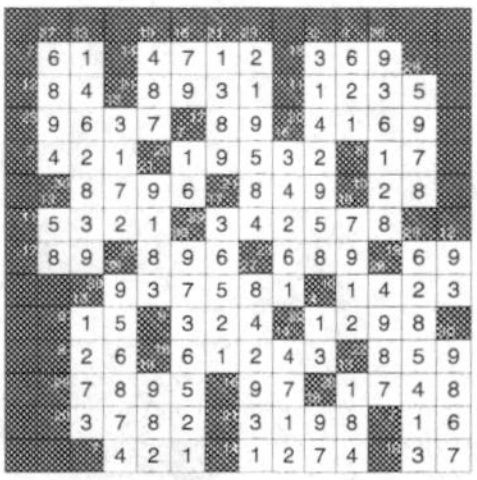

16

17

18

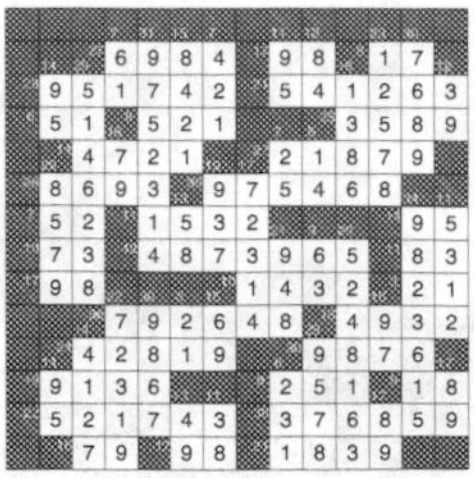

19

20

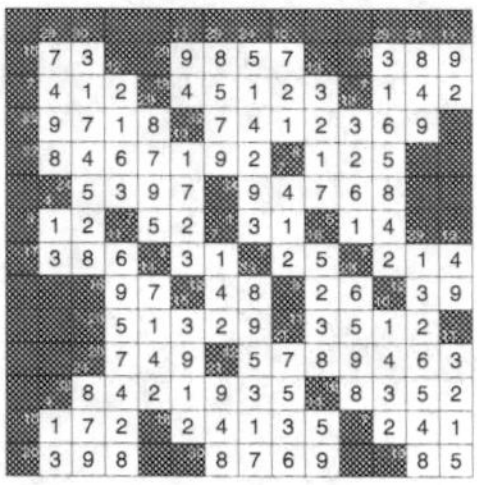

21

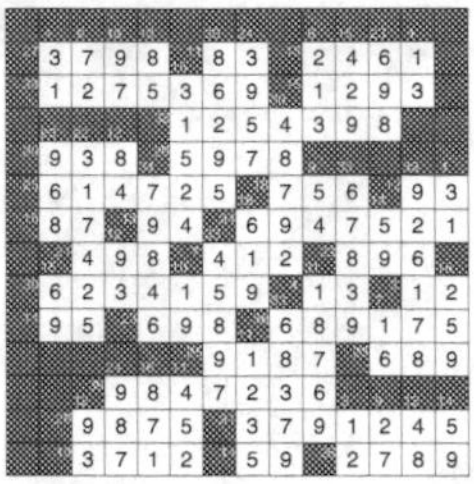

22

23

24

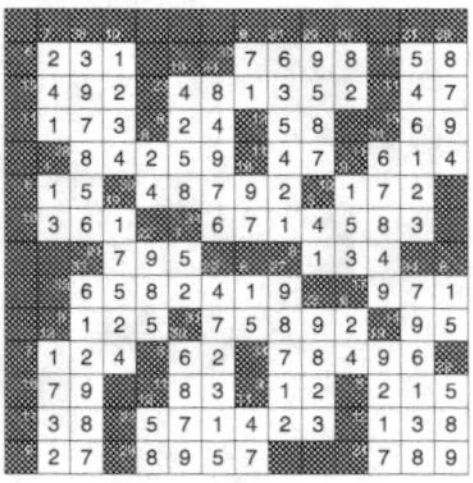

25

26

27

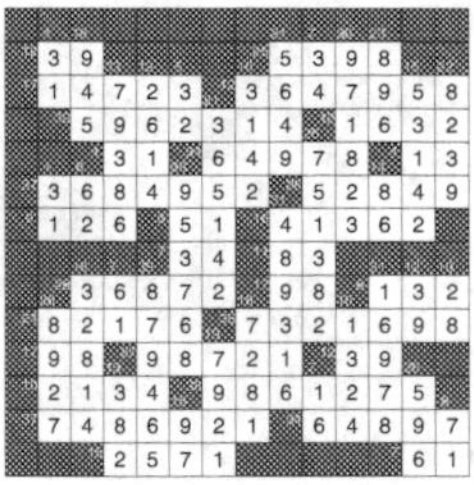

28

29

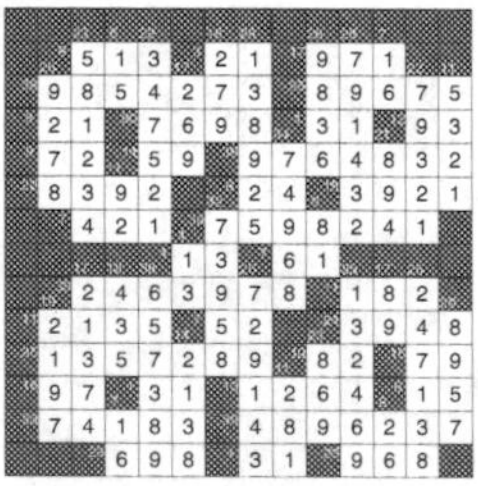

30

31

32

33

34

35

36

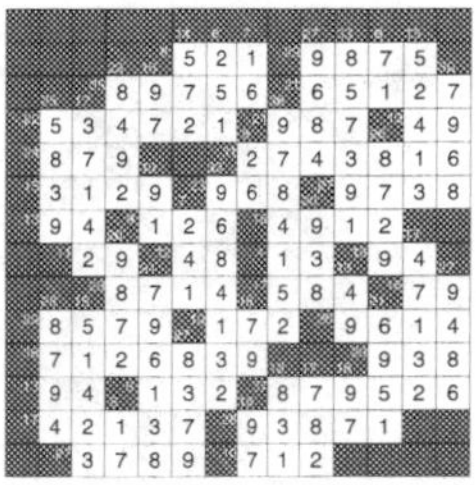

37

38

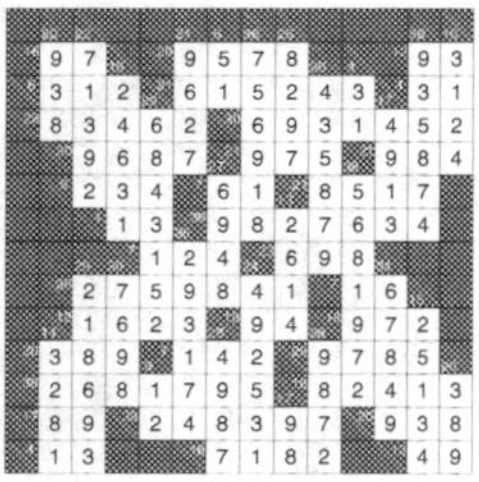

39

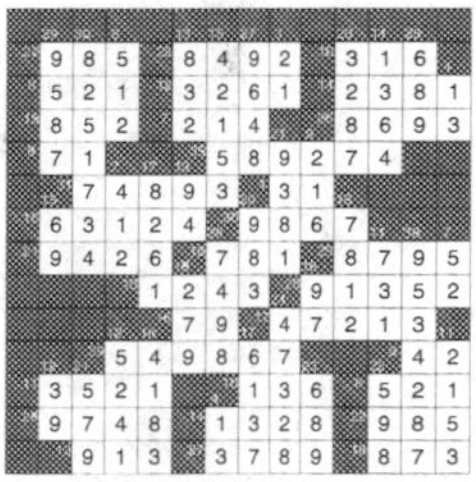

40

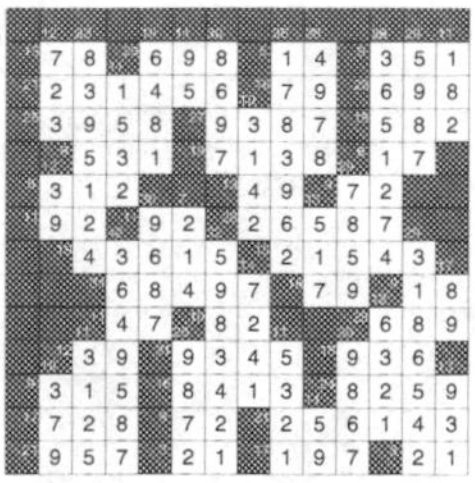

41

42

43

44

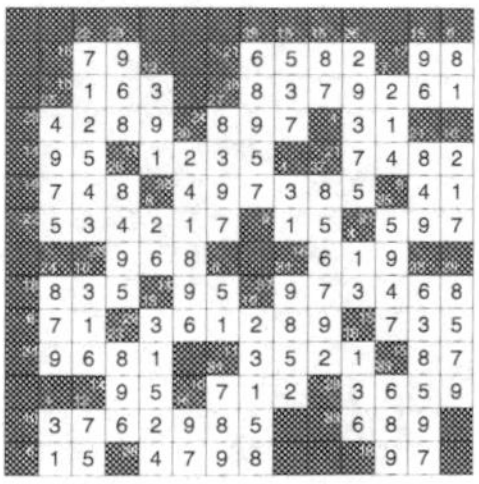

45

46

47

48

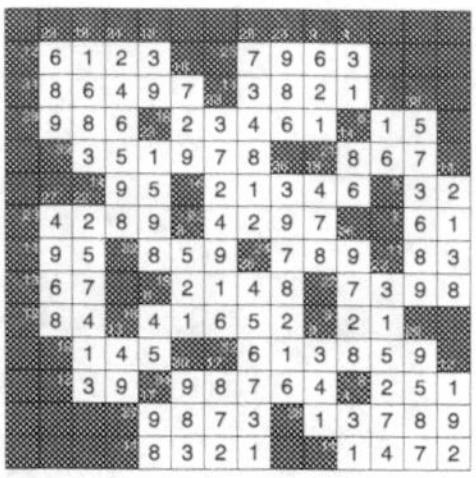

49

50

51

52

53

54

55

56

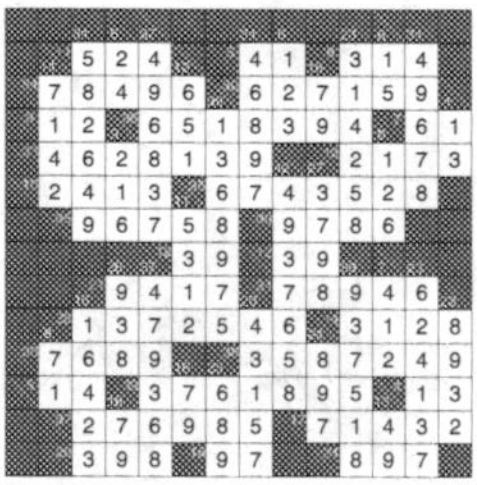

57

58

59

60

61

62

63

64

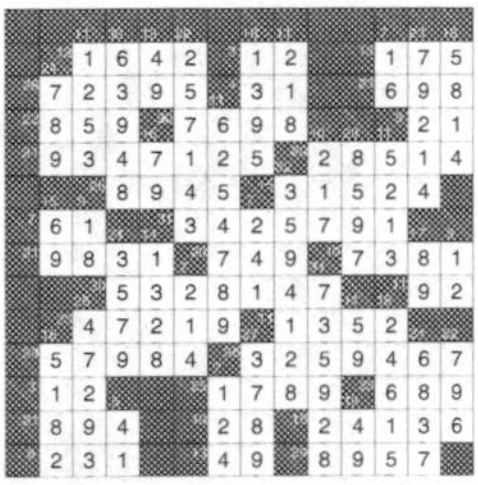

65

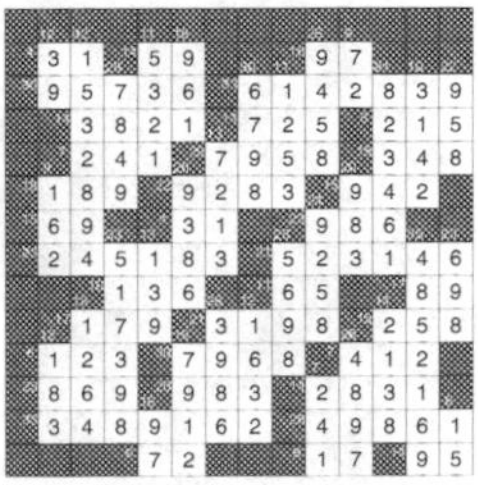

66

67

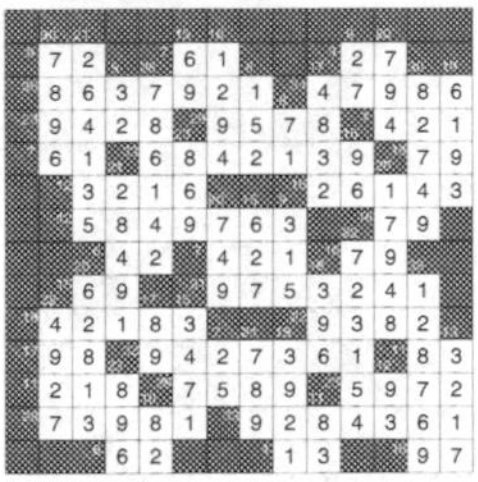

68

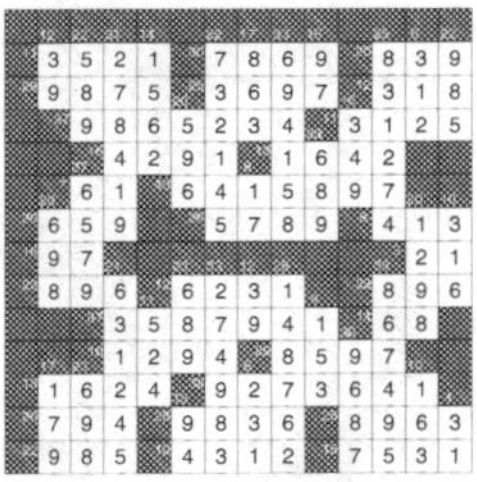

69

70

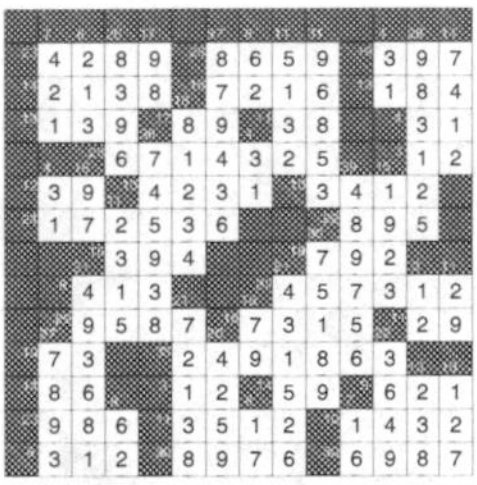

71

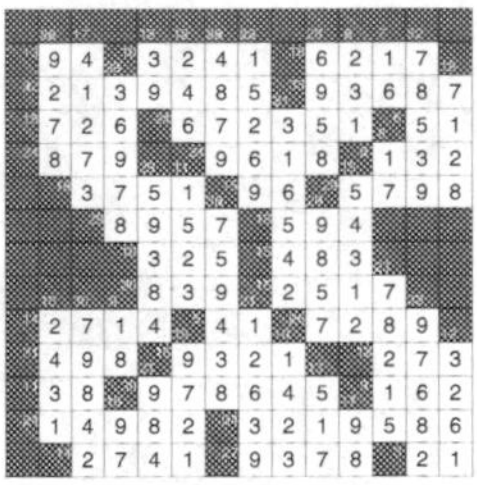

72

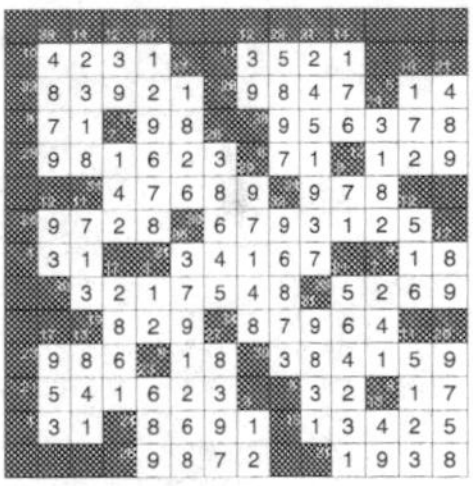

73

74

75

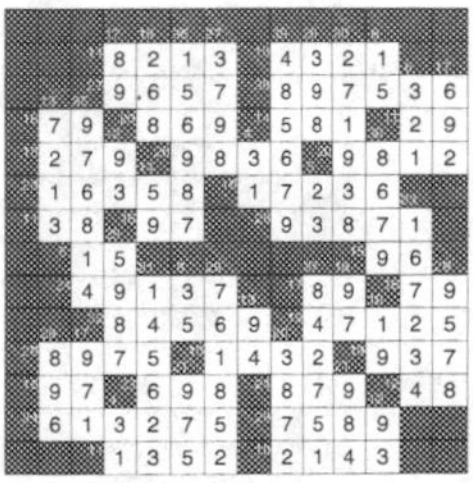

76

77

78

79

80

81

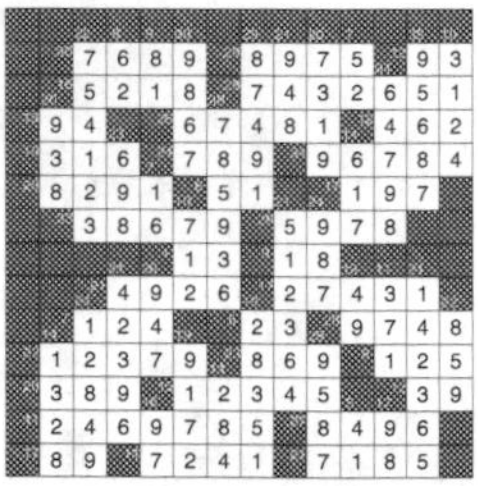

82

83

84

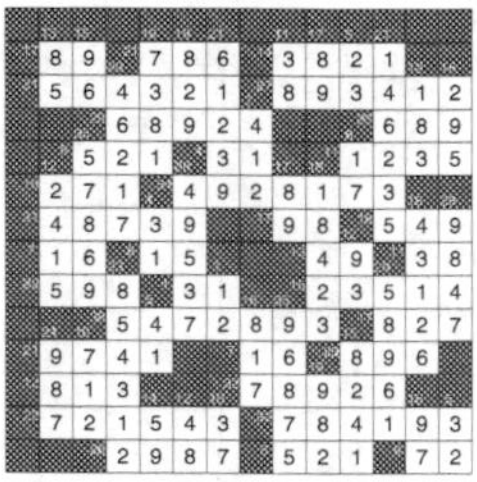

85

86

87

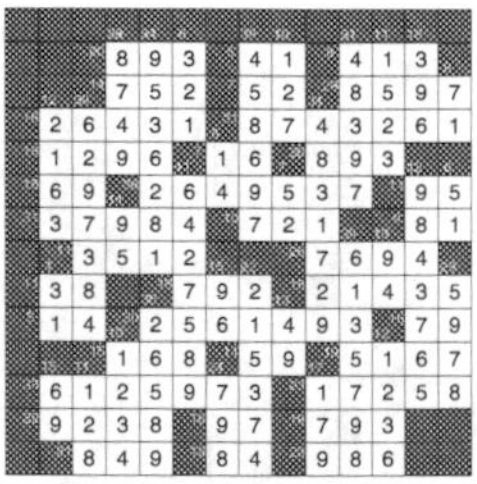

88

89

90

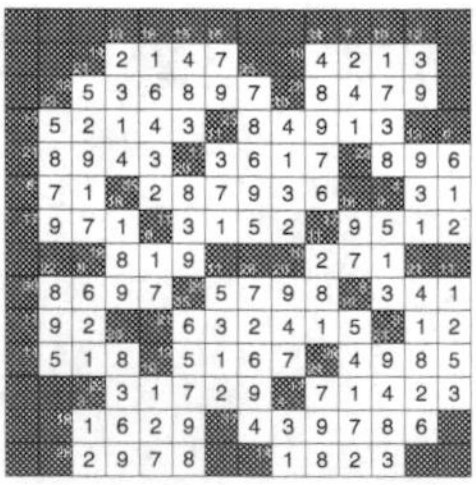

91

92

93

94

95

96

97

98

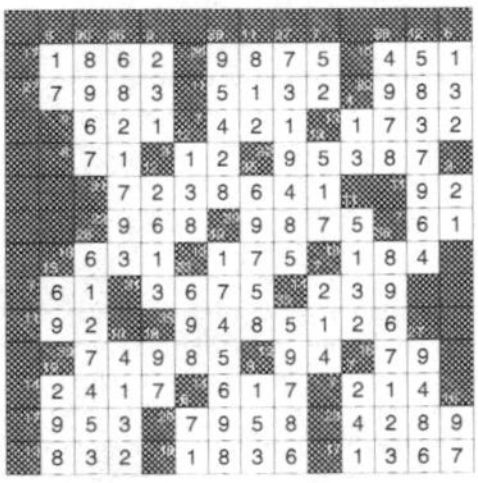

99

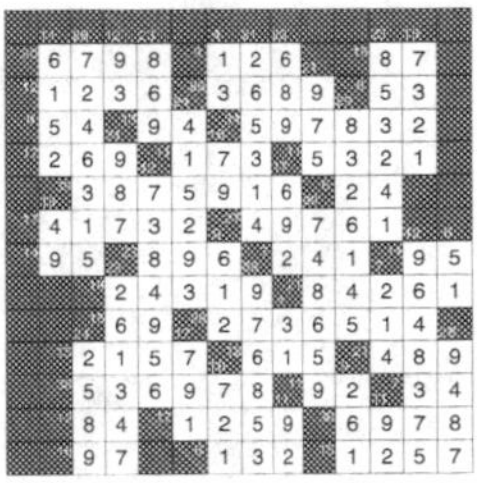

100

101

102

103

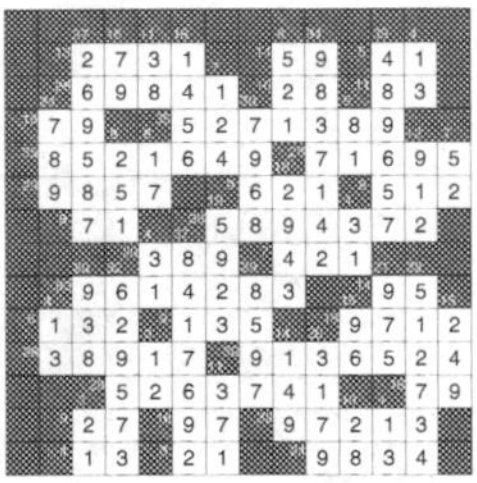

104

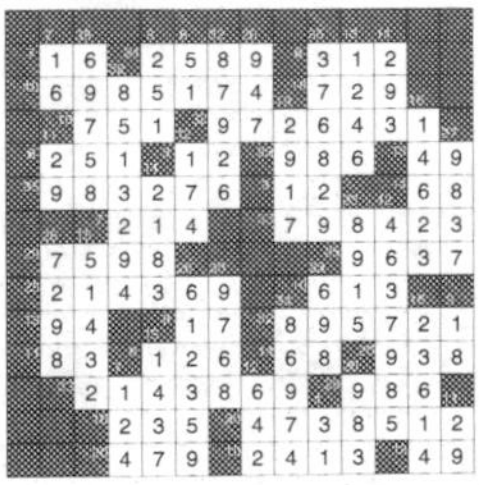

105

106

107

108

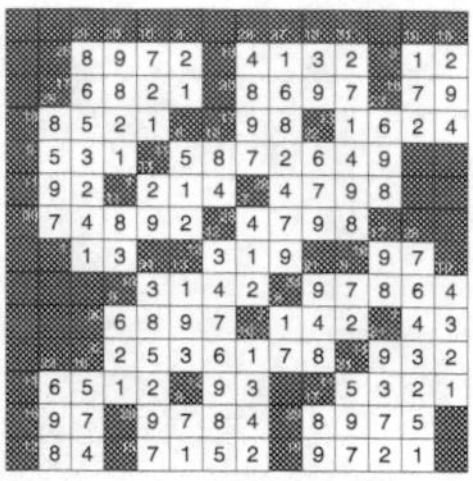

109

110

111

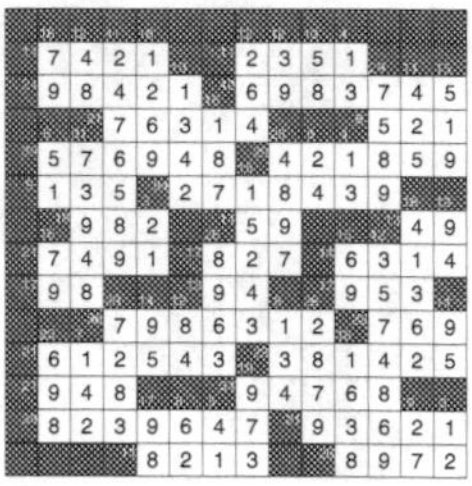

112

Part 3: Extremely Challenging Puzzles

1

2
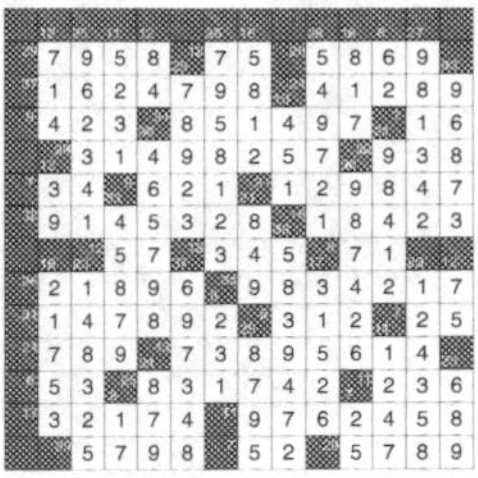

3

4
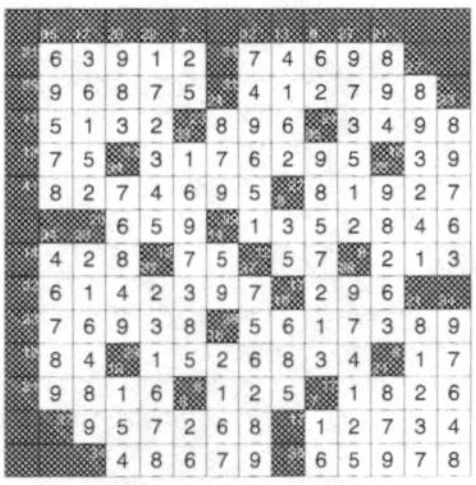

5

6

7
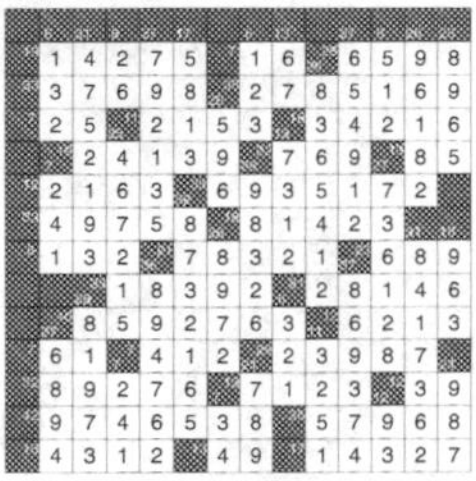

8

9
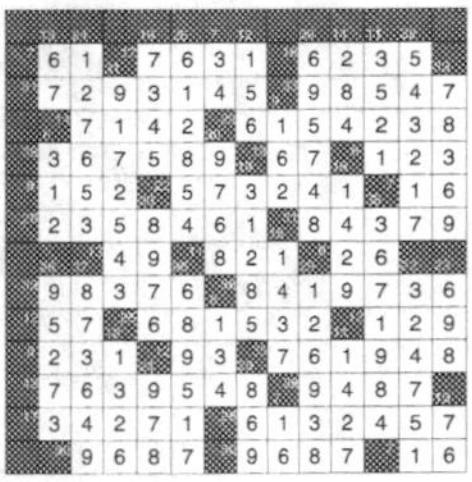

10
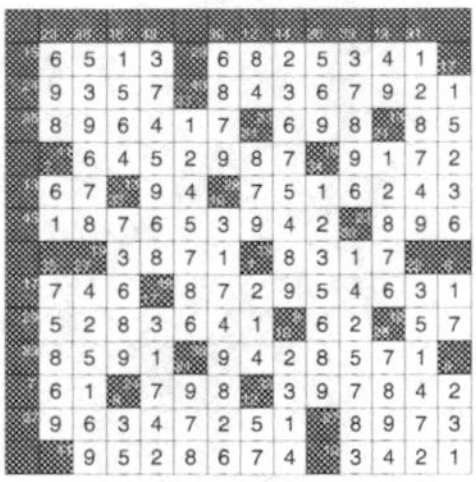

11
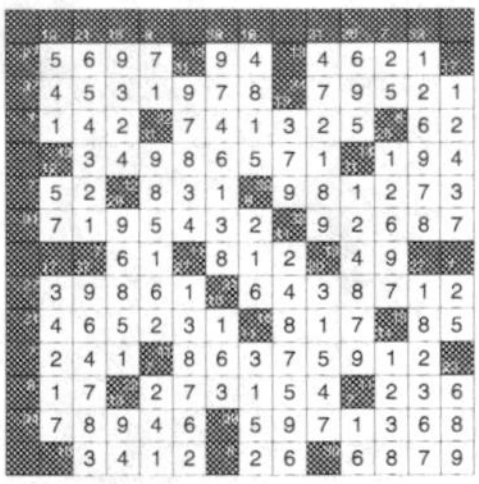

12
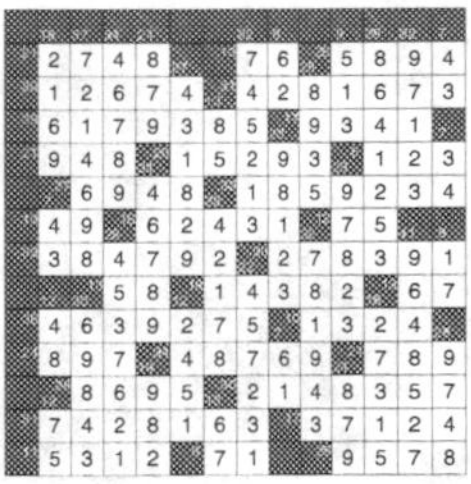

13
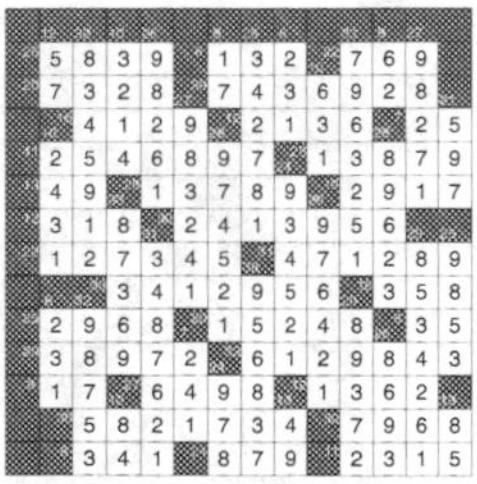

14
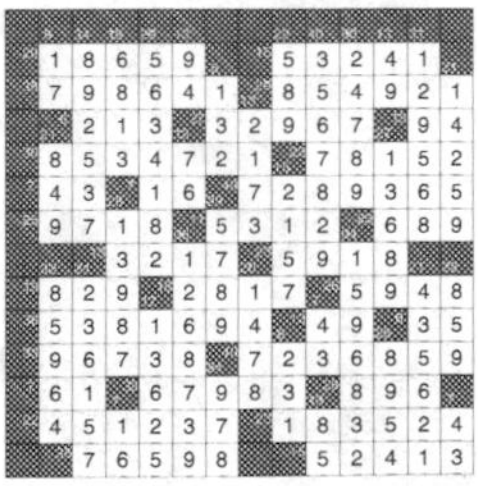

15

16

17

18

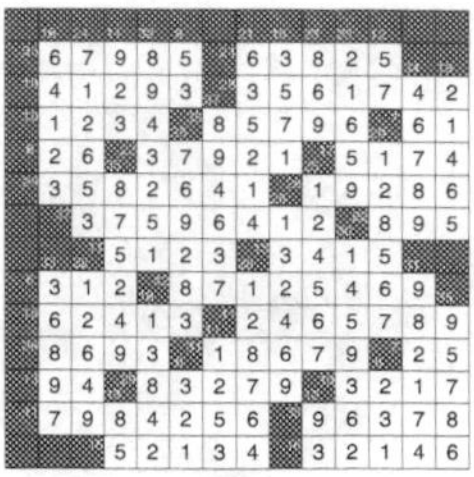

19

20

21

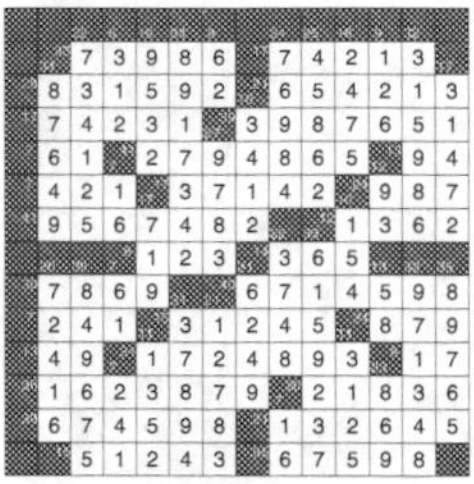

22

23

24

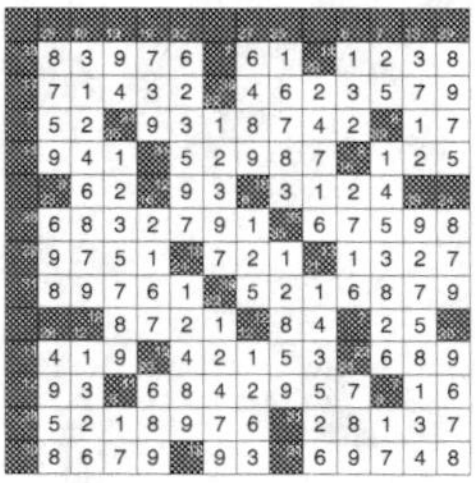

25

26

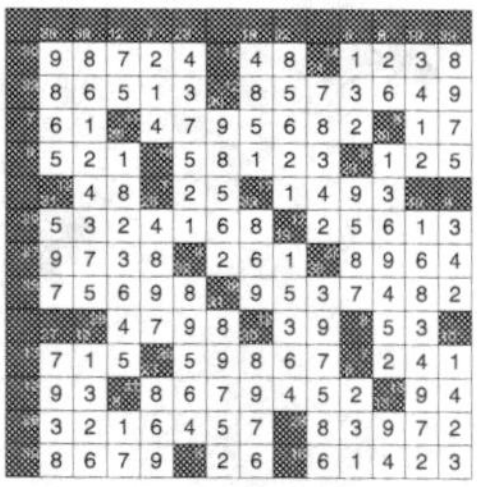

27

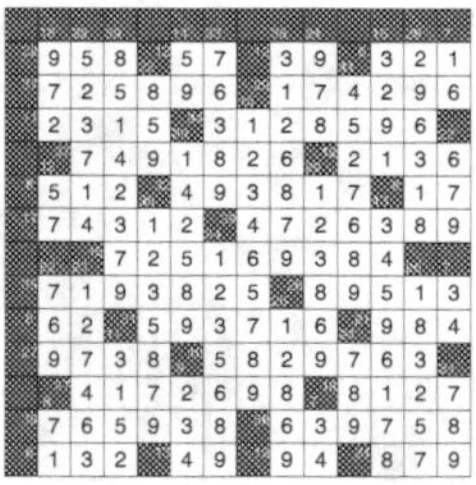

28

29

30

31

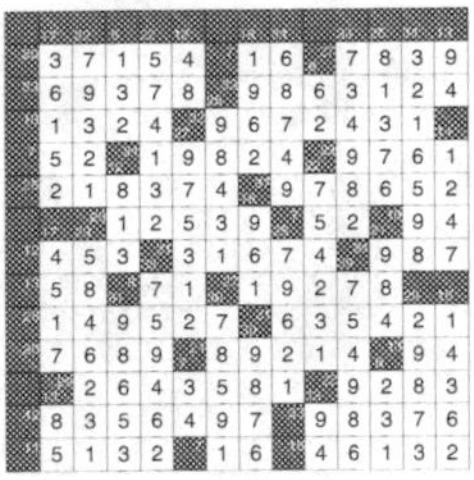

32

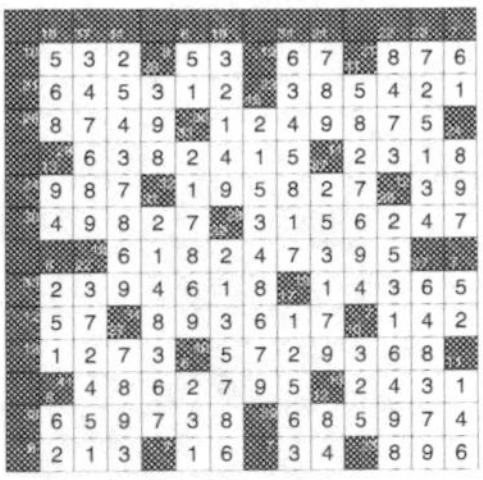

33

34

35

36

37

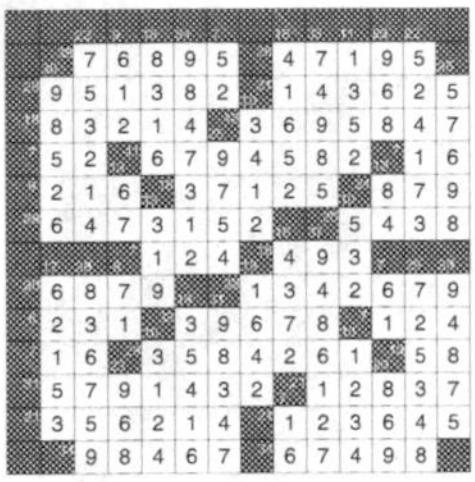

38

39

40

41

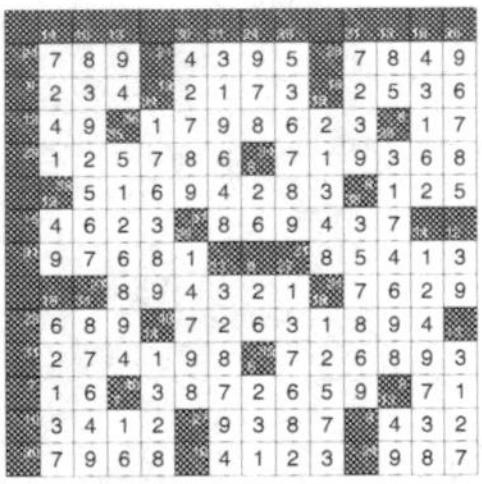

42

43

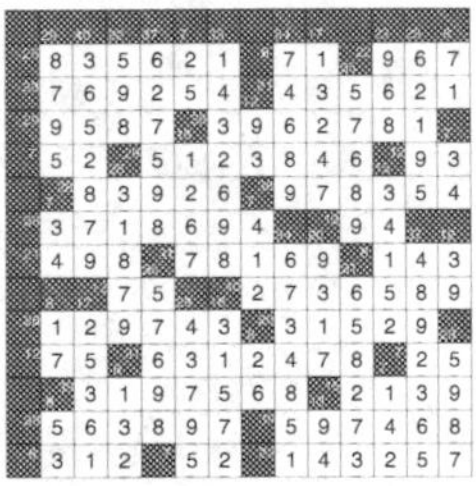

44

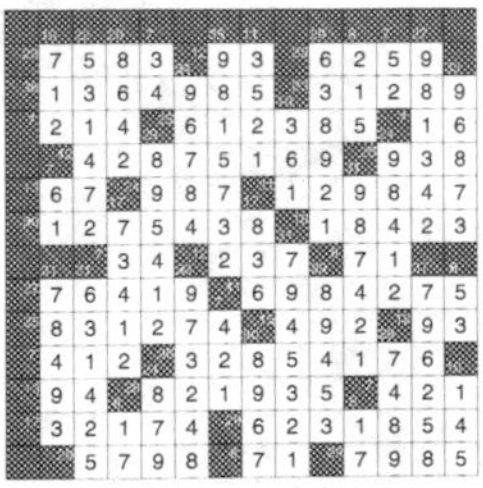

45

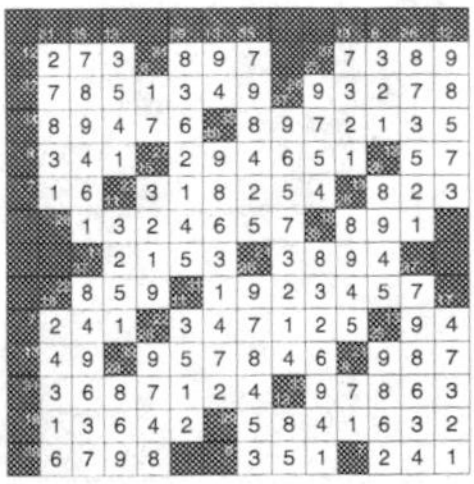

46

47

48

49

50

51

52

53

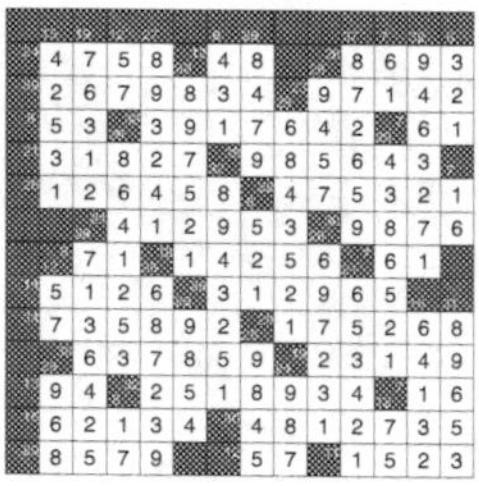

54

55

56

57

58

59

60

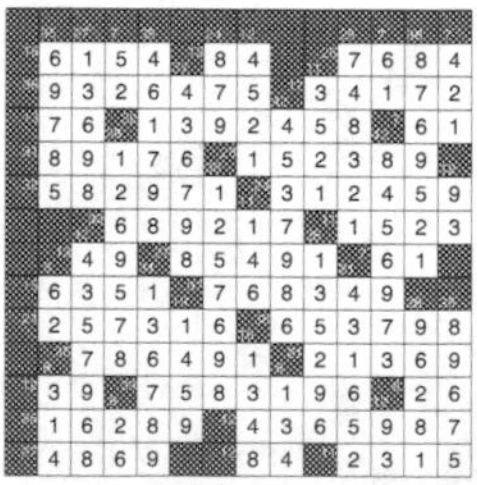

61

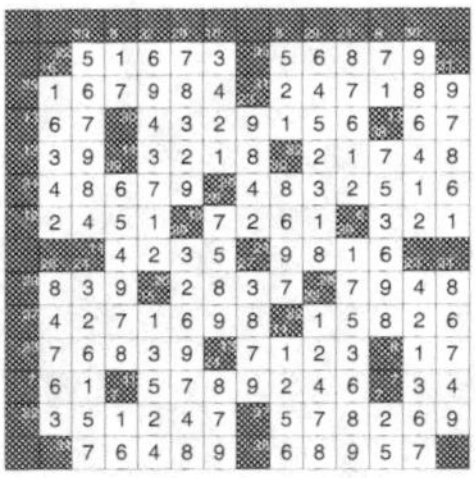

62

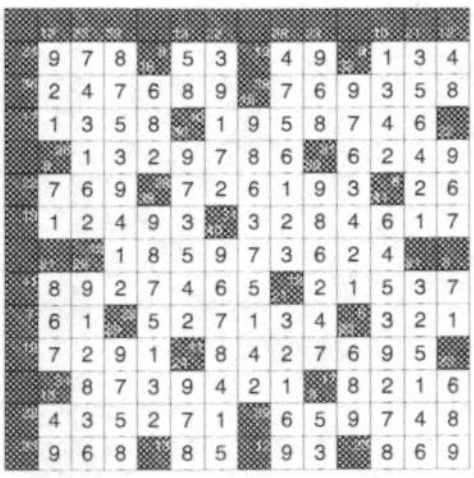

63

64

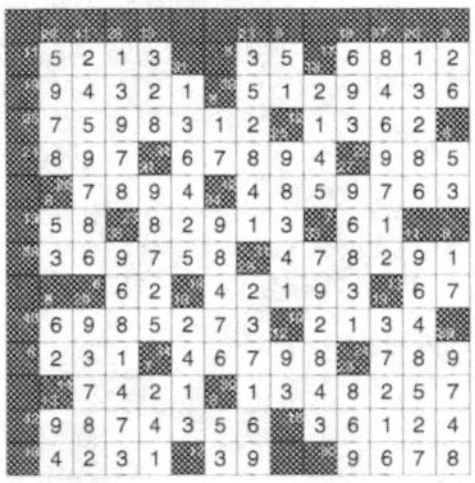

65

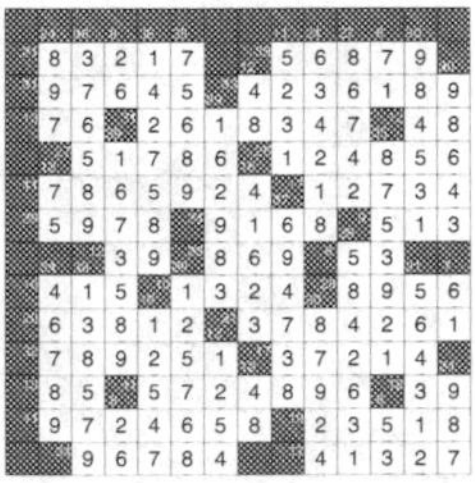

66

67

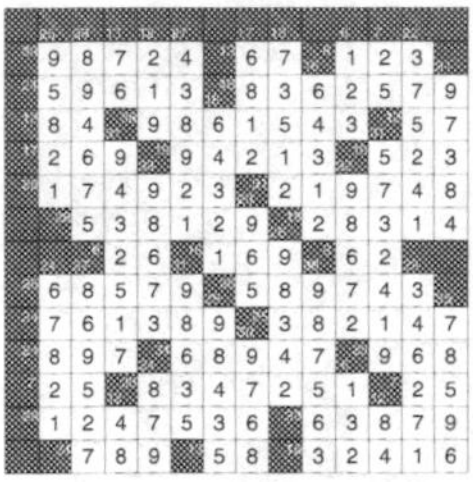

68

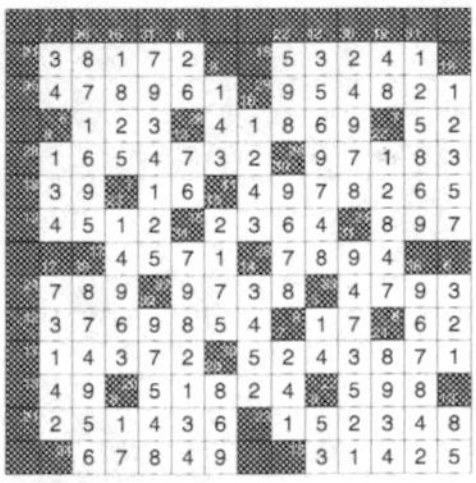

69

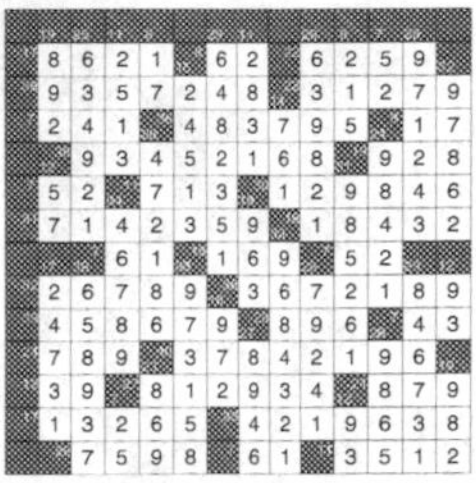

70

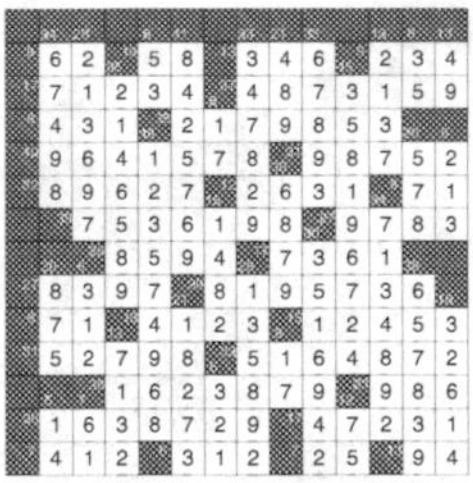

71

72

73

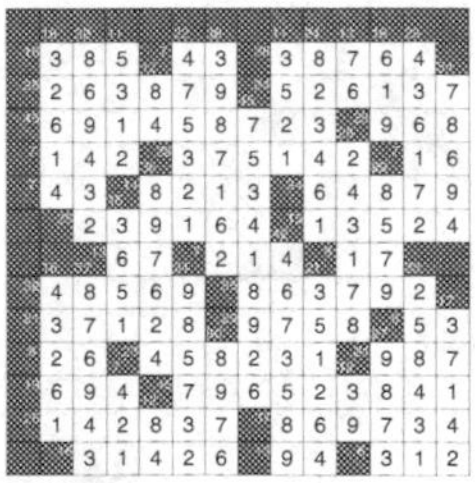

74

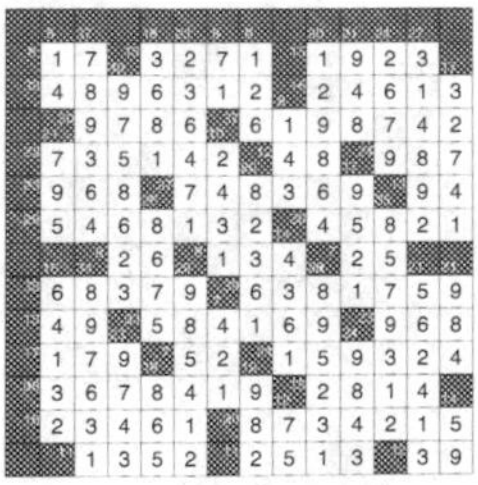

75

76

77

78

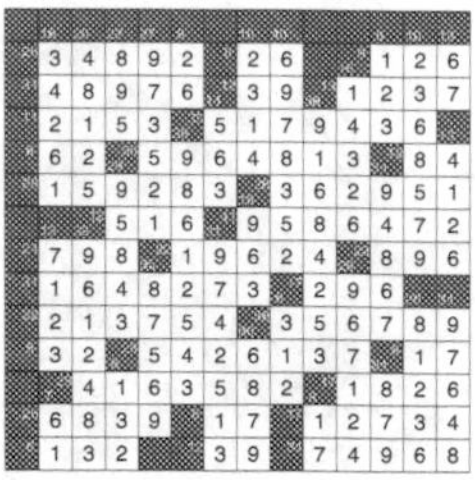

79

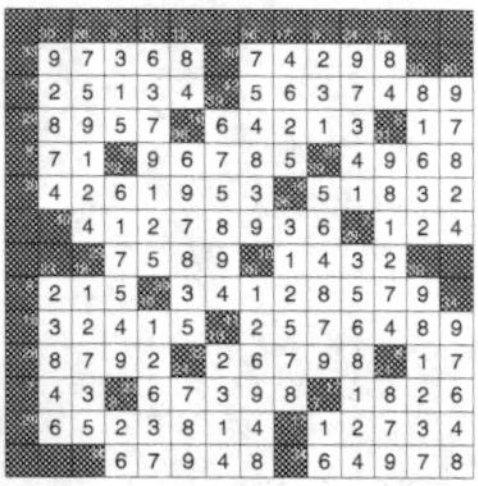

80

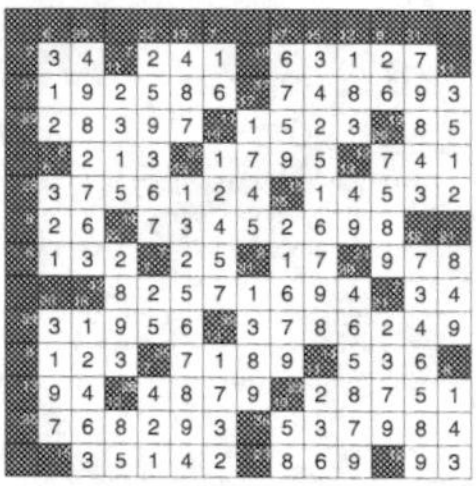

81

82

83

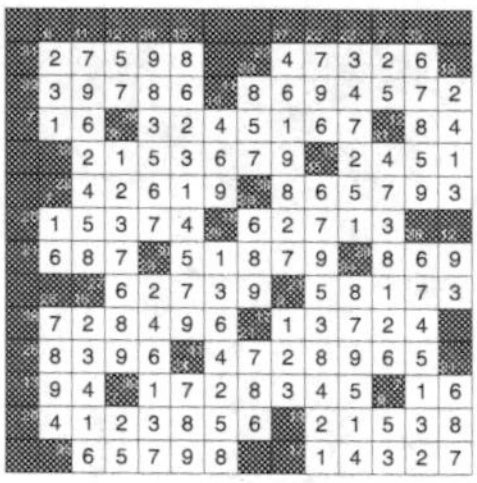

84

85

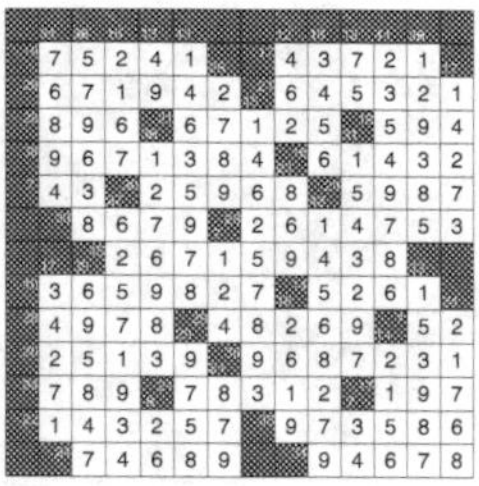

86

87

88

89

90

91

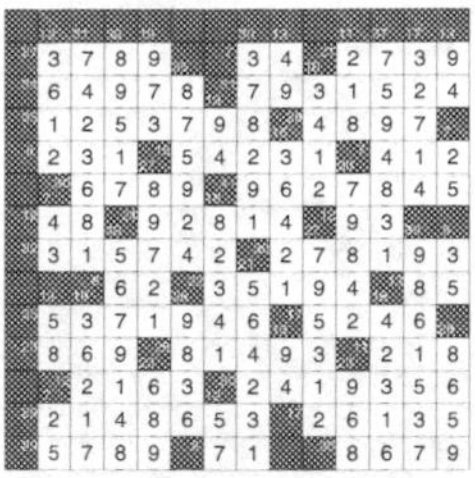

92

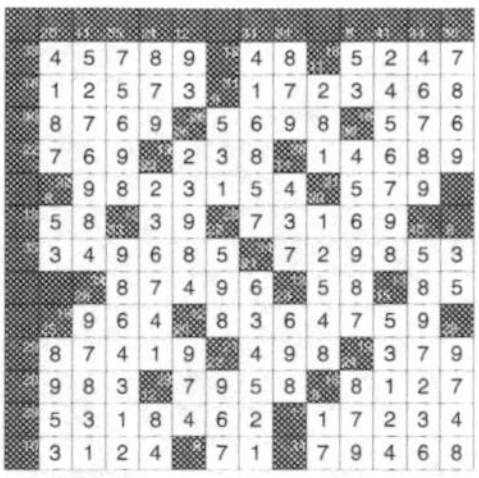

93

94

95

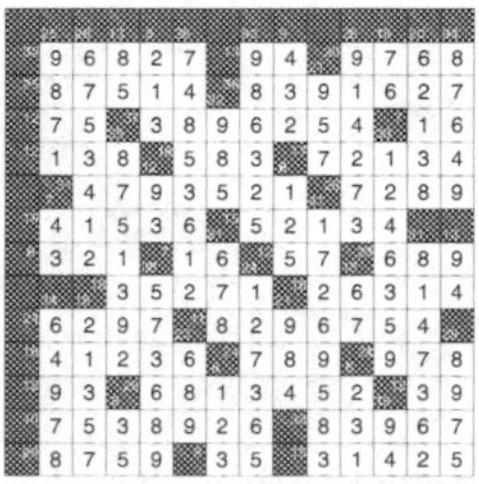

96

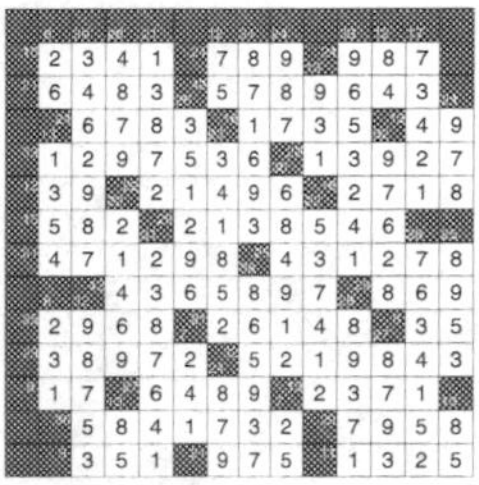

97

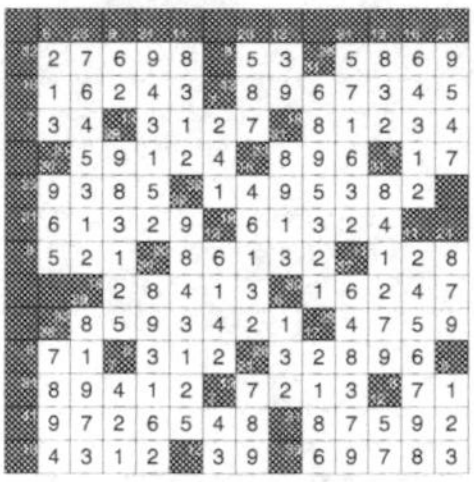

98

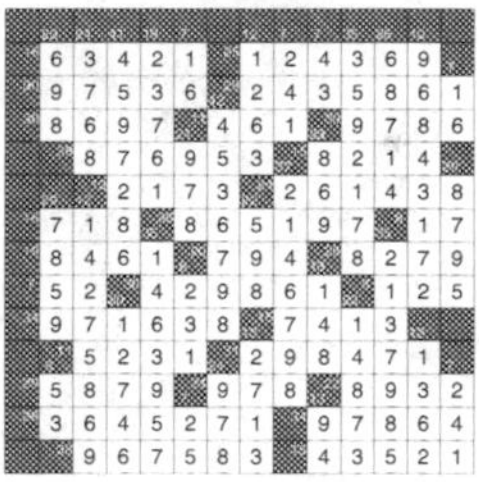

99

100

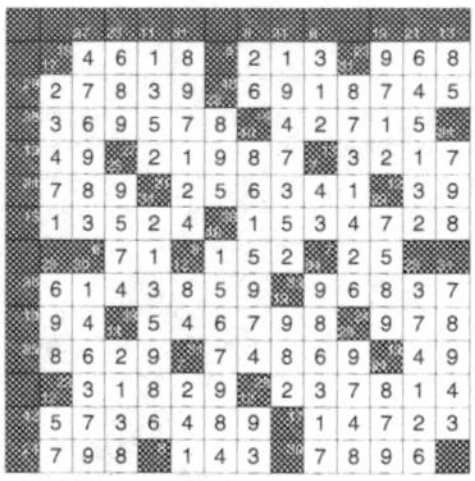

APPENDIX B

Sum Combinations

Sum Combinations

number of spaces	sum	possible combinations
2	3	12
2	4	13
2	5	14, 23
2	6	15, 24
2	7	16, 25, 34
2	8	17, 26, 35
2	9	18, 27, 36, 45
2	10	19, 28, 37, 46
2	11	29, 38, 47, 56
2	12	39, 48, 57
2	13	49, 58, 67
2	14	59, 68
2	15	69, 78
2	16	79
2	17	89
3	6	123
3	7	124
3	8	125, 134
3	9	126, 135, 234
3	10	127, 136, 145, 235
3	11	128, 137, 146, 236, 245
3	12	129, 138, 147, 156, 237, 246, 345

3	13	139, 148, 157, 238, 247, 256, 346
3	14	149, 158, 167, 239, 248, 257, 347, 356
3	15	159, 168, 249, 258, 267, 348, 357, 456
3	16	169, 178, 259, 268, 349, 358, 367, 457
3	17	179, 269, 278, 359, 368, 458, 467
3	18	189, 279, 369, 378, 459, 468, 567
3	19	289, 379, 469, 478, 568
3	20	389, 479, 569, 578
3	21	489, 579, 678
3	22	589, 679
3	23	689
3	24	789

4	10	1234
4	11	1235
4	12	1236, 1245
4	13	1237, 1246, 1345
4	14	1238, 1247, 1256, 1346, 2345
4	15	1239, 1248, 1257, 1347, 1356, 2346
4	16	1249, 1258, 1267, 1348, 1357, 1456, 2347, 2356
4	17	1259, 1268, 1349, 1358, 1367, 1457, 2348, 2357, 2456
4	18	1269, 1278, 1359, 1368, 1458, 1467, 2349, 2358, 2367, 2457, 3456
4	19	1279, 1369, 1378, 1459, 1468, 1567, 2359, 2368, 2458, 2467, 3457
4	20	1289, 1379, 1469, 1478, 1568, 2369, 2378, 2459, 2468, 2567, 3458, 3467
4	21	1389, 1479, 1569, 1578, 2379, 2469, 2478, 2568, 3459, 3468, 3567

4	22	1489, 1579, 1678, 2389, 2479, 2569, 2578, 3469, 3478, 3568, 4567
4	23	1589, 1679, 2489, 2579, 2678, 3479, 3569, 3578, 4568
4	24	1689, 2589, 2679, 3489, 3579, 3678, 4569, 4578
4	25	1789, 2689, 3589, 3679, 4579, 4678
4	26	2789, 3689, 4589, 4679, 5678
4	27	3789, 4689, 5679
4	28	4789, 5689
4	29	5789
4	30	6789

5	15	12345
5	16	12346
5	17	12347, 12356
5	18	12348, 12357, 12456
5	19	12349, 12358, 12367, 12457, 13456
5	20	12359, 12368, 12458, 12467, 13457, 23456
5	21	12369, 12378, 12459, 12468, 12567, 13458, 13467, 23457
5	22	12379, 12469, 12478, 12568, 13459, 13468, 13567, 23458, 23467
5	23	12389, 12479, 12569, 12578, 13469, 13478, 13568, 14567, 23459, 23468, 23567
5	24	12489, 12579, 12678, 13479, 13569, 13578, 14568, 23469, 23478, 23568, 24567

5	25	12589, 12679, 13489, 13579, 13678, 14569, 14578, 23479, 23569, 23578, 24568, 34567
5	26	12689, 13589, 13679, 14579, 14678, 23489, 23579, 23678, 24569, 24578, 34568
5	27	12789, 13689, 14589, 14679, 15678, 23589, 23679, 24579, 24678, 34569, 34578
5	28	13789, 14689, 15679, 23689, 24589, 24679, 25678, 34579, 34678
5	29	14789, 15689, 23789, 24689, 25679, 34589, 34679, 35678
5	30	15789, 24789, 25689, 34689, 35679, 45678
5	31	16789, 25789, 34789, 35689, 45679
5	32	26789, 35789, 45689
5	33	36789, 45789
5	34	46789
5	35	56789

6	21	123456
6	22	123457
6	23	123458, 123467
6	24	123459, 123468, 123567
6	25	123469, 123478, 123568, 124567
6	26	123479, 123569, 123578, 124568, 134567
6	27	123489, 123579, 123678, 124569, 124578, 134568, 234567

6	28	123589, 123679, 124579, 124678, 134569, 134578, 234568
6	29	123689, 124589, 124679, 125678, 134579, 134678, 234569, 234578
6	30	123789, 124689, 125679, 134589, 134679, 135678, 234579, 234678
6	31	124789, 125689, 134689, 135679, 145678, 234589, 234679, 235678
6	32	125789, 134789, 135689, 145679, 234689, 235679, 245678
6	33	126789, 135789, 145689, 234789, 235689, 245679, 345678
6	34	136789, 145789, 235789, 245689, 345679
6	35	146789, 236789, 245789, 345689
6	36	156789, 246789, 345789
6	37	256789, 346789
6	38	356789
6	39	456789

7	28	1234567
7	29	1234568
7	30	1234569, 1234578
7	31	1234579, 1234678
7	32	1234589, 1234679, 1235678
7	33	1234689, 1235679, 1245678
7	34	1234789, 1235689, 1245679, 1345678
7	35	1235789, 1245689, 1345679, 2345678
7	36	1236789, 1245789, 1345689, 2345679
7	37	1246789, 1345789, 2345689
7	38	1256789, 1346789, 2345789

7	39	1356789, 2346789
7	40	1456789, 2356789
7	41	2456789
7	42	3456789
8	36	12345678
8	37	12345679
8	38	12345689
8	39	12345789
8	40	12346789
8	41	12356789
8	42	12456789
8	43	13456789
8	44	23456789
9	45	123456789